Heathen Tribes

A Collection of Essays Concerning the Tribes of Our Folk

by

Mark Ludwig Stinson

Chieftain of Jotun's Bane Kindred
Temple of Our Heathen Gods
Kansas City Area

Written During 2010-2011
First Edition

Published by Jotun's Bane Kindred
Temple of Our Heathen Gods
P.O. Box 618
Liberty, MO 64069
http://Heathengods.com

TABLE OF CONTENTS

ACKNOWLEDGMENTS

This book would not exist without the patience and support of my wife, Jennifer Stinson. She is my partner in all things and I would not be the person I am without the life we have built together.

My children, Nathan, Elizabeth, and Joshua are my inspiration and my joy. They make me laugh. They energize me. They test me and wear me down, and then they make me laugh and energize me all over again. I am proud of them – greatly proud of them. Much of my motivation for writing these essays is to record for them that which I believe, and to narrate for them why I have worked so hard with Jotun's Bane Kindred to build something that can be passed down to them. We will build a Hof and a Hall on tribal land and all of the work I put into these deeds is for them. None of us live forever, but our Blood, our Orlog, and our Deeds live on in our children.

My Tribe, Jotun's Bane Kindred, breathes life into all the essays in this book. We share all of our struggles, our hard work, and our successes in true Frith. These are my trusted friends and sharing strong bonds and oaths with them is clear evidence of my Luck. So many of these essays are based directly on our own experiences and on the conversations we have together of what we want for our families, our Kindred, and our Folk. So, I want to acknowledge Rod Landreth, Craig Winkler, Jamie King, Will Burris, Johnny Hamilton, Kimberly Hamilton, Glen Steveson, Susan Steveson, Jason Grothe, Jennifer Stinson, and all of their families as the best people I know.

I want to acknowledge my Great-Grandfather and name-sake Ludwig Schweiger. He was a Germanic immigrant to the United States, a hard worker, and a beloved family man. My Grandmother and Ludwig's daughter, Elizabeth Shoop, taught me to dream, laugh, and enjoy life. She was my best friend as a child and she left the world too soon.

First among my Ancestors is my father, Glen F. Stinson. He was the best of fathers, and I work hard to pass Orlog to my children that is as good and powerful as the Orlog that my father passed to me.

INTRODUCTION

The essays in this collection were written in the years 2010 and 2011. In their original form they were written as internet essays, message board posts, and as answers to e-mail questions I received. In bringing them together into this book, I have grouped them into categories and put them into an order that gives them context. I have reworked all of the essays to varying degrees. Some required very little refining, while others required extensive reworking.

This book is a very practical book, written in a conversational tone. It is not a scholarly work, heavy with footnotes and quotes from other authors and other sources. There are many amazing books of that nature available, some of the best of which are listed at the end of this book. What you will find within this collection is my approach to various topics and issues within our Folkway – the Folkway that represents the ancestral religion, ways, and worldview of the Northern European people. The essays included here are informed by the experiences of Jotun's Bane Kindred in starting, maintaining, and growing a Heathen Tribe here in the Heartland of the United States.

The scope of these essays is far-reaching, but this collection does not provide a comprehensive examination of Heathenry. If that is what you are seeking, you should buy Our Troth, Volumes 1 and 2. This collection does not serve as a complete introduction to Heathenry, either. Essential Asatru, by Diana Paxon, would better serve you as a brief introduction to our Folkway.

The ways of our Ancestors varied greatly from Tribe to Tribe, location to location, century to century, and even among various levels of society. The same situation exists today within modern Heathenry. These essays are not presented as the one-true-way that things should be done within Heathenry. These essays represent one man's approach – one Tribe's approach – to these issues and topics. It is likely that every reader will find things to both agree with and disagree with in the contents of this book. If nothing else, the essays will hopefully get you thinking about these topics and examining, or re-examining, your own approaches and points-of-view.

Jotun's Bane Kindred draws from Norse, Germanic, Anglo-Saxon, and other Northern European sources for its ways and traditions. For this reason, there is a certain mixing of terminology in the following essays. We do not restrict ourselves to using only Norse terminology or only Anglo-Saxon terminology. If a word or concept accurately reflects what we are doing, then we use that word or concept.

This collection is not an anti-Christian manifesto. Instead the tone is one of starting where our Ancestors left off, reclaiming what was taken from our people, and moving our religion forward into our modern world. Our Kindred and these essays focus on moving *beyond* Christianity. For this reason, I have kept references to Christianity and other religions to a minimum.

Jotun's Bane Kindred is an oathed tribal Kindred in the Heartland of America. We are a Folkish Kindred, at least by our own estimation. These essays reflect a tribal approach to Heathenry. They reflect the importance of Kindreds with committed and hard-working leaders and members. Above all, they reflect the importance of preserving, gathering, and advancing our Folk forward.

This book would not exist if not for Jotun's Bane Kindred. We are a strong and growing Tribe. We work to support and advance each other in Frith, and I would not be the man I am today, without the incredible individuals of worth that occupy my Innangarth. I have said it before, and I will say it again – the thoughts, ideas, and accomplishments of the members of Jotun's Bane Kindred run throughout these essays, culled from our discussions together, and the lessons we have learned working together as a Tribe.

The goal of this collection of essays is not to make money. The goal is to share information. So feel free to share or distribute this material however you wish, as long as you follow the restrictions described in the Open License on the indicia page.

If you wish to contact me in order to discuss or ask questions about any of these writings, please email me at: mark@Heathengods.com.

Mark Ludwig Stinson
December 2011

WE NEED MORE PRACTICAL HEATHEN BOOKS

There are a lot of scholarly Heathen books, and I have no problem with that. I enjoy scholarly books. Part of reconstructing our Folkway, is examining and understanding what our Heathen Ancestors were like, what they did, what they believed, how they viewed the world, and how they viewed themselves. But there are stacks of books about the past written from a scholarly perspective. There are also tons of Asatru 101 books, that describe our Gods and Goddess and basic Heathen concepts.

But there are very few PRACTICAL Heathen books; very few books that say, "here are ways to practically apply these Heathen concepts in real life," written by people who have successfully applied them in real life.

A practical book can include the Lore. It can even have scholarly elements. But, the current trend in Heathenry to raise the scholarly aspects of the Lore above the practical application of the Lore, leaves a large gap in what real Heathens, in real Tribes, working hard to make real progress need in order to inform their efforts. I sometimes use the term "blue collar Heathen," to refer to these real Heathens who are actually focused on living Heathen and building Heathen communities. A practical book is about doing. It is nuts and bolts. It is about what works. "Blue collar Heathens" are starved for practical books on heathen topics.

We talk constantly about Heathenry being all about DOING and all about COMMUNITY. But almost all of our books are scholarly books about ancient texts, interpreting ancient texts, what our Ancestors believed, history, metaphysical aspects, runes, mythological stories, etc. There are so few books that are practical books about living Heathen within a Kindred or Tribe in our modern times.

The 2nd volume of Our Troth (2nd Edition) has some fairly practical information sprinkled through it. True Hearth is a fairly practical book. Way of the Heathen, as outdated as it is, has some excellent chapters that I would consider practical. There are a couple of other books that we could classify as practical heathen books, they are few and far between.

Here are some books I would love to see written. Hopefully someday there will be multiple titles about each of these topics coming from different authors with differing perspectives.

1. Until "Heathen Gods" was written, the largest practical guide on "How to Start a Kindred" was a nine-page PDF that was several years old. So, I think Heathen Gods is an example of a practical book on Heathenry. But, I think more should be written on the topic of how to start and maintain a Kindred and Tribe, from different perspectives and with more ideas. The more good information available on this topic, the better. I would be the first to widely promote such a book by another author.

2. Tribal dynamics. Growing a lasting Tribe. Making it productive. How to ensure that the members are advancing the Tribe forward, while the Tribe is also advancing each of the members forward. How to build collective Luck. Which types of Kindred events build and improve the Kindred. How to judge new members, and how to bring them up-to-speed in the Kindred. How to handle members that are disruptive.

3. A Chieftain's role within a Kindred? How to lead a Kindred. How to handle difficult members, of various types. How to weather a stressful time within a Kindred. How to build consensus. How to assist each member in finding their place or role within the Tribe. The physical, practical steps and actions a Chieftain should take, to be a good Chieftain. There is a lot to be written on this topic.

4. The practical Godhi guide. The books and concepts a Godhi should read and understand. A Godhi's role within a Kindred. The responsibilities of a Godhi. The things a Godhi should know how to do. How a Godhi and a Chieftain work together. How to resolve problems. The problems a Godhi can handle and the problems they should they refer to someone else – a therapist for instance.

5. Developing and maintaining Thew within a Tribe. Explanations of Thew. The role of a Thyle within a Kindred. How does Thew develop and how you can work to develop it within a Tribe. The responsibilities various leadership positions have in maintaining Thew. Many specific practical examples on how to approach, form, and later alter Thew.

6. Regional dynamics. How strong autonomous Tribes come together, work together, and build something greater than the simple sum of their individual parts. How two Tribes approach each other, and treat each other honorably. A description of the boundaries that should be maintained between Tribes. How two Tribes build bonds between each other. How to resolve problems between two Tribes.

7. Heathen Marriage. How it works and its focus. How to resolve problems in the most successful and least disruptive way. How to integrate a marriage within a tight-knit Tribe. The parenting roles that are shared within a tight-knit Tribe. The role of Uncling or Fostering within modern Tribes.

8. Being a Heathen Parent. Methods for educating and involving your children in your Kindred or Tribe. How to prepare children for their transition to adulthood. Specific methods for handling specific problems a Heathen parent will encounter with Heathen children (other children, adults, the messages they get from mass-media, etc.) How and when to handle man-making or woman-making.

So, who will write these practical books? Hopefully Heathens that have had success and Luck in the topics about which they are writing. Practical Heathens writing books for other practical Heathens.

SECTION ONE

ESSAYS FOR
NEW TRIBES

YOUR ANCESTORS WERE HEATHEN

This essay is written for those that know very little about Asatru or Heathenry, or perhaps have not even heard of it.

It is a simple question, really. Did your family come to America from Northern Europe or do you have Northern European Ancestry? Well, if your family does, then your Ancestors were "Heathens."

Many people with Northern European ancestry do not realize that the original religion of our People and our ancient culture was not Christian. If you go back a 1000 years or more, prior to the conversions to Christianity in Europe, our Ancestors had their own native Folk Religion that was rich and meaningful in their lives.

Our People honored their own Gods and Goddesses, their Ancestors, and the spirits in nature. These original Heathens lived in pre-Christian Northern Europe, and included the people of Anglo-Saxon England, Scandinavia, and Germany, among others.

Some of our Ancestors were convinced to convert to Christianity by missionaries. Some were coerced into converting, based on threats of physical violence. Others converted due to political or economic pressures brought on them by Christians. Some of our Ancestors were out-right killed, because they refused to give up the Ways of their People.

THE ORIGIN OF THE WORD "HEATHEN"

If you are just hearing about Heathenry, then you are very likely thinking, "But isn't the word Heathen a word for a bad person or a godless person?"

Well, it is true that Christians frequently use it this way. The word "Heathen" refers to people who do not worship the Christian God or follow the Christian religion. The historical origin of this use of the word "Heathen" is pretty interesting.

The word "Heathen" comes from the fact that the country people (those living on the heath), honored the old Gods for centuries after the city-dwellers were already converted to Christianity.

This is why "Heathen" is a bad word in Christianity. The missionaries and preachers in the cities would rail against the "Heathens" (those living out in the heath), that still honored the old Gods. Today, we embrace the term, for we are proud of those Ancestors that resisted the conversion to a foreign religion, and who remained loyal to the Gods and the Ways of our People.

Another word commonly used for Heathenry is Asatru, meaning "loyalty to the Gods." Though, Asatru is normally used to refer to a more Icelandic-influenced Heathenry, while the word Heathenry itself is a broader term encompassing those focusing on the Icelandic, the Anglo-Saxon, the Frankish, etc.

Our Heathen Ancestors did not refer to themselves as "Heathen" or "Asatru." It is believed they did not have a name for their religion, and simply called it their Way.

HEATHENRY IS A VIABLE OPTION IN OUR MODERN WORLD

So many modern Americans are dissatisfied with what they perceive to be their religious options. Many of the descendants of our Heathen Ancestors have become dissatisfied with Christianity. Many Modern Heathens believe that much of this dissatisfaction comes from the fact that Christianity did not originate with our People. It is a foreign religion that was relentlessly pushed on our Ancestors, until our native Folkway was suppressed, and eventually destroyed, among our People.

Modern Heathens around the world are reviving the Ways of our Ancestors and find that the religion of our Ancestors is truly satisfying and feels "like coming home." Heathenry is very family and community-oriented, and encourages us to live responsible lives of loyalty and honor. A person's word matters greatly, and each person is judged by his/her choices and actions. The Ways of our Ancestors are life-fulfilling and natural to who we are and how we think, and they work to strengthen and enrich our lives.

You will hear modern Heathenry called many things by the people who practice it. You may hear it called Asatru, the Northern Tradition, Odinism, Forn Sed, Germanic Pagan Reconstructionism or, simply, Heathenry. In Iceland, which did not convert to Christianity until the 11th Century, Heathenry has once again become an official (nationally recognized) religion. There are growing numbers of Heathens and Heathen groups across the United States, and that growth seems to be accelerating as more and more people tire of foreign religions.

SOMETHING WORTH CONSIDERING

If you have found yourself dissatisfied with Christianity and organized religion, take a little time to look into modern Heathenry. When your Heathen Ancestors were pestered, coerced, or forced into giving up the Ways of the People, I have to imagine that they wondered if years down the line their descendants would again return to their true religion and way of life. As someone who has returned to the religion of my Ancestors, it is hard to describe how much it has improved my life. In the end, it is something you have to look into yourself and explore whether it makes sense for you and your family.

A good starting place to learn more, is this Heathen FAQ. Reading through all the topics there will give you some idea of what Heathenry is all about:

http://Heathengods.com/temple/modules/xoopsfaq/

For some basic information on Heathenry and how to start and maintain a Heathen group (normally called a Kindred), you might want to read the book, "Heathen Gods," which is available as a free download or in paperback and hardback versions at this site:

http://www.Heathengods.com/library/book/

WE LIVE IN SAGA TIMES

My Godhi, Rod Landreth, was the first to say this to me. I do not know if it is original to him, but I do know it made quite an impact on me.

"We live in Saga times. What is your Saga? Is your Saga worthy of being told around the fire by your descendants?"

This is an interesting question to ask yourself. Once you have asked it and honestly answered it for yourself, it becomes an interesting question to revisit frequently. It is worthwhile self-assessment.

Are you reading and learning about our native Folkway?

Do you teach your children about Heathenry?

Are you living Heathen, and modeling a Heathen way of life for your children?

Do you honor your Gods and Ancestors, and involve your children in you ways?

Are you maintaining and strengthening your marriage and your family?

Are you working as hard as you can at home, at work, and just generally in your life?

Have you taken the time to get to know other Heathens in you area and region?

Do you gather with other Heathens?

Are you a member of a Kindred, and if not, are you working on finding or starting one?

Are you learning new crafts or new skills?

Are you practicing your existing crafts and skills as well as you can?

Do you live your life bravely and with honor?

Are you taking chances and making the effort to make worthwhile things happen?

Do you live a life that would make our Gods and Goddesses proud?

Do you live a life that would make your Ancestors proud?

Let us return to Rod's initial question:

"We live in Saga times, what is your Saga? Is your Saga worthy being told around the fire by your descendants?"

Will your children's children's children tell stories of what you have done to protect and strengthen your family?

Will your children's children's children tell stories of what you have done to grow and advance your Kindred or Tribe?

Will your children's children's children tell stories of what you have done to advance our native Folkway?

In my estimation, we only get one chance at this life. We truly do live in Saga times. What will your Saga say?

GROWING HEATHENRY USING A GRASSROOTS APPROACH

Asatru, or Heathenry, is a reconstruction religion, with just 30+ years of modern history, following a 1000+ year dramatic and unwelcome "interruption." We are not in the same boat as the huge Universalist conversion-focused religions with 1000 to 2500 years of uninterrupted history and growth. The number of our Folk that have returned to their Ancestral Stream number only in the 1,000's. The desert religion's adherents number literally in the billions.

Who exactly is going to grow and advance our native Folkway? Who is going to start and grow our Kindreds into strong and vibrant Heathen Tribes? Who is going to guarantee a future for Asatru? Where are our Hofs and who is going to build them?

Heathen Tribes are going to do these things. YOU are going to do these things.

No one is going to do it for us – no one can. A national organization will not do it for you. Some hypothetical person you have not even met yet will not do it for you. A website or message board will not do it for you. Wishing and dreaming will not do it for you. Sitting around watching reality television shows will not do it for you. The Gods and our Ancestors will not do it for you. Fighting with other Heathens on the internet will not do it for you.

If you want our Folkway to grow and advance, if you want Kindreds and Tribes, if you want our Folkway to have a future, if you want to see Heathen Hofs across the countryside, then you are going to have to make it happen. To succeed, these efforts have to be primarily driven from a grassroots level.

You have 100% control of your own efforts and deeds. If you do not have a Kindred, start one. If you have a Kindred, grow and improve it. Set goals as a Kindred, and work tirelessly to reach those goals. Work towards buying tribal land and building a Hof. Start a savings plan and start collecting dues or donations from your Kindred. Start fund-raising efforts to save money. Make things, sell things, and creatively gather the funds you need. It may take a few years, but if you stay focused and work hard it will happen.

Our Folkway is the religious underdog in this world right now. So, it has never been more important than right now that we struggle, sacrifice, and work as hard as we can. We have to set real goals, and then let nothing stand in our way of achieving those goals. Constantly reassess. Is what you are doing working? Keep what works and change what does not. Our Ancestors were always a practical and hardworking people and we have that within us. Our Ancestors banded together as kin and Tribes, and were able to accomplish great things and we have that within us. Our Ancestors understood what hard work and building one's Luck can accomplish and we have that within us.

As you move forward as a Kindred or Tribe toward your goals, communicate, gather with, and coordinate efforts with other hardworking, focused Kindreds and Tribes in your region. Share ideas with them. If they are doing something that works, take note. Get to know those other Kindreds and Tribes, and form alliances with the ones you come to trust.

This grassroots mindset is perhaps a little different than what we normally hear. I think in a very tribal and regional fashion, and do not put too much thought into "Asatru as a whole." Grassroots efforts are what work.

There is really nothing I can do about "Asatru as a whole." I can control how much work I do personally. I can influence the goals and efforts of my Tribe. I can personally communicate and meet with other Tribes in my region, and we can all influence each other. But I cannot directly affect, or be worried about "Asatru as a whole."

If what our Heathen Tribes accomplish has an indirect impact on "Asatru as a whole," then that is really nothing more than a by-product of what we do locally on behalf of our families, our Tribe, and our descendants.

It seems to me that most efforts that attempt to change "Asatru as a whole" from above, or from a national viewpoint, have not had that much of an impact.

Here in the Heartland I see Kindreds working towards building Hofs. I am seeing Kindreds and outdoor Ve's popping up where there were none. Kindreds and Tribes here in the Midwest are communicating, exchanging ideas, and setting regional goals. We hold one of the largest Heathen gatherings in the world here in the Midwest, and it is at this event that we gather together for a regional Thing.

We need to pass onto the next generation a Folkway that is bigger, stronger, and one that has tribal land and Hofs across the countryside. YOU can make that happen.

Lightning Across the Plains 2011

THE FUTURE OF HEATHENRY - GRASSROOTS OR NATIONAL?

Let us put a finer point on this issue of whether our priorities should be on local grassroots efforts or on a national organization.

I would rather have a new Heathen learning from other Heathens in his area, that he has met face to face, and can physically gather with to learn and to honor our Gods, our Ancestors, and live our way of life.

That is vastly superior to a new Heathen learning from a website, or a message board, or a national organization.

When I work on projects or efforts that will assist our region or all Heathens, I would rather work closely with Heathens in my area or region, that I have met face to face, and with whom I can physically gather. That way, I actually KNOW them and know what to expect from them in the way of collaboration.

That is vastly superior to working with people you have never met, and only know from on-line interactions or because you are both a member of the same national organization.

When I form an alliance with another Heathen or Tribe, I want to make that alliance with Heathens in my area or region, that I have met face to face, and with whom I can physically gather. That way, the alliance is based on a real relationship, and real trust. This is especially true of anyone with whom I am going to enter an oathed or committed alliance.

That is vastly superior to forming alliances with people you have never met, and only know from on-line interactions or because you are both a member of the same national organization.

If my Tribe is going to expend time and resources (including money) assisting anyone, I would rather it be for Heathens in my area or region, that I have met face to face, and with whom I can physically gather. That way I know I am helping an individual or a Tribe that, were the tables turned, would help me or my Tribe.

That is vastly superior to assisting people you have never met, and only know from on-line interactions or because you are both a member of the same national organization.

When I spend my money assisting someone in reaching their goals (building a Hof, buying land, etc.) I would rather it be on Heathens in my area or region, that I have met face to face, and with whom I can physically gather. That way I know my money is going to be spent wisely before I give it.

That is vastly superior to giving your money to people you have never met, and never interacted with face to face. You may like their on-line persona, but do you really know them? Can you really trust them with your gift of treasure?

When I travel with my family and Tribe to a gathering, I would rather it be with Heathens in my area or region. Heathens I can gather with again and again, because we are close enough to gather multiple times throughout the year and form good relationships and strong bonds.

That is vastly superior to traveling across the whole country once a year to meet Heathens you may or may not ever see again due to the vast distances you must travel.

For me, the future of Asatru is self-evident. It is tribal. It is grassroots. It is regional. It is real people meeting face to face, and forming real relationships.

If I am wrong and the future of Heathenry is in the hands of national organizations, let us all pay our $25 membership fees to one of the national organizations, jump on-line and immerse ourselves in internet-Heathenry, and travel once a year to meet with people who live 1000's of miles from us and whom we will likely never see again. To top it all off, we can all develop a completely unreasonable level of loyalty to an organization or a man we have never even met. It that really where the reconstructed world-view of our Ancestors leads us?

No. Let us focus on the real future of Heathenry.

RISING TO THE CHALLENGE

Are efforts to reclaim and reconstruct our native Folkway hopeless?

Recently, over at the Heathengods.com message board, someone started a discussion about feeling hopeless regarding the growth of Asatru or Heathenry. They asked, "*Asatru, and many other ways have been destroyed and forgotten by history. But we have a right to reclaim what once was. But mainstream society's logic instead sees it as 'converting to just some radical fringe movement,' ignoring that everyone in the world once was pagan. So how can we possibly reclaim, in a widespread cultural sense, what once was. What hope is there for paganism in the mainstream world?*"

My answer to this is simple. If I was the only Heathen on earth, I would still be Heathen. If it was illegal to be Heathen, I would still be Heathen. If they were burning Heathens, I would still be Heathen. I do not have a hopeless bone in my body.

Let me explain how this works. It is called Luck. It is probably the most powerful thing that a man can possess and use. Nothing can stand against it. Among our Ancestors, armies would flee if a King known to have Luck was among the opposing force. Men would go to a Chieftain or a Godhi known to have Luck, and ask for a Rede (advice) from that man so that they could travel forth with some of his Luck. A group of people can work hard, make good decisions, and collectively build Luck. Here is a story about Luck, and what it can accomplish.

In 2007, there was no Kindred in Kansas City. There were no study groups, no Heathen Pubmoots. There was nothing Heathen here. It took me over 2 months, just to find one other Heathen here in the area – and he lived an hour from me. Sounds pretty hopeless, does it not? But, I took it as a challenge. Almost everything worth accomplishing is a challenge.

I met with the one other Heathen I had found. We discussed what we wanted and made plans. We scheduled a first meeting, and heavily promoted it. Ten Heathens showed up we had never met before. Five were worthy and stable, and willing to work towards starting a Kindred. These five met, and we made plans, and we worked very hard on getting to know one another and building strong bonds between us. We carefully guarded our efforts from outside disruption and worthless people.

We held open events, and pushed away those that were chaotic, unstable, or not serious about Heathenry. We welcomed in those that had something to contribute to our efforts. We held study group sessions, and learned. We held Fainings to our Gods, and honored them. We sat in Symbel together, and mingled Wyrd. We looked out for each other, and worked to understand how to grow together as a chosen family. We eventually took oaths to one another, and established tribal Thew.

We built the heathengods.com resource website. We put 1000's of hours into gathering materials for the free on-line Temple Library, the Asatru Artwork Archive, and discussing things and answering questions on the message board there. We have published books. Some of these books we wrote, though several were out-of-print and in the public domain. We started a Worldwide Heathen Map, and encouraged others to start new Kindreds in their areas.

Over time, our spouses and children became involved in the Kindred. We attracted more members to our effort. These new members were people who saw we were serious and accomplishing something with our hard work, and who wanted to be apart of what we were doing. Sure we ran into roadblocks, and conflict, and even internal problems. But we kept calm, were Heathen in all things, and worked our way through our problems.

We traveled as a Kindred to meet other Heathens. Traveled 8 hours this way. 4 hours that way. 3 hours the other way. Plus a yearly trip that is 16 hours one way. We gathered with other Kindreds. Got to know them, and built bonds with them face-to-face. We learned from them and they learned from us. We formed alliances with other Kindreds and Tribes. We scheduled and planned our own regional gathering, Lightning Across the Plains, and worked hard to make it well planned, well executed, and well attended. We followed through on everything we have committed to, worked enormously hard, made good decisions, and all of these things built our Luck.

Within three year of starting our kindred, Jotun's Bane Kindred had NINE oathed members. A wonderful number. As of this writing, our Tribe brings together eight households, and 24 people. In 2007, none of this existed.

Just a handful of years since of founding our kindred, the Temple of Our Heathen Gods is one of the largest and most used resource websites by Heathens and Asatruars. The Worldwide Heathen Map is connecting Heathens all over the world. People can go to Amazon or Barnes & Noble and buy the Culture of the Teutons, both volumes of the Saga Hoard, as well as the Heathen Gods, Heathen Families, and

Heathen Tribes books. Over a thousand people have download the free digital version of the Heathen Gods book. In 2007, none of this existed.

Just a handful of years later, Lightning Across the Plains is one of the largest Heathen gatherings in the world. It is regularly attended by 225 to 240 people from across the Midwest. Lightning Across the Plains is the site of the Regional Midwest Thing, which allows heathen individuals, families, and Kindreds to work together for the benefit of our region. In 2007, none of this existed.

Just a handful of years later, we are legally a "church" in the State of Missouri. We are within just a few years of buying and owning land as a Kindred. Then a Hof and Hall will be built. Our Hof and Hall will become a gathering place and a resource for Heathens from across the Midwest. In 2007, none of this existed.

So, what is there to be hopeless about? We are reclaiming what once was. We are working together as a Tribe for our families, our Tribe, and our region. We work enormously hard. We make good decisions. We set goals and reach them. We keep our word. Through these actions, we have built our Luck.

Will Heathenry be a "mainstream" religion before I die? Who really cares? If I based my religious beliefs and world view on what was "Mainstream," I would go to a Lutheran or Baptist church every Sunday. Being Heathen is about honoring the true Gods of our People, and respecting our Ancestors and the Vaettir. We do this, because we know them to be real and worth honoring. They are our Elder Kin. Whether it is Mainstream or Fringe, and what other people think of it, does not really change any of that.

We are facing an enormous challenge in reclaiming our Folkway. There is no room in this effort for sitting around feeling hopeless. When my kids and grand-kids speak of me, they will speak of how I rose to that challenge. They will speak of me, my wife, and the members of Jotun's Bane Kindred, and they will raise horns and toast all of the hard work we put into rebuilding our Faith. Into building our Hof and Hall. Into advancing Heathenry among our Folk.

If you are reading this, I hope your children and grandchildren will have similar good things to say about you. The details will not be the same, of course. But I hope they have the same glow in their eye, as they raise a horn to your efforts and accomplishments on their behalf.

TERMINOLOGY
"KINDRED" VS. "TRIBE"

What is the difference between a Kindred and a Tribe? I am asked this terminology question often enough that I thought a short essay on how we use the terms might be in order.

The term "Kindred" is the commonly used term for a group of Heathens that gather regularly in a particular city or town. The word Kindred refers to the kinship between them. Some Kindreds have an oathed commitment, while others are less defined. Some Heathens refer to their Kindred as their "chosen family." Gathering as a Kindred, allows those involved to work hard together, watch out for each other, and build collective Luck.

Some Kindreds consist of individuals that come together once or twice month. Sometimes we jokingly refer to this as "five guys in a basement," because it consists of 5 individuals who interact together as a Kindred, without their spouses or children really being involved. It is more of a Heathen "club" that individuals join, and it is sort of their "activity" to do separate from their families. Like an over-grown personal hobby.

Other Kindreds bring together whole families into one group. The spouses are there. The children are there. Literally, their Heathen group is a major part of the lives of all the families involved. These Kindreds, I refer to as "Tribes." When a Tribe gathers together, several families are there in their entirety, the adults are talking, cooking, crafting, planning, learning, and laughing, while the kids are running around playing in the background or involved in the Tribe's activities.

For me the word "Kindred" is not really big enough to contain the idea of 20 or 30 Heathens, making up 6 or 7 families, gathered together into a committed group. For me, this is a "Tribe."

Jotun's Bane Kindred grew into a Tribe. We do not plan on changing our name to Jotun's Bane Tribe, but we do consider ourselves a Tribe at this point in our growth.

TO OATH OR NOT TO OATH?

When starting a Kindred, one of the questions that will need to be discussed and fully considered is whether or not it will be an "Oathed Kindred." You can find examples of long-lived and successful Kindreds of both the oathed and unoathed variety. You can also find long and heated debates on the internet as to which is better. This essay will attempt to address some of the issues to consider. Jotun's Bane Kindred is an oathed Kindred, but I realize that this may not be the right way to go for every Kindred.

IT IS YOUR KINDRED

First off, it is your Kindred and your decision as a group as to how it runs and how it is set up. It is always a good idea to look at a variety of existing Kindreds, see how they have approached the issue of Kindred oaths, and how that has worked out for them. But in the end, how your Kindred approaches the issue is up to your Kindred. Each Kindred is different. The people are different. Their needs and expectations are different. So, it is possible that oaths may work for one group, but not work for another.

DEFINING WHO IS "INNANGARTH" AND WHO IS NOT

Before you can even get to the issue of Kindred oaths, you have to examine what defines who is "in the Kindred" and who is not. Ultimately most Kindreds, whether they are oathed or not, have some way of defining who is a member and who is an outsider. Who is invited to private events and who is not. Who is trusted and who is not. Without some sort of line drawn between Innangarth and Utangarth, it is really inaccurate to even call a group a "Kindred." Without a definition of who is a member and who is not, you do not even have a group.

Now, there are some "Kindreds" that do not have a defined membership. Usually there is a person or several people at the heart of things. They announce events. People show up, some frequently, some infrequently, and some randomly. It would be much more accurate to call these loose groups a meet-up or a club, rather than a Kindred. This kind of meet-up can last a very long time, as long as the person or several people at the center of things consistently announce events and continue to attract attendees. But without any sort of commitment, it is hard to get anything done. The "membership" of the group literally shifts and changes from event to event, depending on who shows up. How can one establish Frith, loyalty, or collective

Luck if there is no commitment or strong bonds holding the group together?

So, most long-lived Kindreds – the Kindreds that get something done – have some level of commitment. This normally involves choosing who is allowed to join the group, and who is not allowed to join. It normally involves some process of joining meant to educate new members, and bring them into the culture and ways of the Kindred. There is usually a moment, whether it is a Kindred oath or not, where a person joining the Kindred is told or declared to be a member of the Kindred. This declaration can be as simple as everyone congratulating the new member and welcoming them to the group. Perhaps the Kindred bestows a special hammer to the new member, or puts his/her name and picture on their website as a member. Perhaps it is a commitment oath to the Gods or a Kindred oath to the members or the leadership of the Kindred. But this declaration of membership, defines the moment when they are considered fully a part of the Kindred's Innangarth.

A clear definition of who is in the Kindred and who is not, and an organized process for bringing new members into the Kindred, builds bonds within the Kindred. It encourages loyalty and commitment to one another as members of the group and to the leadership of the group.

WHAT ARE THE ADVANTAGES OF KINDRED OATHS?

Oaths matter to Heathens, and they should. One's honor, one's Luck, and one's Gefrain can all be seriously impacted by how one fulfills one's oaths, either positively or negatively. A man or woman of his/her word is greatly valued as a friend. Marriages are based on oaths. When we marry, we give our word in front of our Gods, our Ancestors, our families, and our friends that we will be loyal and honor our spouse. The marriage oath forms the strong foundation upon which we build our own healthy families. We know going into a marriage that there will be good times and bad times, and that marriages take effort and determination to maintain. We have a clear understanding of just how important the marriage is, so we take an oath to bind and seal that relationship.

A Kindred oath has many of the same features. We give our word in front of our Gods, our Ancestors, our families, and our friends to be loyal and honor the other members of our Kindred. The Kindred oath forms the strong foundation upon which we build our healthy Kindreds and Tribes. We know going into a Kindred oath, that there will be good times and bad times, and that Kindreds take effort and determination to maintain. We have a clear understanding of just how important the Kindred is, so we take an oath to bind and seal those relationships.

Kindred oaths allow the loyalty and consistency that allows Frith to develop within a modern Tribe. Collective Luck can be built, and even used to advance the lives of the Kindred and individual members. Kindred oaths let members know that they can count on the other members to be there through thick and thin. It allows our Heathen children to form relationships with other Heathen children within the Kindred. It facilitates long childhood friendships, that have a real chance at supporting and bolstering that next generation of Heathens for which we have worked so hard. Kindred oaths can be an enormously clear way of defining who is "in the Kindred" and who is not. A very satisfying way of marking that moment when a new member truly becomes a part of the Kindred's trusted Innangarth.

IS EVERY KINDRED OATH FULFILLED?

Nope. Oaths are not always held. Married spouses can fail to uphold their marriage oaths, and Kindred members can fail to uphold their Kindred oaths. Human beings are not perfect. People change. Circumstances can change or directly intervene, and thus undermine a Kindred oath. Some people are not quite as serious about the Kindred or Heathenry as they portrayed themselves to be, though some are very good at faking it for awhile.

One thing to keep in mind about oaths, is the fact that the only oaths you have any control over at all, are your own oaths. You cannot control what other people think and do. You can only control your own choices and your own deeds. You cannot make someone else fulfill an oath.

So again, much like a marriage oath, it is extremely important to get to know the people with which you hope to share a Kindred oath. You should know everything good about them, and everything bad. You should build close friendships with them before taking a Kindred oath with them. You should make sure that everyone involved knows exactly what the oath means, how important it is, and that they are taking it just as seriously as you do.

If someone holds to very few commitments in their life, why would you expect them to treat a Kindred oath any differently? If they are enormously irresponsible or disloyal in other relationships in their life, then why would you expect them to treat you any differently? Before involving yourself in a Kindred oath, be diligent and wise in your choices.

TO OATH OR NOT TO OATH?

When starting a new Kindred, the decision as to how to structure and build your group is something that has to be discussed and approached in a methodical way. The level of commitment that everyone expects from each other should be decided. What you hope to accomplish generally as a Kindred should be worked out. Ultimately, it is each Kindred's choice whether they want to build on the foundation of a Kindred oaths, or if some other approach will work for them.

But with the right people, in the right circumstances, with similar goals and expectations, there is no stronger foundation to build on than a Kindred oath.

DEVELOPING TRIBAL THEW

Every Kindred or Tribe has Thew, whether they realize it not. Thew represents the collective customs, history, traditions, and expectations of the Kindred toward its members, the members toward the Kindred, and the members toward each other. Thew is very fluid and organic, and every decision or action taken by Kindred members or the Kindred as a whole, adds to the depth and complexity of the Kindred's Thew. Whether a Kindred acknowledges they have "Thew" or calls it "Thew," it still plays a role in everything they do, and it is advantageous to understand how it works and how to actively develop it.

Thew is not the same as written rules or bylaws. Rules and bylaws are somewhat static in nature, and by their very nature cover only a limited number of specific circumstances. While a small portion of a Kindred's Thew may be codified within a Kindred's bylaws, the vast majority of Thew remains as unwritten understandings between Kindred members

Thew develops in various ways. Thew develops for small insignificant matters and large important matters. It develops for Kindred-wide issues and inter-personal issues within the Kindred. It develops for secular matters and for matters that are more spiritual in nature. It develops from practical experience and from intellectual study. There is really no area of human interaction, decision-making, or action within a Kindred that is not affected in some way by Thew.

THE INITIAL THEW OF A NEW KINDRED

When a Kindred is in the formational process and still very new, the Thew of that Kindred will be somewhat undeveloped. Nearly every new situation or choice the Kindred faces is something new to them.

On which day of the week should we hold a majority of our events? Where do we meet? What sorts of activities do we do as a group? How do we decide? What if we disagree? When should we hold Blots or Fainings? How do we communicate with or treat someone coming to an event for the first time? Are our Kindred feasts pot-luck or does the host provide everything? Who provides the mead for Symbel? During Symbel, do we toast in turns going around the circle, or raise a horn and wait to be recognized by the Lord of the Hall? Who is the Lord of the Hall? When we travel to a gathering, do we car-pool or travel there individually? On a road trip do we plan for group meals for the Kindred or does each family bring its own food? When a security problem develops at an event who handles it? You can go on and on with these questions. Basically, everything is up-in-the-air when a Kindred is new.

So, very early on some important conversations need to take place within the formational Kindred. Everyone involved in forming the Kindred should be present for these conversations, and some basic understandings need to be formed. Will the Kindred have a Chieftain and/or Godhi and/or Thyle? What responsibilities will each of these positions hold? How will decision-making take place within the Kindred? How will Kindred-related problems we resolved? How will interpersonal problems be resolved? Is your Kindred more of a war-band, a family, or a Tribe? How family-oriented is your Kindred, and what sorts of Kindred events will you hold?

From these conversations and understandings reached within the Kindred, the early Thew of the Kindred is formed. For instance, if the Kindred sits and discusses a certain commitment level they expect from their members, and everyone agrees to a certain level of commitment with specific examples of what actions represent that level of commitment, this becomes Thew. It is an existing understanding between members, and when a member strays from this understanding the Kindred will work to correct the problem and bring that member back in line with the Kindred's Thew.

If the Kindred discusses at length how they will make decisions within the group, what sorts of decisions must be group-wide decisions, and the steps that will be taken to reach those decisions, then this becomes Thew. When the leadership of the Kindred or an individual member strays from this understanding, the Kindred will work to correct the problem and bring its leadership back in line with the Kindred's Thew.

But keep in mind, the Thew of your new Kindred will change and evolve over time.

POSITIVE AND NEGATIVE RESULTS CAN AFFECT THEW

Thew also develops and is changed based on decisions and deeds within the Kindred, and whether those decisions and deeds work well or leave something to be desired. When a certain course-of-action is taken by the group or a member of the group, and it succeeds, it is more likely that when faced with similar circumstances that same course of action will be taken. If the original course-of-action turns out badly, it is very likely that when faced with similar circumstances a different course-of-action will be taken. Past decisions and deeds and their success level tend to inform future decisions and deeds, and this becomes a driving force in the evolution of Thew over time.

For example, if the Kindred allows a new member to join the Kindred after only knowing them a short period of time, and this turns out badly – the Kindred will likely re-examine what led to this bad result and attempt to prevent it in the future. If the Kindred decides that they did not know the new member well enough, they may decide to lengthen the time a new member must know the Kindred before they can ask to join the Kindred. They may lengthen the probationary time period that a new member must complete before he/she can become a full member of the Kindred. They may come up with new ways to interact more frequently with prospective members, thus getting to know them better.

Let us say a Kindred member falls ill and is bedridden for a week, and the Kindred checks on this Kindred member, brings him/her food and other necessities, and helps care for the Kindred member's children. If all of this goes very well, and helps build deeper bonds between everyone in the Kindred – then Thew has been established. The next time a Kindred member falls ill, it is very likely that everyone in the Kindred will follow this Thew, and help in very similar ways. If the next time a Kindred member falls ill, the Kindred does not help that Kindred member in the same way it did before, problems will arise. The fact the Kindred did not follow its own customs and traditions on this matter, is a violation of Thew that is unlikely to go unnoticed.

If the day after hosting a gathering, the Kindred reviews how the gathering went and decides they could have done A, B, and C differently – they will go to great lengths to ensure that during their next event A, B, and C are done differently. In this way Thew is constantly adjusting and changing as new circumstances and problems are faced, and the Kindred learns what works best for them.

This evolution of Thew based on experiencing both successes and failures is constantly on-going. Knowing this, when you recognize that just such a moment has taken place, it can be helpful to articulate that to the rest of your Kindred. This will allow the matter to be discussed, a consensus to be reached, and a clear and carefully considered Thew to be established.

CHANGING CIRCUMSTANCES CREATE CHANGES IN THEW

Over time, Kindreds grow, mature, and evolve. These changing circumstances necessitate the development of additional Thew and adjustments to existing Thew. A formational Kindred's Thew fits the circumstances of that Kindred at that point in time. Every time a new member or a new family become involved with the Kindred, that individual or family brings new skills, personality quirks, preferences, and ways of thinking into the Kindred. While the new member or new family will go through an enculturation process where they will learn and adapt to the Thew of the Kindred, this is a reciprocal process. The inclusion of these new members and new families will also prompt new understandings and new ways of doing things within the Kindred.

A formational Kindred may have five members, none of which are particularly focused on the runes. As such, while they may learn and respect the runes, the formational Kindred may not have a serious interest in holding rune study groups or working the runes into every aspect of what they do. But that same formational Kindred three years later may have added five new members, three of which have studied the runes heavily. It is likely that these three new members will influence how the Kindred views and uses the runes as a Kindred.

A formational Kindred may start with five members, none of which are married or have children. Thew will develop within this Kindred that will fit their circumstances at that moment. But that same formational Kindred three years later may have added several families with children to their membership. In addition, some of the original members may have gotten married and/or had children. Thew will naturally evolve over time within this Kindred that is more family-oriented, and fits their new circumstances.

This evolution of Thew based on the circumstances of the Kindred and its individual members is constantly on-going. If one understands this need for change and adaptation of Thew over time, then you can anticipate changes that will be needed, discuss them within the Kindred, and very purposefully make needed adjustments on a timely basis.

Since every Kindred has different members, different personalities involved, different circumstances, it is not only natural, but also necessary that every Kindred will have its own Thew. No two Kindreds can or should have the same Thew. By acknowledging and accepting that we will all develop our own local traditions and Thew, we allow each Kindred and Tribe to develop exactly the traditions and Thew that works best for them.

STUDY, LEARNING, AND APPLICATION
OF KNOWLEDGE AFFECTS THEW

The knowledge base of a Kindred will also change and expand over time. The members of the Kindred will read more primary sources, secondary sources, contemporary sources, and archeological information. The Kindred will likely gather for study groups and learn collectively. Individual members will also bring to the Kindred information they learn in their individual studies. As this new information and learning is applied in a constructive way to the practices, customs, and traditions of the Kindred, Thew is further altered and advanced.

Nearly all of us were raised in a culture that is thoroughly influenced and shaped by Christianity. Ongoing study and learning is necessary in our attempt to return to a worldview that more closely matches the worldview of our Heathen Ancestors and our native Folkway. Understanding this need, Kindreds should encourage their members to individually read, study, and explore the worldview of our Ancestors, and to develop Thew as a group that not only works well, but also represents traditions and a mindset that our Ancestors would likely recognize and appreciate.

EVERY KINDRED MEMBER IS BOUND BY THEW

We are all bound by the Thew of our Kindred or Tribe. We are all bound by our Tribe's traditions, or collective expectations, and our ways. Our newest member, our most tenured members, and our Kindred's leadership are all bound by Thew. You will sometimes hear someone refer to the leaders of our Kindreds as "dictators" or "cults of personality," or worse. But, a good leader serves his Tribe. A good leader is the least-free of his Tribe. A good leader is the poorest of his Tribe, in both time and treasure. A good leader carries burdens for his Tribe, that no one else in the Tribe is charged with carrying. When the leadership of a good and Frithful Kindred violates Thew, the members of that Kindred will challenge them and demand an explanation for why the leadership is acting outside of their customs and Thew.

One's position as Chieftain, Godhi, Thyle, or other position of leadership within a Kindred does not place you free of Thew. If anything, because of your position of responsibility, any violation of Thew you may commit will be noticed and challenged that much more quickly because all eyes are on you.

TEACHING THEW TO NEW MEMBERS

While WHO you let into your Kindred is important, equally important is HOW you bring them into your Kindred. An existing Kindred shares a certain culture, made up on their history, experiences, traditions, expectations, and even knowledge. They have worked together, honored their Gods and Ancestors together, learned together, suffered together, celebrated together, and all of these commonalities give the Kindred its own culture. These unwritten rules, traditions, and expectations that exist between members is the Kindred's Thew.

When a new member is being brought into your Kindred, it is important that they are brought up to speed regarding the Thew of your Kindred. Much of this they will learn by simply spending time with your Kindred, and interacting with them often over a sufficient period. But there is no reason you cannot actively and purposefully guide them through learning your Kindred's Thew. Jotun's Bane Kindred has a year-long mentoring and educational process in place for new members. An assigned mentor ensures that our Applicant Members are participating, learning, and gaining an understanding of how the Kindred works together. Our Kindred's Thyle plays a role in ensuring new members learn something of our history, experiences, and Thew.

A failure to bring new members up to speed regarding the Kindred's Thew will inevitably lead to problems within the Kindred. While growing-pains will just naturally happen within a Kindred, with a little effort much of them can be avoided.

THE RECIPROCAL EXCHANGE OF THEW FROM TRIBE TO TRIBE

Just as people can learn from one another, so can Kindreds and Tribes. If Jotun's Bane Kindred attends a regional gathering hosted by another Kindred in our region, we have the opportunity to see how they organize themselves, how they interact, what they do during Symbel and Blot, and various other aspects of their Kindred's Thew. If we see something they do that we like, we are very likely to take that home with us and try it ourselves. If it works well, it becomes incorporated into our Kindred's Thew.

This exchange of Thew is reciprocal. The Kindred hosting the event we attended, may very well attend an event hosted by Jotun's Bane Kindred. They may take ideas home with them. With gatherings here in the Midwest regularly attended by anywhere from 6 to 23 Kindreds, and gatherings being held throughout the year, this reciprocal exchange of ideas and Thew is frequent and ongoing. The reciprocal exchange of Thew from Tribe to Tribe is covered in more detail in an essay further into this collection.

IDEAS AND TIPS FOR
OPEN HEATHEN EVENTS

An open event is an event to which everyone is invited. Usually a description of the event and the date, time, and location are announced publicly, so that anyone who is interested can attend. Sometimes the location of the event is not announced publicly, and those that are interested are asked to call a phone number or send an email in order to be told where it will be held. This is a precaution that is taken when the event is at someone's home, and they would rather screen those that are interested before they tell them their address. Some Kindreds also hold "friends-only" events, which are open to people outside of their Kindred, but only people they know well and have specifically invited to attend.

Regardless of the exact type of open event, there are many good reasons for a Heathen individual or group to hold one. For the Heathen individual it is a good way to get to know other Heathens in your area. Since it is announced publicly, the Heathen individual holding an open event has a good chance of attracting some Heathens of which he/she was not even aware. Open Heathen events held by individuals can often lead to the formation of a regular study group or a new Kindred over time. Established Kindreds normally hold open events in order to spend time with other Heathens in their area, and to meet prospective new members for their Kindred.

If a Heathen individual never holds an open event, never attends a Heathen event, and never gets together with other Heathens, they are missing out on the community aspects of our Ancestors world-view. Yes, they may have non-Heathen family members, non-Heathen neighbors, and non-Heathen friends that they interact with, but that cannot fully replace face-to-face relationships with other like-minded Heathens.

If a Kindred never holds open events, and rarely ventures outside of their area to gather with other Heathens, then they tend to stagnate. With little chance of meeting new Heathens face-to-face or of exchanging ideas with other Heathens and Kindreds, they are unlikely to advance forward as a group or to play any real role in advancing our Folkway forward. I am sure there are exceptions, but in this case I believe the exceptions prove the rule.

An open Heathen event can be planned around almost any activity. Obviously, it should be something that the host individual or host

Kindred is interested in, and something that will be fun and/or meaningful. Some thought should go into the sort of person you want to attract to your Heathen event. The activity you plan your open Heathen event around will have a strong impact on who is interested in attending. For instance, if you are trying to attract Heathen families to your open event, then perhaps an open picnic would be a more appropriate choice than an open Pubmoot. What follows are various ideas for open Heathen events you could hold as an individual or a Kindred.

PUBMOOT - A pub or restaurant-bar with good food and a nice selection of beers and ales is a great place to gather, talk, joke around, and have a good time. Choose a place with a great atmosphere and a place that is quiet enough that conversation can take place. Some pubs will even have a private room you can reserve for free, as long as a certain amount of sales are made by you and your guests. Because it is taking place in a pub, it seems completely natural for people to raise a glass and make toasts or even involve everyone in a song. The downside of this sort of open event, is that it is not very family-friendly. Most pubs or restaurant-bars do allow children to be there, but there is usually not a lot for them to do in a pub. For this reason parents usually opt to get babysitters. Regardless, a Pubmoot is nearly always entertaining and a good way to get to know people.

JAVAMOOT - Coffee shops are a good place to meet for conversation, serious discussions, and more of a low key gathering. Especially if you find one that is locally owned and sort of quirky and unique, with lots of couches and personality to the place. A coffee shop is sort of nice because it is fairly casual, and it is maybe a little less intimidating for new people to go to a coffee shop in the afternoon to meet with strangers, than to go to a pub in the evening. If you find a quiet enough coffee shop, you may even be able to hold a workshop there or a discussion group. The one problem you might run into, is if your Javamoot outgrows the establishment where you hold it. Many coffee shops could probably handle 10 to 20 people, but nothing beyond that.

STUDY GROUP OR WORKSHOPS - In my book, Heathen Gods, I discussed how to start and run a Heathen study group. For the Heathen individual this is a great way to meet and get to know other Heathens in their area. The structure, form, and subject matter of the study group can vary widely. The study group can focus on discussions of specific stanzas from the Poetic Edda. Or it could take the form of a book club with open discussions of specific chapters of a specific book. Study groups can cover almost any Heathen topic, including runes, lore, history, crafts, etc. Most established Kindreds prefer to keep their study groups closed, to allow for more in-depth discussions and to build on the knowledge that each of them has gained. A Kindred would probably benefit more from organizing a one-time open workshop on a very specific topic, than attempting to host a series of open workshops.

PICNIC - An open picnic in the park is the perfect venue for families with children to attend. The optimal park will have picnic pavilions or shelters you can reserve in case the weather is less than favorable and a playground area nearby, so the kids can all play and get to know each other as well. If you have a Tafl board or two, setting those up in the shelter so those in attendance can play usually turns out well. There is nothing wrong with making the event a pot-luck feast in the park, with the host providing the main dish and the guests bringing the side dishes. Any event that is held outdoors is a great opportunity to play Kubb, or some other fun outdoor games. We almost always hold a Folk Symbel after the feast when we have an open picnic, and you can also hold a Faining or Blot in the park as part of the open event.

PAINTBALL - Nothing creates instant bonding like shooting at one another and being involved in physical competition. So an open event at a paintball course definitely fills this requirement. There are both indoor and outdoor paintball courses, so plan accordingly for your local weather. Here in Kansas City there is even a paintball field set up in an underground cave. The one problem you might run into is the high cost per person for this sort of event. At our local paintball course it costs $25 per person. That covers your entrance fee, rental on your gun and protective equipment, and your first 100 paintballs. Then you have to buy additional paintballs beyond your first 100.

CAMPING - Camping with people is a great way to get to know them. Choosing the right location for the campout is very important. If you or someone in your Kindred has land to camp on, that would be optimal. But you can also look into pagan campgrounds in your area, State Parks, and other camping opportunities. A camping area where there are things to do (hiking, swimming, sites the see, etc.) will make the event more fun and will attract more participants. Limiting it to two days and one night is probably wise. You can either have people provide their own food or charge a small fee to attend so that you can provide all the food. This option, like the open picnic option, provides a great opportunity for playing Kubb, setting up some Tafl boards, holding a Faining or Blot, and having a Symbel around the campfire at night.

ATTEND A SPORTING EVENT - Going to watch baseball, football, hockey or some other spectator sport can be a fun way to get people out of their house and getting to know one another. If you stick with general admission, you will not have to coordinate reserving a bunch of tickets and asking people to reimburse you. Though, if you get a big enough group together you can get a discount on the tickets and other deals. It is not a bad idea to get everyone together for a meal at a restaurant before or after the event (depending on what time of the day the event is), so that everyone has more of a chance to talk. Most sporting events are pretty loud, and sitting in seats in long rows does not facilitate a lot of conversation.

ATTEND A NORDIC FEST - In some areas, there is an annual Nordic Fest. Sometimes they are fairly small and you will not even know about them unless you actually ask around and do some research on the internet. Attending this sort of event is fun. They usually have traditional Scandinavian foods, dancers, and maybe even a couple of guys dressed up as Vikings. Normally, there are numerous booths featuring traditional Scandinavian crafts. If it is a small Nordic Fest, the additional people you bring to the event will help support it and keep it going.

ATTEND A REN FAIR - Ren Fairs are basically commercial enterprises and I hesitate to suggest this idea, because I have known some people who tend to see what we do as Heathens as something similar to a Ren Fair. This is completely false, and I hate the idea of adding to that confusion by holding an open Heathen event at a Ren Fair. But, Ren Fairs are fun events to attend and there are often craft items available at the Ren Fair that are of interest to Heathens. So, it is an option.

HOST A KUBB TOURNAMENT - You could hold a Kubb tournament in your back yard or a local park. Investing in or making a couple of Kubb sets is not very expensive. Once you get people playing Kubb, it can be rather addicting and a lot of fun. Throw in a pot-luck-dinner afterward and possibly a Folk Symbel, and you have an open event that people will really enjoy.

FAINING/BLOT AND SYMBEL - I am going to discuss holding an open Faining or Blot, and some tips for holding a Symbel at an open event in future essay. But I wanted to at least mention here that holding an open Faining or Blot for the Heathens in your area can help build bonds between them and start them down the path of cooperation and friendship. When we hold an open Faining, we almost always follow it with a pot-luck feast, and then a Folk Symbel.

I think the ideas and tips in this essay just scratch the surface. There is one final thing to keep in mind. Whatever sort of open Heathen event you decide to hold, make sure you are committed to doing it well. It must be well-conceived, planned and organized properly, heavily promoted, and well executed. A quality open event can be the spark that begins a Kindred or pushes an existing Kindred to the next level. A disorganized or poorly done event can have the exact opposite effect.

HOW TO ORGANIZE A
SUCCESSFUL PUBMOOT

Jotun's Bane Kindred holds an open Pubmoot every-other-month so that we can gather with others Heathens from our area and those within driving distance of Kansas City. This allows us to see old friends and to meet Heathens we have never before had the chance to meet. Some of the Heathens that attend our open Pubmoots never intend to join our Kindred, while some of the Heathens that attend do so in order to get to know us better and see if someday they may want to request to join our Kindred. There is the added bonus that our Kindred members enjoy the open Pubmoots quite a lot as well.

I occasionally receive requests for information on how to organize a Pubmoot, and so this essay will cover how we do it and why we do it in that way. I am sure there are other ways to hold a Pubmoot, but what follows is what has worked well for Jotun's Bane Kindred.

CHOOSE AN APPROPRIATE LOCATION – You will want to choose a location that best facilitates what you are trying to accomplish. You should choose a central location that is easy to find. It should be as clean and safe as possible, and have room for your group to sit together. It is better if the location has a nice selection of beers and other spirits, in case attendees want to drink. It is also a good idea to choose a location with good food and it is an extra bonus if they have a really popular food special on the day you choose for your Pubmoot. You are going to want people attending your Pubmoot to be able to converse and joke around, so do not choose a location that is extremely noisy with other people or loud music.

PICK A GOOD DATE AND TIME - Choosing the day, time, and location of the first meeting is very important. We schedule our Pubmoots on Sunday evenings at 6:00 PM since this seems to be a time of the week when not much is happening. We do not want to compete with everyone's Friday and Saturday night plans. But, holding it on a Sunday evening makes it harder for guests to travel even an hour or two to attend the event, because many of them work on Monday morning. These are some of the considerations you have to keep in mind when scheduling your open Pubmoot. It needs to be scheduled at a date and time that works for you and the Heathens you are hoping to attract to your open Pubmoot.

GO THERE ON A DRY-RUN - Once you have chosen a location, a day of the week, and a time, visit the location on a dry-run on that day and time. Make sure the environment on that day and time will work for your Pubmoot. If they have an boisterous Irish Band playing on that day and time every week, you are not going to have much conversation at your Pubmoot. If they have karaoke night on that day and time, you need to change you plans. There is no reason to leave it to chance, when a quick visit from you prior to announcing and promoting the Pubmoot, will let you know if you have made a good choice or not.

CONTACT THE LOCATION - You will want to call the location prior to your event, and let them know what you are planning. If you have a guesstimate as to how many will be attending, it is good to tell them. They may normally under-staff on that evening, and your call might ensure they have enough waiters or waitresses to handle the additional business you are bringing to them. If you want to have some tables or a room reserved, inquire about it when you call and see if it can be arranged. By calling them and making sure they know you are holding a Pubmoot there, it allows them to answer questions about the event or direct people to you, if anyone calls them asking about the Pubmoot.

PROMOTE THE PUBMOOT - You have to do more than just schedule the Pubmoot. You need to promote it. To do this, set the event at least a month in advance. If it is your first open Pubmoot, there is nothing wrong with setting it up to two months in advance. Announce the open Pubmoot in every venue possible. Post it on Yahoo e-lists in your region, set up a Facebook event and invite every Heathen you know in your region to attend, post it on message boards, send out emails, and do everything else you can electronically to make sure every Heathen in your area and region knows about it. You can go further, of course, and put up signs at book stores and coffee shops. You can call and personally invite Heathens you already know in your area. You have nothing to lose and everything to gain from getting creative with how you get the word out about your open Pubmoot.

In your messages about the open Pubmoot, describe the event fully. Make it clear in your announcements and promotions exactly what you are looking for and the purposes of the Pubmoot. Make it very clear that this is a "Heathen" event. You can go further and clearly state that the Pubmoot is for "long-time Heathens, new Heathens, and the Heathen-curious." If you receive inquiries from generalist pagans and Wiccans, tell them very directly that it is a Heathen event. I have seen both Pubmoots and Study Groups destroyed by being overly permissive on who can attend. One enormously pushy non-Heathen who will not shut up and will not go away, will chase off ten serious Heathens if they see that you are allowing that person to continually spoil the event. If 50% of the people who show up for the Pubmoot are non-Heathen and this happens repeatedly, non-Heathens will quickly become 100% of the people who attend the Pubmoot – because the Heathens will find another way to spend their time. Supportive or curious non-Heathens can be allowed to attend in limited numbers, especially if they fully understand and respect that the Pubmoot is a Heathen event.

Once you begin promoting the open Pubmoot, you may get a lot of messages from people asking you to change the day or time of the Pubmoot. Do not change course mid-stream. Once you have set the location, date, and time for that Pubmoot and have begun promoting it, do not start shuffling it around to please people who have scheduling conflicts. Moving the event around after it has already been announced makes people absolutely crazy. Invariably, when you change the day or time for one person who could not make it on the day and time you originally chose, you end up screwing over the people who would have made it on that original day and time.   It will appear enormously disorganized and indecisive to start moving the day and time around when you have already announced it.

If it becomes clear a different day and time would work better and attract many more Heathens, then change the day and time for the next open Pubmoot. The one you have not even announced yet.

THE NIGHT OF THE PUBMOOT - First of all, arrive early for your own event if possible. This will allow you to complete some tasks that will improve the success of your open Pubmoot. When you arrive, make sure the location's hostess, wait staff, manager, and bartenders know you are having a Pubmoot that night, and that they know where in the establishment you will be gathering. When someone comes in looking a little lost, the employees of the location are usually very good about bringing these lost Heathens right over to where you are sitting. But they cannot do this, if you do not tell or remind them about your event.

Grab the tables or area where you will be holding the Pubmoot. If you are holding it in a reserved room or area of the location, set things up the way you want them to look. With the permission of your waiter or waitress, rearrange the tables and chairs if you feel that will help the Pubmoot work better. A restaurant/bar is primarily structured around its retail customers. You are bringing in a group event, so there is the possibility you will be asked to pay a fee to hold your event there.

It is never a bad thing to bring some "Heathen items" to the Pubmoot to show any new Heathens that attend. A copy of the Poetic and Prose

Eddas. A copy of Essential Asatru or Our Troth. You can even bring pamphlets about your Kindred or other topics to distribute.

AT THE PUBMOOT - You know what they say about first impressions. Your Pubmoot will be a first impression situation for some of the Heathens in attendance. So, communicate clearly and get everything across that you want to get across. As the host of the Pubmoot, I always get up and greet everyone in attendance. I welcome them and attempt to set them at ease. I check back with them throughout the night, and make sure they are talking with others in attendance and having a good time. I try to sit down with everyone at some point in the night and have a few words, so that I can connect with everyone there and make sure all of them feel like they have been welcomed and appreciated for showing up. Since our Kindred is hosting the event, other members of the Kindred do many of these same things to get to know any new people and make them feel welcome.

It is never a bad idea to share your contact information and to ask for contact information from the new people that attend. This could be something as simple as your e-mail, but if you are comfortable giving out your phone number, that can be a good idea as well.

Since it is a Heathen Pubmoot, encourage or start discussions about our Gods, our Ancestors, or our Folkway in general. At the very least, you can ask them if they have any questions about Heathenry – especially if they are new.

A Pubmoot that turns into a drunken mess is very likely going to limit the number of return visitors. So, as the host or the hosting Kindred it is important that you keep your drinking reasonable. This keeps your own behavior in check and it sets a tone for the guests that are present. Do all you can to ensure no problems develop, and if you observe or hear of a problem developing address it quickly and fairly. If someone is misbehaving and needs to leave, then ensure they depart with the least amount of disruption and drama.

IT IS JUST AN OPEN PUBMOOT - Keep in mind you are holding an "open" event. So, you are going to get some great Heathens showing up – but you are going to get some odd-balls showing up as well. One of the great benefits of a Pubmoot, is the fact it takes place at a pub and not in your home. So, do not sweat the odd-balls, as long as they behave themselves. Talk to them a bit. Some of them will be a lot more "normal" than your first impression suggested. As odd as some of them can be, they can sometimes be the source of interesting conversation. A Pubmoot is a big fun mess of eating, drinking, talking, and lots of laughter. So, do not get upset if someone shows up you would not have necessarily invited. As long as they behave, go with the flow. If you are setting the proper tone, and making the "Heathen" nature of the event clear, the odd-balls usually take care of themselves by not showing up again.

TAKE SMOKERS INTO CONSIDERATION - Here in Kansas City, all of our bars and restaurants are non-smoking. This can be a problem. Your smokers are going to smoke. Period. This can cause your Pubmoot to become essentially two Pubmoots. You have the non-smokers hanging out inside and the smokers are all out front or on the patio smoking for at least some small part of the evening, and often a large part of the evening. When weather permits, consider holding your open Pubmoot on or near the pub's outdoor patio area, so the non-smokers and smokers can be part of one cohesive and unified Pubmoot. Much of this depends on the location you choose, but I can tell you from experience that it is definitely something to consider.

TOASTING, SONGS, AND POETRY - Something we have encouraged at our open Pubmoots is toasting. Every so often we raise our glasses and someone will loudly say, "A toast is being made," or "A horn is raised." Then we will make a toast to our Gods, to our guests, to our Kindred, or to anything else that seems appropriate at the time. We encourage guests to do the same, if they feel comfortable doing so. We find that new guests rarely do so, but regular attendees will occasionally make a toast. The toasting really seems to improve the focus and meaning of the open Pubmoot, and reminds us why we are all there.

Occasionally we will announce that a specific Pubmoot is going to be focused on poetry. Several of us will prepare Heathen-oriented poems to read or recite from memory and we welcome our guests to bring poems of their own to share. There are times when people will prepare a song to sing at the Pubmoot. The first couple of times you do this it can feel a little awkward or strange. But over time it has become one of my favorite parts of our Pubmoots.

KEEPING THE PUBMOOTS GOING - The most important thing to ensure, is that your Pubmoots are positive, energetic, and organized. Heathens are unlikely to return if your Pubmoots are boring or seem disorganized. Having a regular schedule is a good way to keep attendance regular. Over time, you can have special Pubmoots. We hold a Pubmoot every year that is dedicated to the Einherjar, and the toasts, poems, and songs that are shared that night focus on the brave battle dead. It is fine to experiment and add things to your Pubmoot that will make them more meaningful and entertaining. You should continue the promotion of your Pubmoots even after it has become established. You never quite know who your Yahoo e-list announcement, Facebook Event, or message board post will reach.

DO NOT BECOME DISCOURAGED - Jotun's Bane Kindred's first Pubmoot was attended by the five members of our Kindred at that time, and only three other people. That was a good start. Your open Pubmoots should be organized in a way that they are fun no matter how many or how few people show up. There will be Pubmoots that are sparse in attendance, especially early on in your efforts. If you keep at it, stay on a regular schedule, and ensure that your Pubmoots are fun and worth attending, over time they will grow. We had a Pubmoot this year where 43 Heathens were present and another with 38 Heathens. Most Pubmoots will start small and grow in attendance over time.

Many of the principles and ideas expressed in this essay about a Pubmoot can also be used for other types of open events. It is possible to have an open Javamoot at a local coffee shop or an open picnic at a local park, if a pub environment is not optimal for your members or the Heathens in your area. You can also vary things up a bit, and have a Pubmoot one month, an open Javamoot the next, and an open picnic during months with good weather.

RAISING AWARENESS AMONG "NORMAL" FOLKS

THE PROBLEM AT HAND

I was 37 years old before I even heard of Asatru. I had lived 37 years with no clue that anyone was actively honoring the Northern European Gods. That was 25-plus years of being agnostic – searching, looking, lost, and for the most part, spiritually empty. The way I found Asatru was completely by chance. It is likely I could have lived my entire life without hearing of it. Many people in our culture do live their whole lives without knowing that Asatru or Heathenry even exists. That is not an acceptable situation to my way of thinking.

Heathenry is not mainstream, and in my estimation we are no more mainstream than we were 10 years ago. There are about 1,000,000 people in the Kansas City area. Jotun's Bane Kindred, the only Kindred in the Kansas City area, has 24 people including our spouses and children. If you throw in the Heathens here in Kansas City we know about, at most we are talking an additional 30 Heathens. Many of these additional 30 are not "actively" Heathen, but let us throw them in for illustrative purposes. Even stretching our numbers in this way, we come up with about 54 Heathens among the 1,000,000 people here in the Kansas City area. That is about 0.00005% of the population. Even if we double our numbers, we are still about 0.0001% of the population.

My 10-year-old son Nathan asked me once, "How many other Heathens are their dad?" I told him it was less than 1% of the population. He said, "Oh, my Gosh!" He was shocked. So, what can we do to raise awareness of Heathenry? Our Folk should at least know that Asatru/Heathenry is an option. They should at least know it exists and that it is their native Folkway. Among our own People our Gefrain is minuscule. Non-existent in effect. What can we do today, so that when my grandson asks my son how many Heathens there are, he can answer with a number significantly larger than the answer I gave my son?

Currently, we seem to reach the Wiccan-types just fine. We are pretty good at outreach among the SCA and reenactment enthusiasts. Heathenry is clearly known in our prisons. Many good Heathens have come from Wicca, the SCA, and prison. So, I am not attacking or denigrating these "gateways" into Heathenry. They have existed as a source of new Heathens, and they will continue to serve as a source of new Heathens. As an "alternative" or "fringe" religion, it is natural that we are drawing from "alternative" subcultures of our greater population. We are promoting ourselves within and drawing from fringe groups.

But, we need the blue-collar metal-worker who has been dissatisfied with Christianity for years, and has felt something missing. How do we reach that guy and let him know we exist?

We need the accountant living in the suburbs with a wife and three kids, who has been agnostic for years because he knows Christianity is not for him, but who thinks Christianity is his only real choice. How do we let that guy know he has a better choice, with his native Folkway?

We need the stay-at-home mom with a garden in the backyard, who loves folk-medicine and folklore taught to her by her Pennsylvania Dutch Grandmother. How do we reach this woman, and educate her about how much she is still missing?

We need to find ways to reach people in the mainstream, suburban families, and the great masses of our Folk that we currently do not reach in significant numbers. They are out there. They are dissatisfied with the foreign religions that have been pushed on them. They are leading stable, responsible lives. But their lives would be greatly enriched by a return to the Ways of their Ancestors, if they only knew they were an option. How do we reach these non-Wiccan, non-SCA, non-prison, everyday people and their families? They are members of our Folk, who are feeling that pull to "come home," and some of them do not even know where "home" is yet. How do we let them know?

RAISING AWARENESS IS IMPORTANT

I think our Kindreds would be much healthier if they were drawing from a larger pool of people. The more people you encounter who are interested in Heathenry, the more well-adjusted people you will have to choose from. The more of our Folk that come home to Heathenry, the ratio of well-adjusted people to weirdos within Heathenry will also improve. I know this sounds like a fairly harsh concept, but I believe there is truth in it.

Let us approach this issue from another direction. If you are community building and your group needs two new people, would you rather select these two people from among four people that show up now and again at your open events or from among fifty people that attend your open events? Obviously, all things being equal, you will get better candidates choosing from a pool of fifty people.

Our small numbers are actually a hurdle to our Folk coming home to their native Folkway. There are many towns and cities across our nation that do not have an active Kindred, or even any Heathen individuals living there. Even if one of our Folk learned about Heathenry, their choices for real social interaction with other Heathens can be fairly limited. Yes, they could start their own study group or Kindred. Yes, they could practice our way of life in a solitary fashion. But, the community aspects of our religion are very meaningful and powerful, and it is clear that the sparse population of Heathens affects our ability to grow as a Folkway.

Our small numbers mean that many cities that do have Kindreds, only have one Kindred. If a Heathen does not fit in well with this particular Kindred, the Heathen does not have any other ready options. Our small numbers puts quite a bit of pressure on our children. They go to schools, watch television, and are exposed to wider cultural forces that are 99.9% something other than Heathen. Whether we are willing to face it or not, this has an impact our children. It will assuredly affect the number of our children that will remain with Heathenry as they grow into adults. It just will.

Now, I do not think we need a Heathen mega-church. I am a strong believer in the power of the Kindred and Tribe. There is a built-in critical-mass point for our sort of close-knit oathed Tribe. That critical-mass point lies somewhere between 10 and 20 oathed members. Including unoathed members, such as unoathed spouses and children, this critical-mass is somewhere between 25 to 40 total people involved in the Tribe. When you reach that critical mass point, then other Tribes need to begin growing in that same area. It will be a testament of our success in making Heathenry more mainstream, when there are several Tribes in Kansas City. Perhaps ten Tribes in Kansas City. Of course, the hope is that these Tribes will communicate regularly, and be aligned with each other in some fashion.

POSSIBLE METHODS FOR RAISING AWARENESS

So, what are some ways to increase Heathenry's Gefrain among our Folk that remain ignorant of its existence in the mainstream? What are some ways we can actively reach "normal" people? How do we give more of our People Asatru or Heathenry as a choice? The metal-worker. The accountant. The stay-at-home Mom. The dissatisfied Christian without Faith or satisfaction in that foreign religion, who is unaware there is another legitimate option. How do we reach them?

1. Heathens Living Openly as Heathens - If we hide our Heathenry, then regardless of how good a life we live or how admirable a person we may be, no one will know that a part of our success is our adherence to Heathen values and ways. By living openly as Heathens, we show our extended family, our friends, our neighbors, our co-workers, and anyone else that comes to know us that our way of life is strong, life-affirming, and powerful. By raising strong intact Heathen families, we show that our Folkway is family-oriented. By living openly as Heathens, we show that we do not have anything to be ashamed of or afraid of in declaring our loyalty to our Gods, our Ancestors, the Vaettir, and our native Folkway.

2. Offer Classes on Heathenry or Heathen Topics - There are many places you can organize and hold a class on Heathenry. Most community colleges have a community education component, where they will allow you to come in and teach an Asatru 101 course, or a course on Odin, or perhaps a Heathen concept. Most new age book stores will be happy to arrange a space for you to offer a course on

Heathenry. Sometimes they will charge you to hold the class, but sometimes they are willing to charge your participants for their attendance. Some stores will let you teach a class for free. A class environment is somewhat non-threatening, and often curious people will be willing to attend a class, when they may not have been willing to attend some other sort of Heathen event.

3. Presentation or Lecture at a Local Library, or Similar Venue - Explore and find ways to get your information out to a wider group of people. If you feel inclined to do what everyone else has tried, then go ahead. But also try a bunch of ideas that no one has ever tried. Blaze your own trail. Maybe the library would agree to have you in for a presentation on the Poetic Edda? Maybe you could offer a talk about our traditional Folk Religion at a local Nordic Festival? Look at coffee shops, historical societies, mainstream book stores, and wherever else you can think of for opportunities to talk to people who have perhaps never even heard of Heathenry.

4. Get Television, Radio, Newspaper News Coverage - Television, radio, and newspaper media reaches the mainstream. So, positive media coverage can reach a large number of the people we are seeking to reach. A successful approach to this can be contacting your media of choice during a time of the year when you are holding an event that might be interesting or seen as "quirky" in their eyes. A traditional Yule celebration would make an interesting segment on television. The origins of the Ostara celebration might draw the attention of a newspaper reporter. Some radio stations feature non-denominational religious programming with a rotating cast of ministers, priests, and rabbis. It is possible that you might be able to entice a show like that into having you on for an interview segment about a topic they find interesting.

5. Get a Television or Radio show, or a Newspaper Column - This option is a little more difficult that just getting one-time media coverage. But with a little work, who knows what you might be able to accomplish. Often, the Sunday paper will have a regular column on religion where they will have guest authors from a variety of religions write a religious article. There is a change they might run an article written by you in the paper, especially if it is dynamic and well-written. The radio and television show options are a little more difficult, but college radio channels are often looking for shows or concepts to fill air time, while many areas have public access television that might be an option.

6. Announce Open Events and Classes on Craig's List, an alternative Newspaper, or the Mainstream Newspaper - There are mainstream places you can announce events, such as Craig's List, the events calendar in your local paper, Meetup.com, or other places that the more mainstream members of our Folk visit for information and news. We tend to announce our open events and classes in media and internet venues that are already heavy with Heathens or Wiccans, and this is essentially fishing in that same old pond. Think outside the box, and find strange and ingenious ways to get the word out about your open events and classes.

7. Podcasts or YouTube videos, if They Could be Promoted Outside Pagan Circles - We could use more Heathen podcasts and more Heathen YouTube videos, especially ones that are informative and well-done. But, we really need to figure out some ways to promote these podcasts outside of Heathen and pagan circles, and to make them accessible to people who are just coming home to Heathenry.

8. Advertising of All Sorts, Billboards, Newspaper Ads, Radio Ads, etc. - Advertising costs money. But there are relatively inexpensive advertising options that may work. I know that some of the electronic billboards along heavily traveled stretches of highway in Kansas City, can cost as little as $300 for a full month of advertising. The Heathen advertisement would be in a rotation of advertisements that are flashed on the electronic billboard, but it would provide an enormous amount of exposure. There may be other affordable options in the various types of advertising available.

9. Create a Free Pamphlet or Booklet - One could create a pamphlet or booklet that very clearly and concisely explains our religion, its origins, and why we value it. You could then distribute this material at coffee shops, bookshops, and other locations where it could left lying around as reading material. You could drop it on neighborhoods from an airplane – well, that may be going too far. I realize that pamphlets and little booklets of this nature have been created by the national organizations over the years. But if I was going to do this, I would want to distribute my own information. Not something created by someone I do not even personally know.

10. Write and Publish a Concise Heathenry 101 Book that has Folkish Leanings - Make the book comprehensive, but ensure that it represents the Folkish and tribal approach that is missing in other Asatru 101 and Heathenry 101 books. The key would be to make the case for Heathenry in a format that is very approachable for the average person.

There is a lack of knowledge out there that we even exist. This is a problem, and I have suggested why it is a problem worth solving and shared some possible ways to solve it. What ideas do you have? What would work for your Kindred in your area? There are no right or wrong answers to this. Just be creative and make things happen.

BRINGING OUR FOLK BACK TO THEIR ANCESTRAL WAYS

It is one of those "cardinal rules" of Asatru, that "Heathens do not proselytize." This has always left me with this impression that we, as Heathens, are not allowed to tell people about our religion – and we certainly cannot tell them that our religion would be better for them than whatever they are doing now. This impression is reinforced by the occasionally warnings I will receive that I am either dangerously close to proselytizing or outright proselytizing. But, let us get a little deeper into this issue.

The essay preceding this one was titled, "Raising Awareness of Heathenry Among Normal Folks." It discussed various methods we could use to educate non-Heathen members of our Folk about our Gods and our Ancestral Ways.

Earlier in the book is an essay called, "Your Ancestors Were Heathen," that explained to any non-Heathen members of our Folk, that regardless of their current religious beliefs – their Ancestors were Heathen. It explained that modern Heathenry is attempting to reconstruct our native Folkway.

These are the kinds of essays where I will occasionally receive the knee-jerk reaction from some Heathens, suggesting that what I am suggesting is "proselytizing," and that we as Heathens should never proselytize. Usually the person suggesting this, goes further and suggests that proselytizing is something that Christians do and it is one of the reasons they left Christianity. It is implied that I am crossing a line that should not be crossed.

MYTH #1
PROSELYTIZING IS A DIRTY WORD

First off, let us look at the definition of the word "proselytizing." A proselyte is "a person who has changed from one opinion, religious belief, sect, or the like, to another; a convert." To proselytize is "to convert or attempt to convert as a proselyte; to recruit."

The word itself is very simple and straight-forward. It is the simple act of trying to convince someone to come over to your side of things. It is most often used in relation to religion, but it can also be used in relation to politics, debates, business meetings where sides have been drawn over an issue, etc.

Now many people read all sorts of other meanings into the word. Pushiness. Manipulation. Fear-Mongering. Threats. Passing Judgment "Quoting Scripture." Bothering People. Insulting People. But these meanings that we often see read into the word, have more to do with HOW someone proselytizes – the methods they employ – than it does with the actual meaning of the word.

There was a time when nearly all of our Folk were of our Folkway. But that time was taken away from us. Modern Heathens are but a very small percentage of our Folk, with the vast majority of them being Christians, Agnostics, or Atheists. Most of our Folk do not even know they have a native Folkway as a religious option. Most of them do not even know Heathenry exists. We should communicate to non-Heathens who we are, how much Heathenry means to us, and how well it works for our families and ourselves. I feel it is my obligation to let non-Heathen members of our Folk know about our Gods and our Ancestral Ways. I personally did not even know Heathenry existed, until I was 37 years old. We must do better than that.

Now, that does not mean we should be pushy, manipulative, fear-mongering, threatening, or bothersome in our approach to these non-Heathen members of our Folk. We should be honest, straight-forward, and simply provide the information that our current Christian-dominated culture has completely suppressed.

MYTH #2
EDUCATING PEOPLE WILL OFFEND OR CHASE PEOPLE OFF

Our Ancestors were not a quiet, meek people, constantly worried about stepping on someone's toes with a contrary opinion. They did not constantly bite their tongue for fear of offending people with the truth, and I will not do it either.

I am not suggesting we run about telling people to be Heathen or they "will go to a fiery Hell." I am not suggesting we scare people with fear-mongering that they will not see their beloved family in the afterlife, if they do not convert. I am not suggesting we tell people they are evil or reject them from our lives because they are not Heathen. I do not think we should fire people from jobs or ruin their careers because they are not Heathen. We as Heathens, do not do anything that even slightly resembles what we hate about Christian proselytizing, which happens to be the form of proselytizing with which we are almost exclusively familiar.

I am talking about sharing information with non-Heathens. Letting them know we exist. Explaining the conversion of Northern Europe to them, and the fact their Ancestors were Heathen. Describing to them what our Ways are, and why they work for us. Celebrating our Gods, and letting non-Heathens know how and why we do this. As always, we must be living good lives – lives that illustrate that our Ways truly are natural and healthy for our People.

A hard-core Christian who is satisfied with their Christianity, will likely disregard anything we say. They may even be offended that someone would dare communicate anything to them that was non-Christian. But, the satisfied Christian is really not the target of our communication efforts anyhow. They have "bought-in." They are comfortable with being in servitude to a foreign religion, and getting on their knees to a foreign god.

The target of our communications should be those members of our Folk that are dissatisfied with the foreign religion. Those that are half-living it, out of obligation or habit. Those that will literally come alive when they learn of our Ways and begin to investigate them more deeply. I reject the idea that sharing information about our Folkway with these dissatisfied members of our Folk will offend them or chase them away. We often talk about how Heathenry felt "like coming home." If we truly believe this is spiritually true, should we not trust that those we share information with will eventually feel the same way? Will not the waters of our faith run down familiar courses within them as well?

MYTH #3
CHRISTIANS DO THIS, SO WE SHOULD NOT

There is this automatic reaction among many Heathens against anything even vaguely Christian. To some degree, this automatic reaction extends to any effort to tell any non-Heathen that Heathenry is a good thing and maybe they should look into it. This reaction "against Christianity" is natural and understandable, but we need to get over it.

At some point Heathenry needs to move beyond Christianity, and not in reaction to it. We need to make sound and logical choices about our actions, that are driven by what is good for us and good for our Folk. These choices should be made free of any need to avoid anything that is even vaguely connected in some tenuous way with what Christians do. Who cares what they do? Who cares that they do it badly? That is their problem.

We need to set our own course, and do what is right for our descendents. I want my kids to live in a world where more of their Folk have returned to their ancestral Folkway. I want my grandchildren to see even more Heathens in the world – and my great-grandchildren to see even more. This is something we can do. If we communicate properly, if we work tirelessly, if we live lives that show we walk the walk, as well as talk the talk – then Heathenry will grow as it should. These Ways we follow are natural to our Folk. It stands to reason, that if they know about these Ways and see them as a viable option, then Heathenry will grow.

MYTH #4
HEATHENS MUST BE CALLED BY THE GODS

Occasionally, I will hear Heathens say that new Heathens must be called by the Gods. If the Gods do not call them, then they will not be "coming home" anyhow. This has always confused me.

In almost no other area of our lives as Heathens do we ask the Gods to do it for us. In almost every other area, we say that we must do it ourselves. We accomplish things through our own hard work. We do not beg the Gods to do things for us. We do not sit around waiting for them to save us or do us personal favors. As Heathens, we get up off our duff and make things happen.

Why should it not also be so in bringing our Folk home to their ancestral Folkway? I think the Gods watch us. I think they may give us a nudge now and again. We are a religion that truly believes that the Gods help those that help themselves. If we believe that more of our Folk should be Heathen, then that is something we are going to have to work for and earn – just like everything else in this life.

MYTH #5
WE SHOULD LET WYRD TAKE ITS COURSE

Myth #5 is similar to Myth #4, in that it puts the future of Heathenry in the hands of someone or something else. It diverts responsibility for the health and growth of our ancestral Folkway to some unseen force. It relieves us of any responsibility or fault in the matter. I am just not that kind of person. I do not think our Ancestors were those sort of people. If they wanted something, they made it happen – or wore themselves out trying to make it happen.

Wyrd will take its course, but I am certainly going to make every effort to earn the things I want in this life. I am going to work tirelessly to shape this world through my own hard-work and determination. Of course there will be setbacks, and problems, and bumps in the road, but that should not stop any of us. Perhaps our Wyrd is that we should work very hard and bring more of our Folk home? I certainly reject the idea that our Wyrd is that we will sit on our hands and wait for some unseen force to bring members of our Folk home.

BRINGING OUR FOLK BACK TO THEIR ANCESTRAL FOLKWAY

Really, it all comes down to whether we support educating people that we exist, so they can make their own choices – or whether we want to keep Asatru our secret little club that people have to stumble across by accident.

Communicating to non-Heathen members of our Folk about our Ways, and letting them know that these Ways work well for us will be called proselytizing by some. By definition they are not wrong. We are trying to educate our Folk that their ancestral Folkway is a viable religious option – one that can enrich and improve their lives and their families. We are trying to bring more of our non-Heathen Folk home to the Ways of their Ancestors.

We do so on our own terms. We do not use the manipulative and fear-based techniques the Christians use. We do not bring them this information in an obnoxious or inappropriate manner. We bring them this information in a straight-forward and honest manner, as we try to do in all things.

We should be telling people about our Faith, for knowledge of our Faith has been suppressed. We should be telling them why it works, because as members of our Folk, they deserve to know.

If it is proselytizing to tell non-Heathen members of our Folk that their Ancestors were Heathen and that they would be happier if they returned to the Ways of their Ancestors, then I am happily guiltly as charged. I am just not going to follow that old Heathen chestnut that "Heathens do not proselytize." We have an obligation to communicate to our Folk who their Ancestors were and what they really believed, and to share with them why it works so well for us.

**By Saga Erickson - For Prints Contact Her at
starkravenstudios@yahoo.com**

CLEARING UP MISCONCEPTIONS NEW HEATHENS MAY HAVE

New Heathens almost always encounter other Heathens on-line first, prior to meeting actual Heathens face-to-face in real life. Based on the behavior of many of the Heathens you encounter on-line, it would be easy to falsely conclude that all Heathens are angry, mean people who like to argue and belittle other people. One might mistakenly conclude that the biggest problem facing Heathenry are the "hoards and hoards of racist" people calling themselves Heathen. One might start to incorrectly believe that Heathenry can take place on the internet. One might falsely conclude that the Prose and Poetic Edda are basically the Heathen Bible. One might sadly conclude that there is only one-true-way within Heathenry, and we are debating and working hard to develop and define that one-true-way.

As easy as it would be to come to these conclusions, all of these conclusions would be essentially false.

REAL HEATHENS ARE A GENEROUS AND HOSPITABLE PEOPLE

Our Heathen Ancestors put great importance on their own families and their own local communities. But they held generosity and hospitality as important evidence of a man's worth. A man who knew how to be a generous host and how to treat his guests well, would earn himself great respect among his peers.

Modern Heathens focus on their families and their Kindred, living in Frith and cooperation within their trusted Innangarth, or inner circle. While focus closely on family, Kindred, and friends, they also understand the importance of extending hospitality to Heathens traveling through or visiting their local area or Kindred.

A man's reputation, or Gefrain, is based on his deeds, how much he accomplishes, his generosity, his hospitality, and his honor. There is nothing about Asatru or Heathenry that encourages meaningless anger or pointless confrontations. But, on-line Heathenry is rife with keyboard cowboys that seem to delight in tearing other people down, name-calling, and being as confrontational as possible. This says much more about the nature of the internet and the nature of these people, than it does about Heathenry itself.

THE VAST MAJORITY OF HEATHENS ARE PROUD OF THEIR ANCESTORS

Heathens are proud of their history, their culture, and their Ancestors. We feel that we share a connection with our Ancestors by blood, by culture, and by Orlog (a part of the Heathen soul that is passed from parent to child.) This pride is a positive pride, and does not involve hatred for other cultures or a need to tear down other cultures in favor of our own.

Some mistake this positive pride as somehow being "racist." You will find that most Folkish Heathens do not even use the word "Race," in reference to their beliefs, because pride in one's Ancestors is not about "Race." This on-going "racist" debate and name-calling is decades old within Heathenry, and has gotten us no where. It is an enormous distraction from anything constructive and positive. It should be noted, that this "racist" debate is almost exclusively something that takes place on-line. It is an internet phenomenon and utterly pointless.

Racism is not specifically a Heathen problem. Racism is not the problem of any one particular group. There are Racists within every religion. Christian Racists. Muslim Racists. Jewish Racists. Hindu Racists. Even Wiccan Racists.

Jotun's Bane Kindred has been to scores of face-to-face Heathen gatherings. The topic of "Race" or "Racism" never comes up at these gatherings, and is a complete non-issue within real Heathenry. It is only on-line that self-appointed "crusaders," harp on this topic constantly. In so doing, they give the issue more time and attention that it deserves. Listening to these proverbial "Chicken Littles" on-line, one would think that Racism is a major problem within Heathenry and that the sky is falling. I doubt they realize it, but their constant feeding of attention to this non-issue gives this non-existent internet bogey-man a life of its own.

Rather than running about telling people what we are not, we should be focusing our time on telling people who we are, and why. We should explain why we honor our Ancestors, and how important they are to us. When we ignore and shun what few "racist" Heathens there are as a topic, and focus our time and energy on moving our Folkway forward, these "racist" Heathens cease to have any real impact or importance in Heathenry.

REAL HEATHENRY TAKES PLACE FACE-TO-FACE

Real Heathenry is about community, gathering as a people, shaking a man or woman's hand, looking them in the eye, hearing their voice, telling stories, getting to know each other. It is letting your kids play together. Letting your spouses get to know each other. It is about laughing at dumb jokes, and telling stories from your life. It is about mingling Wyrd, taking the measure of another person, and finding them of worth.

Real Heathenry is about actually DOING something. Reading, scholarship, communication, discussing various beliefs, and even debating approaches to our Folkway are important. But, we are our deeds. What have you done? What are you doing? What will you do?

Starting, growing, and maintaining Kindreds is a way of bringing Heathenry home. You build close-knit bonds of Frith with other Heathens that then become part of your Innangarth, or trusted inner circle. Gathering with other Heathens and living in Frith with them, allows for collective Luck to be built, and for great things to be accomplished. Our children get to know and play with other Heathen children. We establish Heathen communities that draw other members of our Folk home to their ancestral Folkway.

These things can only happen face-to-face. We should never mistake internet interactions and acquaintances as "real." They are just pixels on a screen, and these pixels flicker out when the machine is unplugged.

THE POETIC EDDA AND PROSE EDDA ARE HISTORICAL TEXTS

The Poetic Edda and Prose Edda are both historical texts, written by men. Both texts were actually written down by Christian men. The Poetic Edda was an attempt by Christians to record in writing the old poetry of their oral storytelling culture. The Prose Edda was written by Snorri Sturluson in order to preserve enough knowledge about Norse mythology and the meanings of poetic kennings, to preserve the poetry forms of the North. Heathens understand that these books are not "the word" of our Gods.

We include the Poetic Edda and Prose Edda among our Lore, a collection of primary sources we look to for information about the religion, ways, and world-view of our Ancestors. We also include among this Lore, the Icelandic Sagas, Beowulf, and other contemporary writings of the time. But none of these books are "scripture."

But you will encounter Heathens that read the poetry recorded in the Poetic Edda as scripture. They will quote it, and interpret it as literal truth, without any critical thought as to how and when they were recorded, and by whom. They quote information in the Prose Edda, as if what Snorri Sturluson wrote is exactly what all Heathens throughout history believed of our Gods and Goddesses and the Nine Worlds. Yes, information from both the Poetic and Prose Eddas is important and well worth considering. But both sources are the works of men, and not the works of our Gods.

Other religions have their Holy Books, which they proclaim are the direct "Word" of their god. But our Heathen Ancestors did not have a written tradition, nor a holy book. We, as modern Heathens, also have no holy book.

TRIBAL VARIANCES ARE ACKNOWLEDGED AND EXPECTED

The ways of our Ancestors varied greatly from Tribe to Tribe, location to location, century to century, and even among various levels of society. The same situation exists today within modern Heathenry. There was no "one-true-way" among our Ancestors and there is no "one-true-way" among modern Heathens. We live in different regions, we have different backgrounds and upbringings, we have different life experiences, different personalities, different interests, and different ways of interpreting things we read and learn.

One of the great strengths of grassroots, local Kindred-based, tribal Heathenry is the understanding among various Tribes that they can have unity of purpose and work together, without having unified beliefs or practices.

But, you will encounter Asatruars and Heathens who feel they are right, and everyone else is dreadfully wrong. Heathens who believe that the goal of the Reconstruction of our ancestral Folkway, is to rediscover the "one-true-way" of our Ancestors. These Asatruars and Heathens debate angrily over details, denigrating and insulting all those that do things differently than they do, and they seem completely oblivious to the fact that there never was "one-true-way" of Heathenry.

When you look at the behavior of these elitists who insist there was one-true-way, and that they specifically are the ones that have found it, and that everyone else is wrong – does it not feel eerily familiar of the desert faiths, with their one-true-way?

Our Ancestors did not act in this way, and I am always amazed when people who claim to be the most well-read and learned among us, act in a way that is so contrary to how our Ancestors would have approached their own ancestral Folkway.

BEST WAY TO CLEAR UP MISCONCEPTIONS

The best way to clear up these internet-oriented misconceptions is to meet or gather with other Heathens face-to-face. If there is a Kindred or Tribe within traveling distance of where you live, arrange to visit them or attend one of their meetings. If there is no Kindred or Tribe within traveling distance, do some research on Heathen Gatherings and then attend one. There is nothing like meeting with or gathering with other Heathens, to give you better insight into the reality of Heathenry – rather than what lurks in the internet shadows.

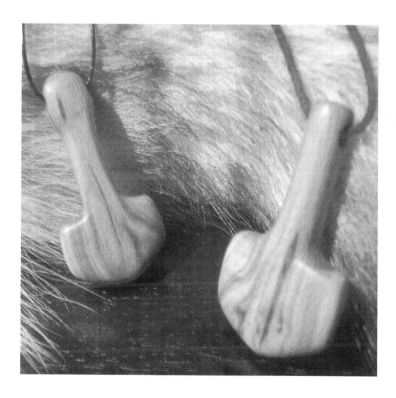

SECTION TWO

MODERN HEATHEN TRIBES

FUNCTIONS
WITHIN A TRIBE

VARIOUS FUNCTIONS AMONG OUR FOLK

People are not all the same. Heathens are not all the same. We have different skills. Different areas of interest. Different functions. Different roles. A Tribe is strongest when there are people within the Tribe that have a variety of skills, interests, functions, and roles.

We have in our Lore, the concept of Jarls, Carls, and Thralls as three different functions established by Rig among mankind in the Rigsthula. We have Georges Dumézil's Trifunctional Hypothesis within the Proto-Indo-European society, with its Priests, Warriors, and Commoners. This categorizes the early Indo-Europeans into functions of sovereignty, military, and productivity. We see this reflected in the Brahmin, Kshatriya, Vaishya, (and Shudra) castes in Hinduism, as well.

VARIOUS FUNCTIONS WITHIN A TRIBE

In a modern Heathen Tribe, we can also categorize the function that each member has within the Tribe. Some people may serve a role in more than one category. I will try to break these categories out, and explain more fully. Try not to get hung up on what I have chosen to call the categories or with the nitty-gritty detail. Obviously real life is a little more complex and varied than any particular model can attempt to capture.

The Leadership - The Gothar and Chieftains clearly fit into this role. Some Tribes have a Gothar and a Chieftain, some only have one or the other. But this group deals with directing the group, and keeping the group focused on its mission and goals. They usually interact the most with other Tribes and outside people on behalf of the Tribe. They often set the tone of the Tribe. They hold and safeguard the Luck of the Tribe. When a problem develops internally within the Tribe, they initiate the actions that will fix that problem. When a threat comes at the Tribe from outside, the rest of the Tribe often looks to them for guidance on how to counter that threat. They are often responsible for most of the education and outreach. They tend to deal with the more intellectual aspects of our Folkway.

The Warriors and Creators - The Thyle and many Thanes clearly fit into this role. These are the strong men and women who defend and safeguard the Tribe. They can be skilled at a craft or art, and are able to create amazing things. These are the Kindred members that make the hand-made Blot-bowl for the Tribe; who carve or craft the hand-made Kindred hammers the Tribe wears. They are the Kindred members who sew or create the Kindred banner. When there is a Heathen gathering, these are the men and women who keep a close eye to ensure Grith is maintained, and who takes steps to protect the Grith. They tend to deal with the more active and creative aspects of our Folkway.

The Workers - These are the men and woman who dependably work hard to get things done. That the food is bought and cooked. That the garden is planted. That the children are tended to and do not get lost. That the Symbel Hall is ready. They tend to deal with the "getting things done" aspects of our Folkway.

This is not to say that someone in the Leadership cannot carve wood, or cook the food, or watch the children, or ensure Grith is maintained.

This is not to say that someone among the Warriors and Creators cannot run a Blot, or help set direction, or plant the garden, or get the Symbel Hall ready.

This is not to say that one of the Workers cannot deal with a problem within the Tribe, or counter an outside threat, or sew a banner, or create something wonderful.

There is definite cross-over between the roles – a blurring of lines – and no one fits perfectly into any of these categories all the time. None of these categories of function can exist and function properly without the existence of the other functions right along side it. No one role is "better" than the other. No one role is "more important" than the other.

But as we approach the issue of advancing and growing our Folk, and ensuring the survival and success of our Folkway, it is important we consider all three of these functions within our Folk, and within our individual Tribes. If we think of the Leadership as the head, the Warrior and Creator as the arms and hands, and the Worker as the legs and feet, you can see we do not have a whole entity, unless they are all present.

A Tribe with very few people serving in the role of Leadership will wander and stray. A chaotic tumble of creativity and hard work that leads no where.

A Tribe with very few people serving in the role of Warrior and Creator will be unprotected and lack the ability to create. It will have a leader and people willing to work, but very little to work on – and what they accomplish will eventually fall.

A Tribe with very few people serving in the role of Worker, will not accomplish much. It will have all sorts of ideas and vision, with no one willing or able to actually make it happen.

THE EXAMPLE OF A HAMMER

The Leadership function on its own, understands what a hammer is. It knows intellectually how to make one, but does not have the skills to do so. It understands how hard steel is, and that an oak handle is best. It even knows all that can be accomplished with a hammer, and that a house needs to be built. But the Leadership function on its own cannot make or use a hammer. The house will not be built.

The Warrior and Creator function knows the skills need to make a hammer. How to shape the steel head and the oak handle, and how to fit them together. How to make sure the right steel is obtained, the right oak, and that no one steals the finished product. But the Warrior and Creator function on its own will not know the house needs to be built, and would rather make more hammers than work on the house. The House will not be built.

The Worker function on its own, knows how to take a hammer and build a house from provided plans. They have the fortitude and the backbone to work all day with that hammer. They are willing to invest their blood, sweat, and tears in raising that house. But the Worker function on its own, does not know the house needs to be built and does not know how to make a hammer. The House will not be Built.

CONCLUSION

Regardless of what you call the functions or how you specifically define them, there are various roles within a Tribe that need to be filled. On the macro level, there are various functions within our Folkway itself that need to be filled.

If our Folkway only has people who fit into the Leadership function, it will not prosper. If it only has Warriors and Creators, it will not prospers If it only has Workers, it will not prosper.

We need to aim our efforts at Tribe-building and Folk-building at all three functions. We need to direct time, effort, and resources toward all three in order to succeed.

61

CLARIFICATIONS

It is hard to put forth an article like this one, because no matter how many times you make it clear in the article that people should not be forced into or stuck within roles, when people read this essay, there is a tendency on the the part of the reader to to put his/her own spin on what is being communicated.

For those of us actually attempting to create strong cohesive Kindreds and Tribes it is important we talk about group dynamics. What are the functions and roles within a Tribe? When do we server in the various roles? How do we do the right thing, at the right time, for the right reasons to advance our Tribe forward? These are things about which it is wise to have discussions.

I am Chieftain of Jotun's Bane Kindred. There are times when someone needs to focus the collective efforts of our kindred, and often that is my job. Sometimes, someone else does it. It depends on the situation, the subject matter, and the timing. Much of the time, I lead by working. If there are 200 chairs to set up for Symbel, you will find me right in the mix setting up chairs. I love to craft and create, and I have carved a large Odin Statue for our Kindred. So, sometimes I am in the Leadership function, sometimes I am a Warrior/Creator, and sometimes I am a Worker. It depends on the situation, and the timing. At a small gathering, there is less need for direction and delegation. At a large gathering, there are sometimes several levels of delegation. That is how things get done, and how you multiply your Tribe's efforts.

This sort of blurring goes on throughout our Tribe. But, despite this blurring, a Tribe works best when its members are playing to their own strengths on behalf of their Tribe. A Tribe works best when its members know and understand each other and, through experience, understand how best to work together.

No one is titled or considered a "Worker" or "Thrall" within our Tribe. Though there are many times that some or all of us are working enormously hard.

Now, not everyone organizes themselves this way. Again, I am simply expressing what we do, and how we look at it.

IS HEATHENRY "TOO INSULAR?"

Recently, I was told that Asatru and much of Heathenry was "too Insular, too Judgmental, and based on a Feudalistic Structure." I have heard this before. Most of the time, it is something I hear from those that are new to Heathenry, but you will hear it from people who have been around awhile as well. I cannot speak for all of Asatru or Heathenry. But I can address each of these areas of complaint, and attempt to shed some light on why Jotun's Bane Kindred is the way that we are. In this essay, I will address the "too insular" portion of the criticism. I will address the other topics in the two essays that follow.

TOO INSULAR? OR PROTECTING THAT WHICH IS MOST IMPORTANT TO US IN THIS WORLD?

Admittedly, as a police officer, my life experience has shown me some of the worst in people. Adults who victimize children. Addicts, who think only of themselves. People going through divorces or major life-changes that are practically out of their mind with grief and stress. Users. Abusers. Thieves. Liars. Drama-Junkies. "Broken People." I wrote an entire essay on the topic of "Broken People" in the Heathen Gods book. While my job may have exposed me to more of these people than most people have to deal with, we all know these people exist.

Our Kindreds are made up of our families. Our Wives. Our Children. Our very best friends in the world. People we are committed to helping, advancing, and protecting. Our most important responsibility in life, is to protect our children and the ones we love. If we are not doing that, then everything else we are doing is practically meaningless. In addition, we invest 1000's of hours of our time to establishing and growing our Kindreds. These Kindreds are something we form for social and religious reasons. They represent our Innangarth, our Inner Circle, and we share our lives, our time, our effort forming and maintaining these Kindreds.

Our Kindreds are our religious communities. They are how we teach our Faith to our Children. The Orlog we share and the Luck we build, is how we hope to bring more of our Folk home to their native Folkway. These Kindreds are our key to acquiring tribal land and building Heathen Hofs. They are how we seek to live in Frith and Honor, as our Ancestors lived. When a Kindred falters or fails, it strikes at our very core as a Germanic people.

So, why would anyone call us "too insular" for protecting our children from "Broken People?" Why would anyone call us "too insular" for carefully screening people we let into our Inner Circle? Why would anyone call us "too insular" for guarding the 1000's of hours of blood, sweat, and tears we have invested into our Kindreds?

Jotun's Bane Kindred holds open events every two months. They are widely announced, and everyone is welcome to attend. Some of our open events are Pubmoots (without our children present). Some are Picnics. Some are Fainings. This represents our outreach. Our invitation of hospitality to those outside of our group, so that we can interact with them, get to know them, and see if we want to get to know them better, or not.

We have had white supremacists show up at events, and try to recruit. We quickly addressed this issue, and protected our children and Kindred by pushing them away. We have had people get sloppy drunk, insulting, and combative at these events. We quickly addressed this behavior, and protected our children and Kindred by pushing them away. We have had people who will not get a job or take responsibility for their lives show up, and we protected our children and our Kindred by pushing them away. We have had unmedicated mentally ill people show up, and we have protected our children and our Kindred by pushing them away. We have had all manner of "Broken People" (emotional vampires, drama-addicts, shit disturbers, etc.) show up, and we have protected our children and Kindred by pushing them away.

We have also met some amazing people at these open events. People who wanted to learn. People who wanted to work within a group. People who were generous and giving. People who were strong and honest. From these good people, our Kindred has grown over time. We have carefully guarded who is added to our Innangarth, and that has served us well.

If you do not guard your Innangarth, then you let people into your group that will weaken it, or who may work to disrupt or destroy it from within. Anyone who has been around Heathenry for a few years, has seen it happen. It has happened over and over and over again.

Most Kindreds I am in contact with, do hold Open Events and other forms of outreach. They are willing to talk to new Heathens that contact them, or old Heathens that have moved into their area. But, these Kindreds also guard carefully who they let into their Kindred.

Usually they are looking for new members that are:

1. Stable, both emotionally and in how they live their life
2. Responsible in their finances and personal life
3. Honest, and Straightforward
4. Willing to work in a group setting
5. Willing to fit into the group as it exists, and not wanting to turn it on its head
6. Loyal to our Gods and their Ancestors

Let us say there is a Kindred out there, that does not hold open events. That does not answer emails from new Heathens. That does not accept new members. Now, we could fairly describe that as an "insular" Kindred. But, even in that case, is it not their right to be this way? If that is how they choose to live their lives, and how they choose to protect what they have, is it not their right to be just as damned insular as they choose to be?

In conclusion, I do not agree that Asatru or Heathenry is "too insular." I see Open Events being held all across the Midwest. I see Kindreds admitting new members and growing all across the Heartland. I would argue, that far too often established Kindreds are not careful enough about who they let into their Innangarth. It is important that we truly KNOW someone before we let them into our Inner Circle. That we truly KNOW them before we give them any sort of power or input over the Kindreds we have fought hard to build and maintain. That we truly KNOW them before we give them access to our homes, our spouses, our children, and our loved ones.

As always, this is simply my view of it. I am sure others will have a different take.

IS HEATHENRY "TOO JUDGMENTAL?"

This is my second essay, in a series of three. Recently, I was told that Asatru and much of Heathenry was "too Insular, too Judgmental, and based on a Feudalistic Structure." I have heard this before. Most of the time, it is something I hear from those that are new to Heathenry, but you will hear it from people who have been around awhile as well. I cannot speak for all of Asatru or Heathenry. But I can address each of these areas of complaint, and attempt to shed some light on why Jotun's Bane Kindred is the way that we are. In this essay, I will address the "too judgmental" portion of the criticism. I have addressed the other topics in separate essays.

TOO JUDGEMENTAL? OR SIMPLY EXERCISING OUR RIGHT TO MAKE JUDGEMENTS?

We say it time and time again. We are our deeds. When we meet someone new to us, we ask ourselves questions about them. Who are you? What do you do? What do you stand for? What do you contribute to the group? Are you stable? Are you safe to have around my children? Are you going to maintain Grith, or do something to hurt us? When we meet someone for the first time or during the process of getting to know them, there is only one way to answer these questions. We interact with the new person. Listen to them. Watch them. Learn about them. Examine their life and their deeds. Then we make a judgment

Our most basic right as human beings, as parents, as adults living within a society..is deciding with whom we will associate and with whom we will not associate. Who will be around our families and who will not be around our families. Having a strong healthy Orlog depends on our ability to judge other men and women, and decide if they are worthy people with whom to associate. Our Luck is directly tied to our knowledge and ability to make these judgments wisely. Sometimes we judge them worthy people with whom to associate. Sometimes not. Sometimes the judgment is about just how much, and to what depth, we are willing to interact with them.

Every choice in life has consequences. When choices and deeds have been put into the well, that is where they stay. So, exercising one's judgment wisely is enormously important.

It is NOT our religion that demands that we "judge not, lest ye be judged." Our religion teaches us the importance of honor. Should I willingly allow dishonorable people into my life? No. Should I allow people that will cause problems and discord into my life? No. Should I follow foreign advice that I should accept all men and women as they are, and not exercise my judgment about them? No.

All that being said, Jotun's Bane Kindred judges people by their deeds. I have written at length in the Heathen Gods book about interacting with those that have done bad things in their past, but who are now leading good, stable, and healthy lives. While all of our deeds remain in the well, a man or woman can change the direction of their life through determination, hard work, and a willingness to learn and change. We have seen it time and again. But, this is our judgment to make. We decide when someone has grown beyond their past ill deeds. They do not get to decide – we decide.

So, if someone is an actively abusing drugs or alcohol, and my Kindred makes a judgment we do not want them around us – that is our judgment to make.

If someone cannot keep a job and seems unwilling to fulfill their obligations, and my Kindred makes a judgment we do not want them around us – that is our judgment to make.

If someone surrounds themselves with drama and discord, and my Kindred makes a judgment we do not want them around us – that is our judgment to make.

If someone does not share the same world view as us, and my Kindred makes a judgment we do not want them around us – that is our judgment to make.

If someone does not keep their oaths, and my Kindred makes a judgment we do not want them around us – that is our judgment to make.

If someone is utterly annoying to be around, or painfully selfish, or unreasonably combative, or has no boundaries, or backstabbing in nature, and my Kindred makes a judgment we do not want them around us – that is our judgment to make.

Honestly, it is our lives. Our families. Our work. Our Kindred. Our Frith. If we for any reason decide we do not want them around us - that is our judgment to make.

Yes, we hold frequent open events. Yes, we hold open gatherings, like

Lightning Across the Plains. Yes, we have outreach, and we give advice, talk with, and meet with new Heathens. But, this level of openness does not require that we abandon our right to make judgments about who we trust, who we work with, and who we associate with at a deeper personal level.

As I ended my last essay, it is important that we truly KNOW someone before we let them into our Innangarth. That we truly KNOW them before we give them any sort of power or input over the Kindreds we have fought hard to build and maintain. That we truly KNOW them before we give them access to our homes, our spouses, our children, and our loved ones. During the process of KNOWING them, we are certainly passing judgment on them. Exercising judgment is how we safeguard our Orlog and our Luck.

As always, this is simply my view of it. I am sure others will have a different take.

ARE HEATHEN KINDREDS "TOO FEUDAL?"

This is my third essay, in a series of three. Recently, I was told that Asatru and much of Heathenry was "too Insular, too Judgmental, and based on a Feudalistic Structure." I have heard this before. Most of the time, it is something I hear from those that are new to Heathenry, but you will hear it from people who have been around awhile as well. I cannot speak for all of Asatru or Heathenry. But I can address each of these areas of complaint, and attempt to shed some light on why Jotun's Bane Kindred is the way that we are. In this essay, I will address the criticism that Heathen Kindreds are "Too Feudal." I have addressed the other topics in the two previous essays.

TOO FEUDAL? OR SIMPLY ORGANIZED IN A WAY THAT WORKS?

Goodness knows, our modern culture is obsessed with "leveling the playing field." Everyone is equal. Cannot have anyone's self-esteem or self-worth being injured by the idea that some people are better at some things, than other people might be. Give every kid a medal or trophy. Anyone who is in a position of authority or leadership, must be out for only themselves, or power, or money, or some other selfish thing. Add to this how disconnected the modern individual is from his extended family and his/her community, and it is easy to understand why people in our modern culture have a hard time understanding what it is to truly be part of something bigger than themselves.

We live in a world where we do not really know our neighbors, though there are 1000's of them living within easy walking distance. Modern families fall apart regularly, with more marriages ending than actually staying together. People go to work, have polite conversation with "work friends," and then come home to the boob tube. Their main social interactions are via the internet or watching other people live their lives on reality television shows. So, we Heathens are very aware that the modern Kindred, with its close-knit bonds, commitments, loyalty, trust, and Frith is a departure from the modern norm. We are happy with that. Those who know history, understand that tribal units are one of the oldest forms of human organization. They work.

Sometimes you will hear it said that Heathenry is "too Feudal," or that we are attempting to bring back an outdated or obsolete social structure. You will also hear complaints about Kindreds that formally recognize the leadership positions, roles, or positions of responsibility that people hold within the Kindred. When we hear this complaint about Jotun's Bane Kindred, it is usually in reference to the fact we have roles of responsibility within our Kindred. We have a Chieftain who handles practical matters, holds and safeguards the Luck of the Tribe, and who helps build consensus within the Tribe on important issues, decisions, and direction. We have a Godhi who serves as a spiritual expert and adviser, and helps keep the Kindred spiritually on-track. We have a Thyle who keeps and maintains records of our oaths and history, and who guards the Orlog of our Tribe. There are other roles and responsibilities that have developed within our Kindred over the time we have existed. The "Too Feudal" comment is normally aimed at these defined roles.

First let me say, that every Heathen Kindred should organize themselves however they see fit. It is none of my business how other Kindreds organize themselves. Different things work for different people, and every Kindred will have its own goals, its own ways, its own Thew. But I can talk about how Jotun's Bane Kindred is organized the way it is, and why it works.

First, we are all bound by our Tribe's Thew. We are all bound by our Tribe's traditions, or collective expectations, and our ways. Our newest member, our most tenured members, and our Chieftain are all bound by Thew. You will hear people refer to leaders of Kindreds as dictators, cults of personality, or worse. But, a good leader serves his Tribe. A good leader is the least free of his Tribe. A good leader is the poorest of his Tribe, in both time and treasure. A good leader carries burdens for his Tribe, that no one else in the Tribe is charged with carrying.

If you look at any successful Tribe with a leader, you will see that leader making decisions that are best for the Tribe – not best for him/her individually. You will see a leader that is right there in the trenches with the members of his Tribe, doing the work with them. You will see a leader that makes decisions that are acceptable to the members of his/her Tribe – not forcing his/her own agenda onto the Tribe. A leader must have Luck, knowledge, wisdom, judgment, and fairness with those that are in his/her Tribe. A good leader has earned that position by deeds and success, and a good leader must maintain that position by continued deeds and success. A good leader has vision, and with the help, cooperation, and input of his/her Tribe, the leader must successfully lead his Tribe toward that vision. In the Heathen Gods book, I wrote an essay on Leadership by Consensus, where I go into this idea more fully.

Now, I know of Kindreds that are proud they have no positions of leadership. But the successful groups of this nature, almost always do have default roles and responsibilities within the Kindred, even though they do not formally recognize these roles. One or several members, tend to lead during times of crisis or at times when a leader is needed, though they do not call themselves a Chieftain. One or two members tend to be responsible for most of the spiritual duties and advice, though they do not call themselves Gothar. One or two members tend to hold other members feet to the fire on oaths and other obligations, though they do not call themselves a Thyle. While these successful groups are proud they have not formalized the roles and responsibilities within their Kindred, in almost all cases there are default roles and responsibilities that have fallen into place over time.

These roles and responsibilities within our Kindreds develop because they are natural to us. As I mentioned above, organizing on a tribal level is one of the oldest and most powerful ways to organize people. It worked for our Ancestors, and it works now. Having roles and responsibilities within that tribal structure is just as natural to us.

If a group of people literally has absolutely no real structure, no leaders, no roles, and no designated responsibilities, then they usually get very little done. What little they get done, is accomplished very slowly. Without structure and organization, it is difficult to build collective Orlog and Luck. What little Luck is built, is not directed in any coherent way. If there are no commitments or loyalty within a group, it is impossible to establish real Frith – in the way our Ancestors understood Frith.

Our Ancestors recognized leaders and roles of responsibilities within their families and Tribes. They understood why they were needed. They also understood that a good leader is not a dictator. A good leader listens and communicates. A good leader is someone who understands Frith, and Honor, and leads in a way that advances his Tribe forward. I know many Tribes personally here in the Midwest, and have witnessed the good leaders among them.

To summarize, our "feudal structure" (their label, not mine) gives us organization. It gives us roles and responsibilities. It allows us to build collective Luck, and to then translate that Luck into success and well-being. It allows an organized way for problems to be resolved, and Frith to be maintained. It allows us to have clear vision and goals, and to plan the work it will take to reach those goals. In our case, it allows a handful of adults to put on an event like Lightning Across the Plains, and have it go well.

Again, other Heathens can organize themselves anyway they like. But, those of us that organize in a tribal fashion, should not accept criticism that the way we organize ourselves is somehow out-dated, obsolete, or oppressive. We do it because it works and because it brings joy to our families and our Folk.

FRITH WITHIN OUR MODERN TRIBES – THE JOY IT BRINGS

In Vilhelm Grönbech's Culture of the Teutons, his first chapter is on Frith. Frith between kinsmen.

Grönbech goes to great lengths to explain that Frith for our Ancestors is not mere "Love." It is not merely "Peace." It is not merely "Cooperation." The concept of Frith is enormously difficult for those of us living in this modern culture to fully understand, let alone exhibit as a trait or value. Yet, the concept of Frith is at the very heart of the Germanic world-view.

In the on-line Temple Library at heathengods.com you can read Culture of the Teutons for free, or you can buy a printed copy if that better suits your reading habits. In this essay I am going to attempt to discuss Frith as it existed among our Ancestors, and then discuss the role it plays in our modern Tribes.

Frith was a deep seated need to, in all things and all actions, consider the "welfare and honor of one's kin." A family was so tightly bound as a group, that not one of them could suffer without the entire group suffering. What one individual did within the group, was seen by others as an action committed by the entire group. A great crime committed by one member of the family, put every family member in jeopardy of paying for that crime either by Shyld or as a subject of vengeance. A great victory or accomplishment performed by one member of the group, was seen as a victory or accomplishment for the entire group.

These bonds within families were the natural state of things. There was nothing that could tempt them away from seeing the family as a whole. A man without kin, had no value. A man who acted in a way outside of Frith, was loosened from the whole and seen as less than nothing. As part of a family, one was fully expected to act in Frith toward other members of the family, and in turn – one fully expected Frith to be shown in return. When one was confronted with a tough situation where one was bound by Frith, there was not even a struggle whether or not to show Frith. To not show Frith was to break the bonds that made you a human being. There was no inner struggle over the matter. You simply did what you did, because this was your family, and this is what families do.

If a family member showed up at your door in the night, and informed you that they had killed a man from another family – you knew immediately that in a sense your entire family had killed that man, and that vengeance would be sought by the entirety of that man's family. There was no question you would defend your kinsman who had done the killing, and the rest of your family was gathered for defense, or in order to make an offer of payment for the act.

So tight were these bonds, that often vengeance for a death would not be sought against the individual killer himself, but instead against a man of the killer's family that closely matched the importance of the dead man. If an important man of one family was killed by a lowly man of another family, it was an insult to the memory of the killed man to seek the vengeance against the lowly killer. Instead an important man of the killer's family would be killed, and thus honor restored to the first victim's family. This practice was completely understood and justified by the tight bonds that existed within families, and the concept of Frith. What one man does, the entire family is considered to have done.

If one killed the cousin of the area's Godhi or Lawspeaker, and then went to this same Lawspeaker for Shyld to be set and the matter settled, it was completely understood that the man deciding the matter would not be "fair" by today's standards. No one would expect him to decide the matter in a balanced way. It was understood that the dead man was the Lawspeaker's cousin, and that as a matter of Frith, the price for this death would be much more than might normally be set. No one would expect or even voice an expectation that the Lawspeaker do anything other than decide the matter with a heavy leaning toward his own family and their loss. That would be the wrong cousin to kill, and now the price would have to be paid.

If the body of one's kinsman was brought home, it did not matter what had led up to his death. Whatever personal quarrels or actions on his part played a role in his death were not even considered. Here was a kinsman, slayed by another, and Frith and Honor demanded that a price be paid.

The Frith between kinsman existed in their very being. To not act in Frith to one's kinsman was something that tore at the very thing that made you human. One who broke this bond, was seen as alone in the world, and thus not even human, in a sense.

Frith means reciprocal loyalty. A complete and utter unwillingness to take action against one's own kin. A disagreement between kinsmen might become loud, and angry, and strongly argued – but the end result must always be the same. In the end, the two kinsmen must work towards an answer that brings unity of purpose between them. Competing or conflicting interests might arise among kin, but in the end, a good kinsman is bound to gather with his kin and come to a conclusion that settles the matter. A quarrel between kinsmen did not have death as a potential result, because Frith demanded that one not take violence against one's kin.

There are even stories in the Lore, of two men meeting in battle, and one suggests that by some illegitimate birth they may be kin. One of the two men would immediately withdraw, even at the merest suggestion that they might be kin, because they could not bring themselves to consider the possibility of killing one of their family.

But Frith goes beyond not hurting one's own kin, or seeking vengeance for a kinsman who was slain. Frith meant you always took your kinsman's side. His side was your side. His side was your entire family's side. Even in cases where you do not like the actions or choices of your kin, you may express privately to them your wishes that they acted differently, but then you back them anyway. It is not a matter of saying "Well, you made your bed," and then standing by neutrally looking on. This is your kin, and you take up his side of every matter.

"All must give way to Frith, all obligations, all considerations." No bond to a non-kinsman can be allowed to interfere with the Frith between kinsmen. No disagreement, no mood, no emotion, nothing at all can stand before Frith.

Frith is not passive. It is based in one's very identity and connection with one's kin. To act in Frith was not a burden. Frith brought joy, security, gladness. One is only truly alive when one lives in Frith with kin.

For modern Heathens, the concept of Frith is at the heart of our modern Tribes. In our culture, extended families barely exist, and even the nuclear family fails more often than it succeeds. Ours is a culture where our kin do not know what it is to be kin. Our kin are often of a Universal religion, that has worked for centuries to break down Frith with kin, in favor of loyalty to one's church or God.

So, we form Kindreds, and these chosen families take many forms. When a Kindred is made up of several families coming together into one group, I prefer to call this social grouping a "Tribe." For these Tribes to succeed, and remain stable, and to bring us joy – we must return to a full and complete

understanding of Frith within our Tribes.

Anyone who is involved in a stable healthy Tribe, knows the joy that comes from the Frith one shares with these people. You love them, you trust them, you have their back no matter what, and they have your back no matter what. You feel like you are truly alive when you are around them, and you feel the loss when you are not around them – though in the depths of your being, you know they are still there and will always be there for you. For those that have experienced true Frith, it is easy to understand why this feeling held such an important place in our Ancestors' lives.

We must make our decisions and take actions that consider the welfare of everyone in our Tribe. What one member of the Tribe does, the entire Tribe is considered to have done. When disagreements arise, it should be the foregone conclusion from the very start that the only result possible is for the disagreement to be resolved in a way that benefits everyone in the Tribe. Bonds with those outside the Tribe cannot stand in the way of Frith within the Tribe. No mood, no emotion, no self-interest, no conflict can stand in the way of Frith.

Does this mean there are never disagreements? That no one ever gets angry? That you never tell anyone in your Tribe that you do not like something they are doing? No, it does not mean any of these things. There will still be disagreements, anger, and people attempting to guide one another away from actions that might be harmful to the Tribe and themselves. But the end result is always the same. Both parties involved know from the start, that Frith must prevail, and the problems must be resolved in a way that benefits all.

These are the people that will "help you hide the body," as the modern saying goes. These are the people that have your side no matter what. Need a place to stay? Their home is yours. Need advice? They are the ones that do not mind the call at 3:00 AM. Moving? They are there with beer, pizza, and a moving truck. In return, you receive the joy of being there for them as well.

The concept of Frith within our Tribes makes it very clear how carefully a Tribe must choose new members. Screening these new members. Getting to know them. Teaching them. The enculturation process become all that more important when one understands the sort of bond you are forming with a new member. If the Tribe allows in a troublesome new member, Frith will be regularly tested. If the Tribe lets in a new member who does not understand Frith or is not willing to be bound by Frith, the security, gladness, and joy that comes from Frith will be diminished or lost.

On the eve of a road-trip with our Kindred to go to a Heathen gathering here in the region, Jamie King, one of my Kindred-sisters called me and said she was just "High on Heathenry." We laughed, and then we talked about how amazing it feels to know we were going to be with members of our Kindred throughout the weekend. Traveling together, working together, meeting with other Tribes together. Knowing that you are part of a group, and that you have complete loyalty and Frith within that group, is truly a feeling of Joy. It is so different from what we face in our modern culture, that the Joy is almost overwhelming in its intensity. It is foreign when compared with what we face in this culture, but it is the most natural thing to the ways of our Ancestors. The ways of our Folk.

Frith is at the very heart of a Tribe. It is at the very heart of the Germanic World-View. Once it is understood and established, it feels completely natural. One quickly realizes why our current culture is failing. Why depression is at incredible levels. Why so many people are medicated. Why families fail. Why our culture is failing. Our modern culture has purposely moved away from the very heart of our people. Modern men and women are individuals first. Seeking out their own interests and their own pleasures, with very little regard to their kin, or those they choose as kin.

Our Germanic Ancestors understood that without Frith, an individual was completely alone in the world. Without Frith, a man was nothing. Less than nothing. Yet, our modern culture seeks this state of nothingness as a goal!

In reconstructing the ways of our Ancestors, we must form Kindreds and Tribes. We must establish Frith within those Kindreds and Tribes. Then the energy, the work, and the Luck that is created will drive our Folk forward.

ESTABLISHING TRUE FRITH IN OUR LIVES

Our Ancestors, pre-Christianity understood what it was to be in a large interconnected family. What it was to show reciprocal Frith and Loyalty. What it meant to preserve the Honor of one's family. The idea of a relative acting against Frith or against honor, was a terrifying concept. To violate Frith was to be completely alone. A man without kin and Tribe, had no value. To lose one's Honor was like a bleeding wound, and until one had addressed the situation and regained one's honor, that wound would continue to bleed.

In our modern culture, the concepts of true Frith and Honor in most families has become so decayed, that it must be completely rebuilt. There is a lack of understanding regarding Frith and Honor, and the bonds that once held extended families tightly together have diminished. A problem modern Heathens will often encounter, is the absolutely selfish rotten relative, that lies, steals, cheats, and lets everyone down (including his family), but then comes to family members for help and says, "But we are family – you have to help me." I will speak more about that situation in the latter half of this essay.

So, how do we as modern Heathens build and reestablish Frith with those people we count among our Innangarth (our trusted inner-circle)? How do we insert Frith back into our lives?

It starts with our own households. As a father or mother of a family, a modern Heathen must teach the concepts of Frith and Honor to one's children. This teaching must overcome the enculturation that takes place from the culture at large, through television, school-age peers, teachers, and even the actions of extended family members. Marriages must be about advancing both spouses forward, coming to a consensus on decisions, and both spouses doing what is best for the entire household. The household or Hearth is the heart of Heathenry. If we work to establish Frith in our own homes with our closest family members, then it has a place from which it can grow.

A modern Heathen can also establish true Frith within their Kindreds and Tribes. Frith should be discussed, taught, and shown by example. Everyone within the Kindred or Tribe should have a working understanding of Frith, and a consensus should be built that true Frith is something the various families within the Kindred or Tribe want to share between their households. In a sense, a Kindred or Tribe then becomes a "chosen" extended family. The commitment within the Kindred or Tribe becomes one of kinship, and Frith makes that commitment and everyone involved stronger or more productive.

A modern Heathen can also start rebuilding true Frith with good-hearted and honorable relatives that are not within their household, and not necessarily even Heathen. Understanding can be built with sisters, brothers, cousins, and others that are teachable. This can be taught by example, and showing Frith towards these good relatives. It can be taught through holding family reunions and gatherings. It can be taught through conversations and building face-to-face bonds with these extended family members.

But there is a reciprocity to Frith. A back and forth. Frith offered in one direction toward a family member that neither understands nor practices Frith, can be counterproductive. It can be enabling of bad or selfish behavior.

So, in modern times, you will often encounter absolutely selfish rotten relatives, that care not one bit about their family, or maintaining Frith, or upholding the family's honor - UNLESS IT BENEFITS THEM IN THAT MOMENT.

They act contrary to Frith in every instance, but then demand the family show Frith toward them. They act with zero concern for their honor or the honor of their family, but then question the honor of any family member that will not SAVE THEM when they suffer the repercussions of their own selfish actions.

We must protect our Innangarth from those that would harm it intentionally and repeatedly. The selfish rotten relative that shows by consistent bad action that they have absolutely no concern for Frith, or family, or anything except their own selfish interests, is someone Heathens must guard against.

At the very least, Heathens should understand that they do not have an obligation to show Frith to the rotten family member that would selfishly harm their close Innangarth. If they choose to show Frith to this person, that is their choice. But it is not an obligation during our reconstruction process.

It is most important that we focus on establishing and maintaining Frith in our households, our Kindreds or Tribes, and among those non-Heathen family members that are willing and capable of showing Frith in a reciprocal manner.

THE BARE BASICS
ON "LUCK"

Sometimes we as Heathens, use terms that not everyone understands. Or terms that do not mean today, what they used to mean to our Ancestors. I received a message the other day from a new Heathen, asking me to explain what I was talking about when I referred to "Luck." I thought I would share that response in an essay for anyone else that is not familiar with how our Ancestors viewed and defined the concept of "Luck."

Luck is something that was very important to our Ancestors. It is not "dumb luck" or "random luck," as many think of luck today.

Luck was something some people had and some people did not. Those that had Luck were almost always successful in everything to which they dedicated their efforts. But Luck was earned. Luck came from right-action, experience, hard-learned lessons, knowledge, wisdom, and especially hard work. The leader (whether it was the head of a family, the Chieftain of a Tribe, or the King) held and safeguarded the Luck of his people.

Luck could also be lost. Poor decisions, inaction, or dishonorable deeds could all have a large negative impact on one's Luck, and thus affect a person's ability to succeed on future efforts.

It is said that an army without its King, when facing an army led by a King, would often flee prior to the battle because they knew they could not stand against the Luck of the man leading the other army.

Men would go to a leader, and ask for advice on an important matter. That advice (Rede) was considered to contain some of the Luck of that leader. His advice, if followed, was likely to lead to success because of that Luck.

Men would go to a leader, and actually ask for Luck. The leader would give them advice and give them his Luck. They would then go to other men to recruit them to their cause, and say, "I come with the Luck of King so-and-so." That held weight with our Ancestors, because they understood the importance of Luck.

Among modern Heathens you will see the one's who have Luck. They are stable, knowledgeable, strong, and willing to work their tirelessly to make something happen. This combination of traits results in them having success, and this is Luck in action.

That Luck builds on itself. Success in and of itself brings more Luck and makes the next effort even more likely to succeed. A string of successes builds such Luck that failure becomes very unlikely.

A disorganized Kindred, that has no leadership (official or implied in nature), no direction, no work ethic, no focus, no real Frith, naturally has no Luck and will succeed at very little.

But a group working together, in a committed Kindred, brings together collective Luck. That Luck is held and safeguarded by their leader, but it advances the entire Kindred and all the individuals in that Kindred. A Kindred with Luck can accomplish almost anything they set their minds to.

GROWING FOLK COMMUNITIES AROUND OUR KINDREDS

This essay is specifically for Heathens who are in an established Kindred, or those who someday plan to be the member of an established Kindred.

Once a Kindred has established itself, grown, and maintained a stable existence, it is likely that it will begin to attract additional Heathens or the Heathen-curious from its surrounding local community. These non-Kindred Heathens come to all or some of the Kindred's open events. Some of these non-Kindred Heathens will lose interest over time, and stop coming around. Others will start to form friendships with members of the Kindred, and eventually begin inquiring about how to join the Kindred. Others will develop a fondness and loyalty for the Kindred, without any real interest on their part in actually joining the Kindred. This ever-shifting group of non-Kindred Heathens associated with the Kindred can be called that Kindred's Folk Community.

Having non-Kindred Heathens gravitate towards an established Kindred, attending their open events and forming friendships with the

Kindred, is just a natural result of having an active and vital Kindred. But, Kindreds can engage in certain efforts to grow and improve the Folk Community that gathers around their Kindred. This benefits everyone involved in both the Kindred and the Kindred's Folk Community.

WHAT A FOLK COMMUNITY IS AND IS NOT

The people that comprise the Folk Community around a Kindred, live in the local area, attend the Kindred's open events, and are on friendly terms with the Kindred and its members. The Kindred likely does nice things for the members of the Folk Community, and the members of the Folk Community likely do nice things for the Kindred on occasion. But the members of the Folk Community are not truly a part of that Kindred's Innangarth. They are not members of the Kindred, and the bonds, true Frith, and obligations that each Kindred member owes the Kindred and its members, do not extend to the members of the Folk Community.

A Kindred's Folk Community is made up of people that the Kindred knows face-to-face, through real interaction in real-life. People that the Kindred only knows from on-line interaction, are not part of the Kindred's Folk Community.

Most Kindreds will very loosely define their Folk Community, having no official designation as to who is a member of the Folk Community and who is not. Kindreds may also call this group of people many names other than "Folk Community." Some Kindreds may call these people "Friends of the Kindred" or do not really call them anything at all. But over time, some Kindred's may see a value in having a more formally recognized Folk Community, with clearer definitions as to who is a member of that group and who is not. This will vary greatly from Kindred to Kindred.

THE SORTS OF PEOPLE THAT
COMPRISE YOUR FOLK COMMUNITY

There are many categories of people that comprise a Kindred's Folk Community, and people can move from category to category over time. Labeling in this way is somewhat artificial, but it helps to understand who is attracted into the orbit of an established Kindred, and why they are there.

The Heathen-curious are naturally drawn to a Kindred's Folk Community. They hear about Heathenry from a friend, on-line, or from a book, and they begin looking for open Heathen events, Asatru

101 classes, or other "beginners" activities in their area. This naturally brings them into contact with a Kindred that hosts these kinds of events in their local area. The Heathen-curious are there to learn more and to figure out whether Heathenry is something they want to fully commit to as a religion, belief-system, and world-view.

New Heathens have committed to Heathenry as a religion, belief-system, and world-view, but they are not members of a Kindred yet. They very likely do not quite understand how a Kindred works or how it will benefit them and their families. So, they attend a Kindred's open Heathen events, Asatru classes, and other activities in an attempt to not only learn more about Heathenry, but also to figure out if they want to join the Kindred or not. A new Heathen will also attend open Blots/Fainings so that they can honor their Gods and Goddesses along side other Heathens. Over time, some of these new Heathens will become interested in joining the Kindred and inquire about it. Others will remain comfortable not being part of the Kindred, but will continue to come to the Kindred's open events.

A Kindred's Folk Community is also made up of established Heathens who are not interested in joining the Kindred. They may not have the time they feel it would require. They may be uncomfortable committing at that level to other people. They may be married to a non-Heathen who has pressured them heavily to not join the Kindred. There are many different reasons why these established Heathens may want to remain part of a Kindred' Folk Community without joining the Kindred. These Heathens stick around and attend events, because they want to honor their Gods with other Heathens. They want to share friendship and fellowship with other Heathens, and usually have come to like the Kindred and its members quite a bit. Over time, some of these established Heathens will reach a point where they do want to join the Kindred, but others may never take that step.

A Kindred's Folk Community is also made up of established Heathens that the Kindred is not comfortable having as part of their Kindred. They may be going through a large life crisis, and the Kindred may feel they need to get their life back on track before they can join. They may be the sort of person that is fine to be around, but not the sort of person you would want to depend on in a time of need. They may have a somewhat anti-social or grating personality that would not make them a good fit within the Kindred. There are many different reasons, both temporary and permanent, that a Kindred may want to keep an established Heathen out of their Innangarth. These Heathens attend open events, because they want to honor their Gods with other Heathens. They want to share friendship and fellowship with other Heathens, and usually have come to like the Kindred and its members quite a bit. Over time, some of these established Heathens will reach a point where the Kindred is interested in letting them join the Kindred. But others may never reach that point.

Many Folk Communities include non-Heathens, who have great respect for our ancestral ways, but who are not Heathen themselves. Most often these people are agnostics who enjoy close friendships with members of the Kindred, but just cannot move beyond their agnostic point-of-view regarding religious beliefs. Over time, these non-Heathens usually begin sounding and acting more Heathen than many Heathens do, because they accept the cultural values and worldview of our Ancestors, even if they have not accepted their spirituality or their Gods. These non-Heathens attend the Kindred's open events to share in fellowship with people they respect and enjoy being around, and they are almost always enormously respectful of our ways and beneficial to have present. These non-Heathens rarely ask to join the Kindred, understanding that a component of Kindred membership is Faith and Loyalty to the Aesir.

Because the Kindred's Folk Community is not directly a part of their Innangarth, there will be people in their Folk Community that the Kindred would not necessarily let into their Kindred. There are times, when a person's involvement in the Folk Community causes them to change and evolve over time into someone the Kindred would want as a member. But, a Kindred must tend to its Folk Community, weeding out disruptive people and or anyone who seems bent on hurting the Kindred. Removing disruptive people is as simple as letting them know they are no longer welcome at the Kindred's open events, Asatru classes, open Blots/Fainings, etc. This effectively jettisons the disruptive person out of the Kindred's orbit, and prevents the disruptive person from working against the Kindred at the events they host.

BENEFITS OF HAVING A FOLK COMMUNITY

Having a healthy Folk Community surrounding your Kindred has many benefits, to both your Kindred as well as the members of your Folk Community.

If fellowship with 5 or 10 quality Heathens is enjoyable and productive, then fellowship with 20 to 30 quality Heathens is more of a very good thing. When the Kindred works together with its Folk Community, much more can be done – and done faster. Organizing an event or a Heathen gathering is an excellent example of this. If a Kindred of 10 members is organizing a Heathen Gathering, their is only so much they will be able to accomplish. If a Kindred of 10 members is also directly assisted by 10 members of their Folk Community, now 20 people are working on the Heathen gathering. Over time, this level of collaboration and cooperation between the Kindred and members of its Folk Community becomes almost second nature. The Kindred learns who in its Folk Community it can really depend on, and those members of the Folk Community learn the benefits of being part of a larger effort in conjunction with the Kindred.

In times of crisis, a healthy Folk Community can help immensely and/or be helped immensely. While the members of the Folk Community are not a part of the Kindred's Innangarth, there are obviously times of crisis when the Kindred would gladly come to the aid of members of its Folk Community. In return, at times of crisis for the Kindred, it is only natural that members of the Folk Community would offer help when they can.

This relationship we have described between the Kindred and the Folk Community, serves as a perfect testing mechanism for whether someone in the Folk Community would make a good addition to the Kindred. If a member of the Folk Community is at nearly every open event, assisting when they can, and following through on anything they offer to help with, it goes a long way toward showing what sort of person they are. This contact between the Kindred and its Folk Community can serve to transition a new Heathen that knows very little about Heathenry or the Kindred, into a knowledgeable Heathen who is enormously familiar with the Kindred.

One benefit of a healthy Folk Community, is the possibility that if a sufficient number of Heathens become involved in the local area, additional Kindreds may grow from a Kindred's existing Folk Community. If familiarity and friendships are maintained between the Kindred and its Folk Community, these additional Kindreds can form peacefully and with good will toward the original Kindred. Taking Jotun's Bane Kindred as an example, there are currently about 40 Heathens in the Kansas City area and Jotun's Bane Kindred is currently made up of 9 oathed adults. What if in the next 10 years the number of Heathens in Kansas City grows to 300? Would it not be natural that there would be several Kindreds in Kansas City at that point? Would it not be best, if those Kindreds knew each other, communicated regularly, and looked out for one another? As Heathenry grows among our Folk, Maintaining a good relationship with your Kindred's Folk Community can lead to just such a result.

WAYS TO IMPROVE YOUR KINDRED'S FOLK COMMUNITY

Many Heathens argue that we should allow everything to take place naturally, or as "organically" as possible. I understand this inclination, but I feel that if you want something, and you can plan for it and work for it, you should. As my Godhi Rod Landreth would say, "If you want a garden in your backyard, you have to till the earth, plan out your plantings, plant the seeds, weed the garden, water the plants that need it, and protect the garden from animals or bugs that want to eat up the results of all your hard work." You cannot just stare at your backyard and hope a garden grows. You cannot plant seeds, and just hope they grow and are not eaten by animals or bugs. A little hard work can get a lot done.

One way to develop and maintain a Folk Community around your Kindred is to hold regular open events and Asatru classes. The events and classes should be announced loudly and effectively, to reach the maximum number of potentially interested people. The events and classes should be organized, interesting, welcoming, and all guests should be shown generosity and hospitality. Worthy events will attract worthy people, and when they go well, people are more likely to return. Include our spirituality in your Kindred's open events, by scheduling open Blots/Fainings and Folk Symbels.

Plan at least some of your Kindred's open events to the needs of the non-Kindred Heathens you are encountering. If many of these non-Kindred Heathens have never been in a Symbel before, then host one for them and show them how to do it properly. If they are new to Heathenry, then plan a series of Asatru 101 classes for them on various topics. It is also good to listen to input from non-Kindred members as to what sort of open events they would be interested in attending. The goal should be to grow the size of your Kindred's Folk Community, while also educating them, enculturating them, and assisting them in becoming better Heathens. It is possible to work toward a larger Folk Community and a quality Folk Community at the same time. You just have to work at it.

Like all friendships and relationships, the more that your Kindred members communicate and gather with potential members of your Kindred's Folk Community, the stronger the bonds will be built. Having members of your Kindred's Folk Community over for dinner, going to a ball game or concert with them, or just hanging out in a pub are all ways to get to know one another better. The giving of gifts can also build bonds. Books on Heathenry that your Kindred really like make excellent gifts to new Heathens that begin coming to your open events.

Over time, your Kindred can begin holding events to which known and valued members of your Folk Community are invited. These "friends only" events are not "open to anyone" or announced publicly. They are specifically scheduled and planned for just the Kindred and proven members of the Kindred's Folk Community to attend. Most often these events might be a special Blot/Faining, feast, or a series of study group sessions.

Another way to grow stronger bonds between your Kindred and the members of your Kindred's Folk Community, is to invite their involvement in the planning and/or organization of some of your events, or even a Heathen gathering that your Kindred hosts. This is an excellent way to get to know people better, and to develop some common efforts and goals.

GROWING FOLK COMMUNITIES AROUND OUR KINDREDS

Most active and established Kindreds that hold open events will naturally develop over time a group of non-Kindred members that regularly attend their open events. If you grasp the benefits of having such a Folk Community around your Kindred, you can plan and take steps to increase the size and knowledge-level of this Folk Community. You can work to form closer bonds between your Kindred and these non-kinrded Heathens. If done right, these efforts benefit everyone involved and strengthen our grassroots efforts to advance our Folkway forward.

BRINGING NEW MEMBERS INTO A KINDRED

For an existing Kindred, bringing new members into the Kindred can greatly strengthen and improve the group. If done carelessly, it can greatly weaken and injure the group. In other essays I address the topic of carefully screening new members to a Kindred, taking the time to properly get to know them first, and having firm standards to prevent "broken" or troublesome people from getting into your group. After all, this is your Innangarth – your inner circle – and you will share loyalty and Frith with these people. You must be discerning about new members.

No one even starts Jotun's Bane Kindred's year-long applicant process until every single member of our Kindred believes they would make a good member of our Kindred. This only happens if the potential new member has regularly attended our open events, has been coming around awhile, and is serious about our Folkway.

While WHO you let into your Kindred is important, equally important is HOW you bring them into your Kindred. An existing Kindred shares a certain culture, made up of their history, experiences, traditions, expectations, and even knowledge. They have worked together, honored their Gods and Ancestors together, learned together, suffered together, celebrated together, and all of these commonalities give the Kindred its own culture. These unwritten rules, traditions, and expectations that exist between members is the Kindred's Thew.

When you bring a new member into that existing group, they need to be brought into that culture in a methodical and thoughtful way. If a new member is brought in without learning the Thew of the Kindred, the Kindred and the new member will face a series of problems, misunderstandings, and failed expectations that will bring strife and drama into the Kindred. It is important that an existing Kindred have an enculturation process to fully educated a new member as to the Kindred's Thew.

Some Kindreds call these new members Applicants, others call them Probationary, or Prospects, and the Theodish call them Thralls. For the purpose of this essay, I will refer to them as "applicant members" Each Kindred's process of enculturation will vary greatly in detail, and even at times, in purpose. The given culture and Thew of each Kindred will have a large impact on how they bring new members "up to speed" within that culture. But, there are some common features of nearly every Kindred's enculturation process that we can talk about in general terms.

BOTH SIDES OF THE EQUATION ARE CHANGED

When talking about bringing a new member into a Kindred, there is this presumption that everything is on the applicant. That the applicant must learn. The applicant must change. The applicant must work to fit into the kindred. The applicant must acclimate., etc.

But, an applicant process is a back and forth. The Kindred must also learn about the applicant. The Kindred will change based on their contact with the applicant as well. The Kindred must find a way to fit the applicant into their existing group. The Kindred must acclimate to having the applicant as part of the group as well.

Every new member that is brought into a Kindred, alters that Kindred to varying degrees. This is a natural process of growth for the group, and if the applicant was chosen well and the applicant process is designed well, then the growth and change will be in a positive direction.

IT TAKES TIME

You cannot take someone outside a group and make them truly a part of that group overnight. Or even in a couple of weeks or a couple of months. An existing Heathen Kindred should have deeply held bonds between its members and a fairly developed and complex Thew. It should be built on a strong foundation of loyalty and friendship. It should have its fair share of stories, experiences, ways of doing things, and even inside jokes that are shared within the group. It takes time for an applicant member to develop the bonds between the group's existing members that are necessary to truly say the applicant member is "part of the group." It takes time for an applicant member to learn the ways of a group, and what is expected of each member in a wide variety of circumstances.

The period of time might be six months, a year, or it may not be a set amount of time. It may have some other mechanism for deciding when the applicant process is over with other than time. Jotun's Bane Kindred's applicant process is one year, though it can be extended if the Kindred or the applicant needs a little more time. Our year-long process gives the Kindred time to truly get to know the applicant member, and ensure they are someone we want as part of our Kindred. The year-long process also gives the applicant member time to truly get to know us, and ensure they still want to be part of our group. With effort, a year is a sufficient amount of time for a group of people and a new applicant member to fully involve themselves in each other's lives.

ASSIGNED MENTOR

It is a good idea to have an assigned mentor or contact person for the applicant member. This mentor can serve as a guide to learning the ways of a group, answer questions, give direction, and keep the applicant on task and focused on what they need to learn. Having a mentor assigned ensures that the applicant gets consistent input from the group through one stable source.

The mentor can also keep close tabs on the applicant member, ensuring that the applicant is doing the work they need to complete in order to become a full member of the Kindred. Within Jotun's Bane Kindred, an applicant member's mentor is first to speak for or against him/her at the meeting where we decide whether to allow an applicant member to become a full member. While everyone should have a fairly good idea of whether an applicant member is ready, it is acknowledged that the applicant's mentor should have the most informed view on the matter.

REGULAR PARTICIPATION

Having an applicant process is fairly pointless, if an applicant member is not expected to participate regularly in the activities of the Kindred. This includes events on the Kindred's official schedule and those events of a more social nature that are hosted at the homes of Kindred members. It is only through direct participation, interaction, and observation that an applicant member can become a full member of the group.

If an applicant member has complications or problems with participating with the group during the applicant process, those complications or problems will only get worse if the applicant is made a full member of the Kindred. It is a little like dating. Any problem the applicant has during the applicant process, will only be aggravated once the applicant is made a full member. So, these problems should be addressed and corrected during the applicant process.

LEARNING GOALS

There is a certain level of knowledge that each Kindred will expect of a new member. They can work this into their applicant process by requiring certain books be read, certain deeds be completed, and they can even work some level of testing into their process if they feel that is necessary.

Jotun's Bane Kindred requires all applicant members to read the Poetic and Prose Eddas. We feel that without this very basic exposure to the Lore, an applicant member cannot become a well-informed full member of our Kindred. We also require that they read certain chapters of the Heathen Gods book, since these chapters describe in very practical terms how Jotun's Bane Kindred views and approaches certain matters within our Kindred. We also require each applicant member to write and prepare for a Faining, and then lead that Faining for our Kindred. These three areas of learning represent, at a minimum, what we would expect a new member to know prior to becoming a full member of our Kindred.

DECISION TO ACCEPT THEM AS FULL MEMBER

Every applicant process must have a conclusion, and a method for determining whether the applicant member will be accepted as a full member of the Kindred. This decision can be triggered by a time-limit on their applicant process, or a judgment call by the Kindred's leadership or the applicant's mentor. It is good to have rules in place, as to how the Kindred makes this decision regarding all applicant members.

Jotun's Bane Kindred discusses the matter without the applicant present. The applicant's mentor speaks first, giving his or her opinion on the matter. Then everyone in encouraged to offer their opinions. The discussion continues in an orderly way, until the Kindred can come to a consensus on how to continue. We demand a unanimous consensus among the Kindred, because bringing a new member into the Kindred without the full agreement of the Kindred can cause long-term strife and discontent among your members.

FORMAL TRANSITION TO FULL MEMBER

That moment when an applicant member becomes a full member is an very important moment. If you are an oathed Kindred, then the transition to full member of the Kindred is marked with the taking of an oath. But even if you are not an oathed Kindred, it can be a powerful thing to mark or ritualize that transition in a meaningful way.

There can be other signs of acknowledgment of their transition from applicant member to full member of the Kindred. Perhaps you give them a formal Kindred hammer, that signifies their inclusion in the Kindred. Perhaps you give them a specific spot at the table during

High Symbel. Perhaps you give them a gift, that you have given to all the other full members of the Kindred. Perhaps they have certain perks and privileges that they did not have before. Every Kindred will mark this transition differently, but it is important that the transition be marked.

JOTUN'S BANE KINDRED'S APPLICANT PROCESS

Every Kindred's process will differ to varying degrees. But, in the interest of sharing information, I have included at the back of this book a copy of our Kindred's by-laws. To read the written guidelines for our process, read "Article III – The Applicant Process" in our Kindred by-laws.

IntentionaL migration -An ill-Conceived idea

When we discuss Heathen communities – and actually working to establish physical Heathen communities – there are several ways to go. Jotun's Bane Kindred is working enormously hard at gathering the funds necessary to buy tribal land here in the Midwest. We will then build a Hof and Hall on our land and some of our kindred will live there as part of an intentional community. This plan has a local grassroots focus, but will also provide a resource here in the Midwest for heathens in our region. It is based on the strength of our tribe and the Frith we share with one another.

Currently, there are Heathens on Facebook and the internet, proposing several different versions of what I would call a "planned heathen migration." Basically, the concept is to choose a location somewhere in the country or the world, and then a bunch of Heathens move there and sort of slowly take over the town or county. Some of these plans involve forming a "Heathen Homeland." This concept does not have a local grassroots focus, and is somewhat ill-conceived.

Personally, I would not and could not uproot myself to move to such a community or "homeland" for the following reasons:

1. My Kindred is here in Kansas City. I would never leave that.
2. My kids go to good schools here. I moved to my current house

specifically so they could go to these schools.
3. My career is here. I have been a police officer since 2003, and I am less than a decade from retiring.
4. Our families and friends are here. We have roots, connections, and bonds here in Kansas City.

Jotun's Bane Kindred does plan on establishing a Heathen community right here where we are. But, it will be based on knowing one another and having close bonds. In other words, it will be as safe and stable as we can possibly make it for our families. We all have history with one another. Other Heathens can get to know us over time, and join the community, but again, that takes bond-building, time, and trust.

One of most important decisions about establishing an intentional community, is deciding how it will be populated. If it is on private property, and some controlling authority (an owner, a Kindred, etc.) decides who moves there and who does not, then it is possible something like this could work.

But the "planned migration" model proposed so often on the internet seems to have a "build it and they will come" mentality to it. It is this idea that you can announce a town or county, and then a bunch of Heathens move there and sort of take over. In this model, I do not see how anyone could control the sorts of people who move there. It is completely a throw of the dice..

Who will come to this sort of community? Let us assume for a minute that people really put their money where their mouth is, and move there. Let us move beyond the wishful thinking and internet-commitments, and assume there are Heathens that actually pack up everything they own and move there. What sort of people will they be? We cannot say for sure.

But, my first worry is that it will be mainly people who are rootless. People without jobs – or at least good jobs – where they currently are. People without families. People without any real ties, or friends, or Kindred where they are currently located. What good will come from a Heathen community or nation made up of rootless people who were incapable of forming or maintaining a stable life of worth prior to their migration?

My second worry, is that many of the people we will not associate with will move there. People who currently work to twist and misuse our ancestral Folkway would certainly be interested in taking advantage of such an open invitation. White supremacists, chaos-bringing Jotun worshipers, and people of little worth. The wide-open model of populating such a Heathen community, has no real way of preventing these elements from flooding to the area.

My final worry, is that withdrawing from the world by planned migration into a purely heathen community or nation, we are withdrawing from the world and reinforcing our position as a "fringe" religion. Our ancestors did not withdraw from the world. They were constantly traveling out into the world, interacting and trading with others, exploring, and adopting ideas and concepts they liked. They had a clear idea of Innangarth and Utangarth, but they did not withdraw from the world.

Based on these three concerns, I would not be able to participate in such a wide-open effort at populating a community, or purposely migrating to a community or nation. I will not expose my family or children to that. I do not gamble with them. The intentional community we build in the Midwest, will be people we know personally. People we trust, and who trust us. But that is our choice. Our approach.

Obviously, other heathens will have differing points-of-view on this. So, this post should not be considered a personal attack on those putting forward plans for a "planned migration." I simply wanted to share my concerns and ideas about the various "planned heathen migration" models, and illustrate how our plans for an intentional community are enormously different. If the "planned migration" concept is a good idea, I am sure my thoughts and concerns about it will not really have any impact on it what-so-ever.

One thing I do worry about regarding the various grandiose internet plans and efforts that are constantly starting and failing on Facebook or the internet, is that they burn people out. One month people are all fired up about a "new national organization" that is starting, and the next month that effort has faded away or completely self-destructed. A couple of months later, people get all fired up about a "new Heathen Nation" that is going to be formed, and the next month no one is posting on that Facebook page anymore. And as each grand, grand effort starts (on the internet only) and crashes on the digital reef of meaninglessness, I think it has the tendency of disillusioning Heathens and making them cynical.

The key to success for any Heathen effort, is building something meaningful and real, with flesh & blood people whom you actually know and trust.

ESTABLISHING A HEATHEN HOF AND HALL

Our Hof and Hall Fund was set up so that we could accumulate money from our own efforts, our own donations, our own profits (the sale of the book Culture of the Teutons for instance), and the contributions and gifts of others, so that we can buy tribal land.

We would likely buy 15 to 35 acres. It would be far enough from the city and suburbs as to be affordable. But close enough to the city and suburbs for people to easily travel to it for gatherings, commuting, etc. I currently live about 20 to 25 minutes from downtown Kansas City. I believe our tribal land will be about 40 to 50 minutes from downtown Kansas City.

We will need to keep in mind how many utilities and amenities are already available on the land at the time we buy it. We could get some fairly rustic land for a cheaper price, but end up spending a large amount of money getting power, water, and other amenities to it; or we could spend a little more for land that already has these utilities at hand.

We will also have to consider the quality of the road that accesses the property. Land on a paved road or within a 1/2 miles of a paved road costs more. Land 5 miles down a dirt road is a lot cheaper.

On the 15 of 35 acres, we would probably first build a pavilion of sorts. A long roofed pavilion in the general shape of a long hall. Sturdy poles holding up a roof, with no walls, and a concrete floor. Over time, we would enclose this building and make it more of a long hall. A Hof may be included in the end of this hall, or later built onto it, depending on our needs. This is all very preliminary, but the idea is that over time, we would invest more time and money into structures and infrastructure on the tribal land.

We would want to add animals over time. We would likely start with some chickens. Then add goats or sheep. etc. We would also like to plant large gardens.

We would create an outdoor Ve and a camping area, hopefully large enough to hold a large gathering right on the tribal land. We would set aside an area as a burial ground.

While the land is owned by our "church," the legal entity that we have established as Jotun's Bane Kindred, we would figure out a way that those Kindred members that chose to live on the land could do so. Perhaps they would lease space for a trailer. Or land would be partitioned off for the building of homes. That is all to be decided. But the option of living there exists for Kindred members.

While all of this is going on, I intend to keep my job. I intend to keep living where I am living. My kids will still go to school. But I will spend a lot of time at the tribal land. Perhaps I'll build a very small cabin there, in which to spend the night on weekends.

In other words, the fact our Kindred is buying this land, building on this land, and some of us even living on the land, does not mean we are isolating ourselves from society or the world.

But, since this is owned and controlled by our Kindred, the project goes as we want it to go, and our Innangarth is protected.

I suspect, that as our Hof and Hall plans go forward, there are Heathens that may move to the Kansas City area to be closer to our Heartland Hof and Hall. We will have regular open Fainings, religious and culture classes open to the public, and other events that might attract Heathens from other places. Some may move here with the some intention on their part to join Jotun's Bane Kindred.

But as always, that is a matter of getting to know them, them getting to know us, and everyone seeing how that works out.

SECTION THREE

TRIBAL ROLES AND RESPONSIBILITIES

MODERN EGALITARIANISM TAKEN TO THE EXTREME

The term Egalitarianism is derived from the French word égal, meaning "equal," and it refers to various philosophies, that to differing degrees assert that human being should be held as equal to on another. As in all things, it is a matter of degrees. It can refer to an equality of worth as a human being. Sometimes people use the term when referring to equality of opportunity, while others use it while demanding an equality of results. This essay will focus very specifically on the concept of egalitarianism as it is sometimes applied to Heathen Kindreds and Tribes.

A balanced egalitarian approach can be healthy. For instance, there is great value in everyone within a Kindred being able to express their ideas and opinions. When Kindred members feel that have a role in the decision-making process of the Kindred, they are more likely to support the final decisions that are made. An opportunity for each Kindred member to serve in a role for the Kindred that takes advantage of their personal interests, their areas of knowledge, and their natural talent makes each Kindred member happier and more involved.

In some cases though, an extreme egalitarian approach can cause problems. Sometimes it makes people feel good, or makes them feel more "enlightened," to insist that we are all "the same." Other groups will brag about having no acknowledged leaders within their group, for they are all "100% equal." I have seen groups unwilling to make any value judgments about who to let into their group and who not to let into their group, because to do otherwise would be "elitist and judgmental." Below, I address some of these pitfalls.

TREATING EVERYONE EXACTLY THE SAME

None of us are identical. Even identical twins are not truly identical. Knowing this, it completely ignores reality to insist that we are all the same.

Some members of a Kindred are more out-going. Some members are smarter. Some members are more emotionally stable. Some members are more empathetic. Some are better at planning. Some are better at making decisions. Some are more determined. Some are more logical. Some are more skilled with their hands. Some have more artistic skills and potential. Some are very practical while others are very spiritual. Some are stronger. In more ways that we can count, the members of a Kindred are not the same.

If a Kindred makes the mistake of taking an extreme view of "equality" within their ranks, they ignore the strengths and the weaknesses of each member. Taken to its extreme, it is possible to ignore the various talents, interests, skills, and experience that each member of the Kindred possesses.

A more balanced approach acknowledges these differences, and in the best case scenario, exploits these differences for the benefit of the group and its members. Over time, Kindred members gravitate to what they do best, and what they enjoy most. Over time, the rest of the Kindred comes to recognize that Kindred member's role within the Kindred, and the benefits of having them serve in that role. The pieces of the puzzle come together into a Kindred that is truly greater than the sum of its parts.

NO LEADERSHIP

There are some that take the egalitarian approach to the extreme of having no leaders within the Kindred. These group are usually very proud of the fact that they have no Chieftain, no Lord, no Godhi, and that "all the members of the Kindred are equal." This leads to the idea that everyone in the Kindred must be involved in every decision that is made regarding the Kindred, which can become in the worst cases, "leadership by committee."

Imagine for a moment the extremely egalitarian Kindred, where they proudly proclaim that "no on is in charge." Heathen gatherings hosted by such Kindreds can be very dysfunctional. Events are on the schedule, and perhaps a Kindred member has been tasked with coordinating that event, but no one is in a position to ensure the events happen or start on time. Events start late, if they start at all. Other events, not even on the schedule, sometimes pop up randomly without any real rhyme or reason. Guests are never quite sure who to go to within the hosting Kindred, because no one is really in charge. When a guest does ask a member of the hosting Kindred a question about the event, they can be hesitant to answer the question on their own, for fear that the other members of their Kindred might take offense at them answering the question "without consulting the group."

Decision making within such a group can be an arduous process. Even the smallest decisions become difficult to make, and even the simplest matters require a huddle of the entire group just to move forward.

When will dinner be? What should we have for dinner? Will Symbel start right after dinner, or will there be a break? In day to day matters this is time-consuming, but in any sort of crisis or in a situation where timely decision-making is crucial this can quickly lead to disaster.

A tendency can develop in such a Kindred to punish or rebuke anyone within the Kindred that begins to show a little more initiative or a little more leadership than any of the other members. Potential new members with any sort of leadership abilities or initiative, are either driven away for not fitting in or being too pushy, or the potential new members get frustrated by the slow pace of things and lack of initiative and stop coming.

Now, I feel obliged to add here that I have seen Kindreds with no acknowledged leadership that worked really well. But I feel they are the exception to the rule.

NO RECOGNITION

It is possible to take the egalitarian ideal so far, that regardless of what a Kindred member does or does not do, he must be treated the same. The Kindred member that comes to every event, works harder than anyone else on Kindred projects, and is loyal to a fault is treated exactly the same as the Kindred member who shows up now and again, never works very hard on anything, and seems to have a healthy indifference to the Kindred.

While the concept of Frith does dictate that we are loyal and stand by all of our Kindred brothers and sisters, our Ancestors did value some people more than they did others. Some members of a family had more Gefrain or Luck than others. Some were more respected than others. If the patriarch of the family was killed, the vengeance exacted from the killer's family would be much more severe than the vengeance exacted if "drunk uncle Bob" was killed. Vengeance or payment was required in either case, but it was a matter of degrees depending on the quality and value of the person.

I have seen Kindreds where one or two people do most or all of the work, and receive little or no recognition from the other members of the Kindred. Their efforts are almost completely taken for granted. Usually the other members of the Kindred allow these one or two workers to do the work and make decisions, as long as it is convenient to them. As soon as the going gets a little tough or the decisions do not agree completely with what the others think, suddenly the default leaders/workers are warned they are a getting "a little too big for their britches."

There are Kindreds where one Kindred member essentially serves as the unrecognized Chieftain, arranging things, communicating on behalf of the Kindred with other Kindreds, and making decisions. But due to the egalitarian ideal, there is this refusal to acknowledge or call this person the Chieftain. If this arrangement works for everyone, then so be it. But it can lead to confusion among those outside this Kindred as to who to speak with regarding the Kindred, and it can lead to frustration on the part of the "default" Chieftain. Again, it seems like everyone is fine with letting that person serve quietly as a "default" Chieftain, until the going gets tough, and then the rest of the group shuts them down.

Having some defined areas of responsibility and titles, based on the skills, talent, knowledge, and interests of the people who take on those positions of responsibility tends to clarify things, and keep Kindred matters structured and organized.

NO VALUE JUDGEMENTS

If one takes the egalitarian ideal to the extreme, then making any sort of value judgment regarding potential new members that show an interest in the Kindred becomes very difficult. After all, "who are we to judge other people." Taken to the extreme, anyone who shows up to an event is considered a member of the group. I have seen starting Kindreds do this more often than established Kindreds. There is this fallacy that they must allow everyone and anyone to come to their events. I have seen one Kindred-building effort that continually invited several people from the local Heathen community that were heartily opposed to the Kindred ever being established. These nay-sayers would come to event after event, disrupting any effort being made to establish a new Kindred – and eventually the effort failed. Right up the end of things, the organizers of the Kindred-building effort resisted strong recommendations to stop inviting those that opposed their efforts.

Life is about value judgments We judge situations, people, and ideas constantly. Some situations, people, and ideas are bad for us, while other situations, people, and ideas are good for us. Taken to the extreme, the urge to be overly egalitarian leads to a failure to protect one's self from those situations, people, and ideas that are bad for us.

A BALANCED APPROACH

As in all things, too much of a good thing leads to bad results. Taking modern egalitarianism to its ridiculous extreme can be enormously hurtful to anything and everything you are trying to accomplish as a Kindred.

A balanced amount of egalitarianism can be very productive. It is important we acknowledge that there are differences between people, and that we allow people to develop roles for themselves within the group dynamic that play to their strengths, while limiting the damage caused by their weaknesses. It is important we establish a leadership structure for our Kindreds, that allows wise decision-making to happen in a timely fashion. Acknowledging and formalizing these roles and positions of responsibility in a way that works for the group, clarifies matters and helps avoid unnecessary conflict. Finally, the willingness to make value judgments about situations, people, and ideas allows us to protect our hard work, our families, and our Kindred from those people or things which will cause damage or destroy what we have built.

Frigga

EARNING ONE'S ROLE
WITHIN A KINDRED

There are various roles within modern Heathen Kindreds and Tribes. Some Kindreds have one or two of these roles, while other Kindreds have more. Chieftain. Godhi. Thyle. Skald. Loremaster. Lawspeaker. Valkyrie. Secretary. Treasurer. A Trusted Thane. These are just some of the roles you will find here and there within modern Kindreds. Some of these roles are official titles within the Kindred, defined in their by-laws and officially bestowed upon a Kindred member by the Kindred. Some of these roles are simply default positions that people have earned, and are unofficially recognized by the Kindred as that Kindred member's role within the group.

HAVE YOU EARNED THE ROLE?

For these roles to have any sort of meaning, they have to be earned by the person holding that position of responsibility. Often, Kindred members will have an interest in a certain area of responsibility, but they will not have really done any work toward earning that role within the Kindred. They may become very motivated about being bestowed with a title, without having really earned it. The worst thing a Kindred can do in this situation is bestow the title or recognize the role, without the Kindred member having worked for it. The best thing they can do in this situation, is be honest and straight-forward about the fact the Kindred member has not earned that recognition, and then clearly state what he/she should do to earn that role.

For instance, if a Kindred member that rarely reads the Lore, almost never begins or engages in conversations about the Lore, and has never even touched the Sagas steps forward at a Kindred meeting and says, "I want to be the Loremaster of the Kindred," the Kindred will react in couple of ways:

1. The Kindred may choose, in an attempt to be nice, to agree with the request and assign the person the role of Loremaster. In this worst case scenario, they do this just to keep from hurting the person's feelings or with little understanding of why we have roles of responsibility within a Kindred. They assign the role without putting any conditions upon the person, and in most cases the person who showed little interest in the Lore in the first place, will continue to show little interest in the Lore. In this scenario, the role of Loremaster has been assigned or recognized by the Kindred, but it has not been earned, and it means absolutely nothing.

2. The Kindred may choose to express their concerns to the person requesting to be the Loremaster, the fact that they have seen this person show little interest in the Lore. They may after some conversation with him or her, agree to bestow the role upon the person, but with some conditions. The new Loremaster may be required to set up a regular study group. They may ask the new Loremaster to start discussions about the Lore on their Yahoo Group or Message Board on a regular basis. They may ask the new Loremaster to begin reading the Sagas, and to encourage other Kindred members to read them as well. If all goes well, the new Loremaster will step it up, live up to the expectations put upon him or her, and the role will have meaning. If things go poorly, the new Loremaster will do very little to live up to the Kindred's expectations, and the Kindred will remove him or her from the role they gave him or her. The need to remove someone from a role they never earned in the first place, causes unnecessary drama in my opinion.

3. In the best case scenario, the Kindred will very candidly explain to the Kindred member requesting the role of Loremaster, that they have not earned such a role within a Kindred. In very straightforward and honest terms, they will explain exactly how the Kindred member falls short of being recognized in this role. They will decline the request, but show the Kindred member a clear path as to how he or she can earn that role and that recognition. In the long run, this third option causes the least amount of drama. The person requesting to be Loremaster will either step it up and earn that role within the Kindred, or they will not. Regardless, they will learn a valuable lesson in reality. If you do not have the knowledge or the talent, and you have not done the work to earn a position of responsibility within the Kindred, then the Kindred is not going to recognize you in that position.

ARE YOU ALREADY SERVING IN THAT ROLE?

In the simplest terms, the best way to be recognized in a particular role within a Kindred, is to serve in that role in every way, prior to being officially recognized in that position.

If prior to a Kindred having a bank account or a treasurer, there is one Kindred member who is always handing everything money-oriented in the Kindred, then when the time comes to recognize a treasurer, that Kindred member is the natural choice. After all, they helped collect all the money for Holiday feasts, they are the one who collected the money for the Kindred t-shirts, and they coordinated all the Kindred members' registrations to a big Heathen gathering. So, when it is time to name a Treasurer, they already are the Treasurer, in a sense.

If prior to the Kindred officially forming, or recognizing a leader or Chieftain, there is one man or woman who is always scheduling the meetings, leading the discussions, and building consensus among the new Kindred's membership, then when it comes time to choose a leader or Chieftain, that Kindred member is the natural choice. After all, they are already leading. It is not a stretch at all to simply take that default position, and make it something recognized.

If prior to the Kindred recognizing a Thyle, there is one man or woman that keeps things on task. This person seems to be very concerned with the Kindred's direction, the fulfillment of oaths, the attainment of Kindred goals, and they keep notes on what is discussed at meetings and what occurs at Kindred events, then when the time comes to recognize a Thyle, that Kindred member is the natural choice.

The converse of this is true as well. If you try to picture a certain Kindred member in a specific role, and all you can do is chuckle at how badly they fit into that role, then obviously they are a poor choice for the role.

ARE YOU SHOVING A SQUARE PEG INTO A ROUND HOLE?

While this all seems like common sense, there are various reasons that an individual would attempt to take on a role within a Kindred for which they are a bad fit. Perhaps they seek some sort of recognition. Perhaps they are having trouble finding exactly how they fit into the Kindred, and they believe having a position of responsibility (even a poorly chosen one) will help them fit in. Perhaps they are not very good at ascertaining their own strengths and talents.

There are multiple reasons a Kindred would recognize a Kindred member in a role for which they are a bad fit. Perhaps there is a role they feel they need filled, but no one currently in the Kindred fits that role. Perhaps they agree to bestow the role on someone requesting it, in order to avoid hurting their feelings. Perhaps the Kindred is not very good at ascertaining the strengths and talents of its members.

Giving a Kindred member a new role within a Kindred is always a leap of trust. Everyone involved in the decision, needs to examine carefully the past actions, interests, knowledge, skills, talents, and dedication of the member that is being recognized within a new role. If they are a good fit, it is an easy leap of trust. If the fit is a little more tenuous, it is a perfectly good option to give the matter some more time.

ARE YOU SEEKING TO SERVE IN A SPECIFIC ROLE?

So, let us assume for a moment that you want to serve in a specific role in your Kindred. Maybe your Kindred does not have a Thyle, and you not only think you Kindred could use a Thyle, but you feel you would fit well into the role. Or maybe your Kindred does not have a Loremaster, or a Secretary, or a Treasurer, or some other position you feel you could do well. How exactly do you earn that role for yourself?

First, learn everything you can about the role. Read what you can about whatever historical background there is on the role. Read about how people serve in that role in modern times. Befriend and talk with Kindreds who have someone in the role, and find out what they do, why they do it, how they do it, and everything else you can directly from someone serving in that role for another Kindred.

Put some thought into how you would serve in that role. What changes would you make in what you have learned about, to make it fit within your Kindred better. Ascertain if you have the knowledge, skills, and talent to fulfill that role. If you are deficient in some areas, then do what you can to fill the gap. If you want to be Treasurer, then would it hurt to take some courses on accounting at your local community college? If you want to be Loremaster, and you have not read many (or any) Sagas, then would it hurt to start reading some Sagas and brushing up on your Lore knowledge?

If you Kindred has established leadership, have some conversations with the members of that leadership about what they think of the role in which you are interested. Share with them the information you have learned about how the role is dealt with in other Kindreds. Ask for their advice regarding how they see the role fitting into your existing Kindred, and how they would like you to move forward.

Armed with this advice, look for opportunities to implement or try out the role within the Kindred. Look for authentically helpful ways to step forward to take action in ways that prove you to the rest of the Kindred as someone who fits into that role within the Kindred. It is important to do this in a way that is natural and fits well within the Kindred. If you are disruptive in these efforts, then you are actually working against your own goals.

THE BOTTOM LINE?

Kindreds should only recognize or bestow roles and positions of responsibility upon those that have earned them. In the best case scenario, the person should for all practical purposes already be serving in the role prior to asking to be recognized within that role. For someone with an interest in serving in a specific role within a Kindred, there are steps they can and should take to earn that role within the Kindred. If they ask to serve in a role prior to earning it, the Kindred should decline to recognize them in that role, and then give them honest and straight-forward advice about how to move forward and possibly earn that role in the future.

THE ROLE OF LUCK IN RECOGNIZING KINDRED LEADERSHIP

To summarize, Luck is something that was very important to our Ancestors. It is not "dumb luck" or "random luck," like it is viewed in today's modern culture. For Heathens, Luck is something some people have a lot of and some people did not. Those that have a lot of Luck are almost always successful in everything they set their mind to. But Luck is earned. Luck comes from right-action, experience, hard-learned lessons, knowledge, wisdom, and especially hard work. The leader (whether it is the head of a family or the Chieftain of a Tribe) holds and safeguards the Luck of his people. Luck can also be lost or even squandered. Poor decisions, inaction, or dishonorable deeds can all have a large negative impact on one's Luck, and thus affect a person's ability to succeed at future efforts.

Since our Heathen Ancestors believed that their leaders held and safeguarded the Luck of his/her followers, men chose leaders that were seen as having Luck. Obviously, if a man's decisions and actions are successful more often than not, then this is a man whose advice, support, and leadership you would want. The same is true today. When choosing the leadership of your modern Kindred or Tribe, would you rather choose a successful leader or an unsuccessful leader? Would you rather choose leadership that makes good decisions most of the time or bad decisions most of the time?

Among our Heathen Ancestors, when people looked to someone else for advice (Rede), they looked to someone who was seen as having Luck. A man with Luck, had the knowledge, experience, wisdom, insight, and the sort of contacts that allowed him to give Rede that was immensely valuable. When you asked a man for Rede, some of his Luck was considered to go with this Rede. If you were facing a big decision or problem, and you asked a man with Luck for Rede, then following that Rede was seen as enormously likely to help you make the right decision or solve the problem successfully. Common sense would dictate that this is true today as well. When choosing someone to ask for advice, do you go to the man who has repeatedly succeeded or the man who seems to repeatedly fail? Do you ask for marriage advice from a man who has been divorced three times? Do you ask for advice about work-politics from a man who has been fired four times due to work politics?

So, as we talk of what qualities we look for in a Chieftain or a Godhi, one quality that cannot be ignored is Luck. The leadership of a Kindred helps to keep the Kindred focused on its goals, helps build consensus within the Kindred on important decisions, and at times of strife or serious problems, the leadership of the Kindred must sometimes act quickly to solve problems and move the Kindred beyond hardships. Every member of a Kindred is important for different reasons. Each member has a crucial role in making the Kindred what it is. The role of Kindred leadership is one of holding and safeguarding the collective Luck of that Kindred. In order to do this, it is important that those considered for Kindred leadership have Luck of their own.

Let us take the example of a 45 year old man, divorced twice and estranged from his kids, who has started and then run four different Kindreds into the ground, who never goes to Heathen gatherings because he was laid-off from work a year ago, and still has no job, and he is behind on his child support – when this man says he is a Chieftain of a new Kindred (his fifth Kindred, by the way), it is just natural for us as Heathens to see this as rather silly. This man has made many wrong choices, his life is a hot mess, and he has no Luck. What good is his Rede or his Leadership?

When a 17 year old boy with no Kindred who has never read the Eddas or Sagas, never had a family, never had a career, never owned a home, and who lives in with his parents or in the basement of a friend's house, says he is a Godhi, it is just natural for us as Heathens to see this as lacking credibility. This boy has no experience, little knowledge, and no Luck. What good is his Rede or his Leadership?

When a 32 year old woman who spent 15 years as a Wiccan and converted to Heathenry a year ago, who lost her children to the State, who picks fights with every Heathen she meets online, and who avoids Heathen gatherings because people might find out what a mess she is, says she is a Gythia, then it is just natural for us as Heathens to see this as rather sad. This woman has no knowledge base, makes bad decisions, and has no Luck. What good is her Rede or Leadership?

I have given somewhat ridiculous hypothetical examples on purpose. First, I do not want anyone to mistakenly think I am describing them. Second, sometimes exaggerating a bit helps make the point a little sharper. One must consider the life, the Gefrain, the Honor, and most certainly the Luck of the man or woman whom you accept Rede from, or whom you decide to recognize in a leadership role within your Kindred. Do they have experience and knowledge in the matters you need advice about? Have they succeeded at the very things you are asking advice about? Do they make good decisions and do they have more successes in their life than failures?

The positions of Chieftain or Godhi are given by the people who know and respect that man or woman who would serve in these roles. Each time a man or woman trusts in the decision-making or guidance of their Chieftain, his/her position and "authority" is reaffirmed. Each time a man or woman trusts the Rede given to them by their Godhi, his/her position and "authority" as a Godhi is reaffirmed. This is much different than the source of "authority" that exists in many other religions. The people in leadership over our Kindreds earn their authority, and their authority is bestowed on them by those that respect their decisions, guidance, and advice. It is very much a reciprocal relationship.

108

CHIEFTAIN, GODHI, AND THYLE LEADERSHIP STRUCTURE

If a Kindred attempts to organize and structure itself based on the structure of sociological groups among our Ancestors, there are many choices to make. Should you structure your Kindred more like a small family, a large family, a village, a warband, or a Tribe? What time period do you look at for your example? What geographic area? What socio-economic status? Even if you have answered all of these questions, you then have to decide what might need to be tweaked or changed to make that structure work in our modern world and with the people you have in your Kindred.

As you can see, there are various ways to structure a modern Kindred. A structure that works for one group, may not work as well for another group. Every Kindred is made up of different people, with different personalities, different goals, and different life circumstances. That being said, there are some structures that tend to not be very effective in the majority of cases, while there are other structures that tend to be very effective in the majority of cases. So, let us look at some of the things to consider.

A man can be measured by his deeds, and in a similar fashion a Kindred or Tribe can be measured by its deeds. So it is important to put in place or evolve a Kindred structure that allows your Kindred to make good decisions and get things done.

A Kindred needs to be able to weather whatever difficulties and disagreements may occur within the group. So, it is important to put in place or evolve a Kindred structure that allows your Kindred to handle internal disagreements in a Frithful manner.

A Kindred needs to be able to build strong positive Orlog, and collective Luck. So, it is important to put in place or evolve a Kindred structure that can protect its Orlog, and hold and safeguard its Luck.

The structure of Jotun's Bane Kindred includes a Chieftain, a Godhi, and a Thyle. These roles and their responsibilities are described in more detail in the essays that follow. The Chieftain holds and safeguards the Kindred's Luck and shapes and guides decisions within the Kindred. The Godhi tends to the spiritual direction of the Kindred. The Thyle guards the Orlog of the Kindred, and helps the Chieftain in safeguarding its Luck.

Working together, this leadership structure works to ensure that our Kindred makes good decisions and gets things done. This structure allows our Kindred to handle internal disagreements in a Frithful manner. Finally, this structure serves to protect our Kindred's Orlog, and safeguards our Luck.

There are other roles and positions of responsibility within our Kindred, and everyone in the Kindred is important and plays their own important role in making us who we are.

THE ROLE AND RESPONSIBILITIES OF A MODERN CHIEFTAIN

The position of Chieftain is a responsibility recognized and bestowed upon a member of their Kindred or Tribe, by the other members of that Kindred or Tribe. In bestowing this responsibility upon one of its members, the Kindred or Tribe is recognizing the Luck, knowledge, stability, force of character, decision-making, skills, and ability to "get things done" of that particular member. The relationship between the Chieftain and his Tribe is a reciprocal one.

The Kindred goes as its Chieftain goes. A Kindred without a Chieftain can often lack focus, direction, and the ability to wisely come to important decisions or get things done. A Chieftain without a Kindred, is essentially nothing, and certainly not a Chieftain.

In the interest of simplicity, I have referred to the Chieftain throughout this essay using masculine pronouns. There is no reason that a woman could not be a Chieftain. I know too many strong and knowledgeable women of Luck and worth to hold the opinion that only men can serve in the role of Chieftain.

BOUND BY THEW

A Chieftain is bound by the Kindred's Thew, perhaps more than any other member of the Kindred. Due to the vast responsibilities that rest with the Chieftain, the Kindred's eyes are always on him, and the Chieftain's actions and decisions rarely go without notice. Many of the most basic and practical matters of Kindred Thew, affect and are affected by the Chieftain. The customs and traditions of a Kindred, establish many understandings and expectations between the Chieftain and the Kindred's membership, and this Thew helps preserve and maintain the reciprocal relationship between the Chieftain and the Kindred's members.

To be successful, the Chieftain must have a strong working knowledge of Kindred Thew, and an understanding of how his actions and decisions will be perceived by the members of his Kindred. When the Chieftain acts or chooses a course of action within established Thew, the Kindred will quickly and naturally agree and follow his course of action. If the Chieftain acts or chooses a course of action for which no Thew has yet been developed, the Chieftain must ensure that the Kindred's members fully understand the situation and his decision. If the Chieftain acts or chooses a course of action which is contrary to Kindred Thew, then the Chieftain should expect to be challenged and be ready to explain in a compelling manner why acting contrary to Thew was necessary. The Thyle plays a role in advising the Chieftain in a manner consistent with Kindred's Thew, and also in challenging the Chieftain when he acts outside of Thew.

This dynamic within the Kindred, described above, will often result in new Thew being developed or in Thew being adjusted or expanded to fit new situations as the Kindred encounters them. One of the roles of the Chieftain is to act within the bounds of Thew, or to build consensus regarding adjustment or expansions in the Kindred's Thew.

As in all things involving the Chieftain, success in his actions and decisions play a large role in the development of trust between the Chieftain and his Kindred. A Kindred will follow the decisions of a person who has shown great Luck in the past, and a Kindred will continue to follow his decisions as his Luck holds, and as it grows.

It is completely false to think that a Chieftain can dictate whatever he wants to his Kindred. A Chieftain is bound by Thew, and must always actively consider Thew when making decisions. To do otherwise reduces the trust between the Chieftain and his Kindred, and will surely unbalance the reciprocal relationship between the Kindred's members and its leadership. If the Chieftain is allowed to continue along this course, distrust and dissension will develop, disrupting the Frith shared within the Kindred. This in turn will negatively affect the collective Orlog and Luck of the Kindred. If a Chieftain regularly acts in ways contrary to Kindred Thew, and overrides all attempts to challenge him regarding these actions, it is likely that he will be removed from his position or some or all of the Kindred will walk away.

CONSENSUS BUILDER

The strongest way for any group to move forward and accomplish something, is to move forward with a consensus of what to do, how to do it, and why you are doing it. Moving forward with a consensus means that everyone's ideas and opinions have been voiced, discussed, and evaluated. Having a consensus means that you have examined the way forward and discussed it to a point that everyone is in agreement with the plan. A consensus means the entire Kindred has "bought in," and will do their best to make the proposed plan of action succeed.

Consensus is completely different than majority rule. In majority rule, it is possible for half-the-Kindred-plus-one to love the plan for moving forward, while half-the-Kindred-minus-one does not like it at all. This can cause division within the Kindred and result in a disruption of Frith.

Consensus is also different from compromise. Compromise suggests that several courses of action were proposed, and discussions were held until such time as the Kindred decides on a hybrid plan with bits and pieces of the opposing plans. There can be quite a lot of deal-making in compromise. "I will agree to this thing I do not like, if you agree to this other thing that you do not like." Often compromise can lead to a plan for moving forward with which no one is particularly happy.

Consensus is also completely different from having a dictator. If one person dictates and all the rest are just expected to follow, then you do not have everyone's input and ideas, and you have very little true "buy in" from the members of the Kindred.

For consensus to work the Kindred must share true Frith, and the use of consensus further develops and deepens the feelings of Frith between Kindred members. The goal of having a consensus, is to talk about a course of action in a free and Frithful way, until the best parts of everyone's ideas make it into the plan. The process also involves the exposure of flaws in the plan, and efforts as a group to adjust the plan to remove those flaws. The goal of building a consensus, is to develop a plan that everyone "buys into," and values as a healthy way of moving forward. A plan based on consensus is almost always a better plan than any one person in the Kindred could have developed on their own.

When the Kindred faces a serious problem or a large disagreement exists within the Kindred regarding how to move forward, it falls on the Chieftain more than any other member of the Kindred, to move the Kindred toward a consensus. Within a Frithful Kindred, the Chieftain should not spend all his time politicking for his own ideas or his own side of an issue. An inexperienced Chieftain will use the power of his position and the force of his personality to make things go "his way." An experienced Chieftain listens to everyone's ideas, fully evaluates all the pluses and minuses, and then communicates a course of action about which everyone can be supportive and excited.

If the Chieftain wants to enact a new program for bringing in new members, or wants the Kindred to host a new gathering, or wants to purchase something substantial with the Kindred's money, it is not enough that he just dictate this new direction. When a Chieftain wants to takes his Kindred in a new direction or wants the Kindred to tackle a new project, it is the Chieftain's role to elicit suggestions and input from the Kindred's membership, and to communicate his plan in such a way that a consensus successfully forms to move forward with the new idea.

An experienced Chieftain knows the Thew of his Kindred and he knows the members of his Kindred very well. The Chieftain must look ahead to problems, challenges, or decisions that the Kindred will likely face in the future, and works to build consensus and Thew regarding these future problems, challenges, and decisions before they even occur. This ability to look forward and anticipate issues where a consensus among the Kindred will be necessary to move forward, ensures the smooth operation of a Kindred and reinforces the Frith that they share.

DECISION MAKER

Ultimately, a Kindred's Chieftain is respected in that role by his people, based on his own Luck, knowledge, decision-making, and skill with dealing with the world. The need to build consensus within a group does not mean that a Chieftain does not make decisions. The need to build consensus with a group does not amount to some sort of "leadership by committee." A Chieftain is constantly making decisions.

Based on the Chieftain's knowledge of his Kindred and its Thew, the Chieftain can make decisions without consulting with the Kindred when he knows that his decision will be accepted as being within the Kindred's Thew. For example, if the same or similar situation has come up two times and both times the Kindred handled it in the same way, the third time that situation comes up the Chieftain can simply handle it according to Thew, and no one will question it. Actually the Kindred will appreciate the fact that their Chieftain knows what to do in that situation in a decisive way, based on established Thew.

In emergency or any situation where a decision must be made immediately or quickly, the Chieftain is expected to make a wise decision at that moment. The Kindred will understand and appreciate their Chieftain being able to handle that situation quickly and wisely, without having to call a Kindred-meeting or form a committee. It is for this very purpose that a Kindred has chosen to recognize one of their own as Chieftain, and hopefully they have picked someone to fill that role that has the Luck to make good decisions under pressure.

Even for small details, the Kindred will often look to the Chieftain for decisions. What time will dinner be served at an event? Who will set up tables and who will cook? What time are we leaving for a trip to visit another Kindred? What time do we need to break camp and start packing up? Should we do our study group first and the Faining later, or the Faining first and study afterward? These decisions are not always made by the Chieftain, but there are times when the Kindred simply looks to the Chieftain to make some easy decisions regarding what the Kindred should be doing, and in what order we should be doing it. It is not that Kindred members cannot decide these things for themselves. They are all strong and intelligent individuals with a will of their own. But there is a convenience and efficiency to having someone willing to make a quick decision about a small matter that affects the entire Kindred. The last thing a Kindred wants or needs is a full Kindred discussion or a committee meeting to decide what time the Kindred should start cooking dinner.

Another time that the Chieftain may have to take control and simply make a decision for the group, is in any situation where a decision must be made but the Kindred cannot come to a consensus. If it is clear that no consensus can be found, but a decision must be made, the Chieftain must take everything into consideration and make the wisest decision possible. It is important that the Kindred understand that this will sometimes be necessary, and trust in their Chieftain and support his final decision on such a matter. If the Chieftain is good at building consensus and everyone in the Kindred approaches these discussions in a Frithful manner, it should be fairly rare that the Kindred cannot reach a consensus.

The Chieftain is constantly making decisions regarding what matters deserve priority, interactions with Heathens outside the Kindred and other Kindreds, and regarding the basic internal operations of the Kindred. He must know what is going on in the lives of his Kindred members, and decide what actions he can take to advance them forward in their own lives, and collectively as a group. Good decisions and successful results help build Luck for the Chieftain and his Kindred, and further develop and deepen the complexity of the Kindred's Thew.

EXAMPLE SETTER

One way that a Chieftain serves as an example to his Kindred, is in his work ethic. If the Kindred sees the Chieftain working hard, they are more than willing to work hard by his side. If the Chieftain is working hard, and asks someone in the Kindred to assist him or to take on the completion of some other important task, the direction given by the Chieftain will be welcome. Often, if the Kindred sees the Chieftain working hard, they will busy themselves with work of their own out of obligation and loyalty to their Chieftain.

As an example, if at the end of a camping trip the Chieftain walks over and begins packing gear and loading it into the vehicles for the trip home, the rest of the Kindred will also begin packing and loading their gear and the Kindred's gear. The Chieftain does not even have to say a word. They follow his example, and they would feel shame to sit quietly off to the side while their Chieftain works alone.

As a contrary example, if the Chieftain hardly works at all, but instead sits on his rear constantly telling other people what to do, this can very quickly lead to resentment among the Kindred's members. They will quickly recognize his laziness and either join in on the laziness or quickly develop anger at the work they are having to do on his behalf.

The Chieftain sets an example for his Kindred in many areas besides his work ethic. It is true that as the Chieftain goes, the Kindred goes. If the Chieftain is generous, honorable, works hard, shows Frith towards everyone in the Kindred, and has a strong sense of responsibility, this behavior sets a tone and expectations within the Kindred that its members also be generous, honorable, work hard, show Frith toward others in the Kindred, and have a strong sense of responsibility. The opposite is true as well. If a Chieftain is stingy, dishonorable, lazy, disloyal, and has no sense of responsibility, then it is enormously likely that his Kindred will eventually turn into a mirror image of their Chieftain's failings.

This happens in two ways. First, the Chieftain can set a tone within the Kindred and inspire existing members to be the best they can be, or conversely the worst they can be. Secondly, a strong Chieftain of worth, will attract new people willing to join the Kindred that are also strong and worthy. A weak and dishonorable Chieftain will by his nature, drive away every new person of worth that comes around the Kindred.

When choosing a Chieftain for your Kindred, consider the fact that within several years the Kindred as a whole will very likely have many of the same qualities the Chieftain has, for good or ill. If you serve in the role of Chieftain for your Kindred, you must understand that your every action and decision will have an effect on the nature of your Kindred.

HOLDER OF THE KINDRED'S LUCK

To understand this portion of the essay, you must understand that Luck is something we earn. Our hard work, our knowledge, our skills at dealing with people, our ability to overcome hardship and conflict, our decision-making, and all that we accomplish honorably in this world is part of our Luck. Over time, the more successful one is the more Luck he/she gains. When something goes wrong, the Luck we have built can make the problem easier to overcome. When someone attacks us, the Luck we have built can turn their attack away. Our Luck encourages unanticipated positive events and opportunities to develop for us.

Collectively, the same things that constitute the Luck of an individual, can also be attributed to the Luck of a Kindred. When a Kindred performs great and honorable deeds, builds its collective knowledge and skills, and learns to work together in true Frith, then they begin to build collective Luck. When something goes wrong, that Luck makes the problem easier to overcome. When someone attacks the Kindred, the Luck they have built can turn the attack away. The collective Luck of the Kindred encourages unanticipated positive events and opportunities to develop for the Kindred and its members.

Our Ancestors understood that the collective Luck of a group was held by its leader. It is simply common sense that this same concept is true and applicable today. If a Kindred or Tribe is led by a person who is knowledgeable, focused, makes good decisions, stable, a hard worker, knows how to work with others, and determined to succeed, then the Kindred or Tribe will do well. It will experience Luck in its efforts in a positive way, and will be able to take advantage of all the positive opportunities for moving forward that are generated.

If a Kindred or Tribe is led by a person who is ignorant, unfocused, makes poor decisions, unstable, lazy, unable to work with others, or lacks determination, then the Kindred or Tribe will likely have no Luck at all. Many bad things will happen. When problems do occur the problems will be more difficult to overcome. The group will be so busy dealing with the problems their poor leader causes or allows to happen, that very few positive opportunities will come along, and even when they do, they will be squandered.

Without quality leadership, any group will have very little Luck. Individual members of the group can attempt to make up for this bad leadership, but they spend all their time essentially swimming upstream as long as the bad leadership remains in place. This not only goes for Heathen Kindreds and Tribes. It is also true of Heathen organizations, study groups, Pubmoot efforts, and it is also true for groups outside of Heathenry, like corporations, organizations, small businesses, charities, and clubs.

In order to effectively hold the Luck of their Kindred, a Chieftain must have Luck of his own. He must know how to generate Luck, how to protect his Luck, and how to use his Luck. Having this knowledge personally in his own life, such a Chieftain knows what the Kindred must do to generate Luck, protect its Luck, and how to use the Kindred's Luck to its maximum benefit.

The Chieftain should also understand that a Kindred that accepts Luckless individuals into its Innangarth, is putting its own collective Luck at risk, and a Chieftain should do everything he can to prevent this.

GUARDIAN OF THE KINDRED'S ORLOG

The past deeds of an individual do have an effect on the opportunities and possibilities that come their way. This feature of individual Orlog, also plays a role in a Kindred's combined Orlog. The past deeds of every individual in the Kindred and the past deeds of the Kindred itself do have an effect on the opportunities and possibilities that come the Kindred's way.

As a consensus-builder and a decision-maker within the Kindred, a Chieftain must always keep the Kindred's combined Orlog in mind. What will be the results of the Kindred's deeds and actions? Are these deeds and actions honorable? Are these deeds and actions pleasing to our Gods? Do these deeds and actions make our Ancestors proud? Will these deeds and actions show the respect and consideration of the Vaettir that is due to them? How will these deeds and actions affect the Kindred's Gefrain (reputation)?

The Kindred's Thyle should work very closely with the Chieftain in this regard, and they should communicate regularly about such matters.

If the Kindred appears to be moving toward a course of action that the Chieftain believes will be damaging to the Kindred's Orlog, it is his obligation to communicate, convince, and build consensus that his judgment is correct. He must use everything in his power to steer the Kindred away from this damaging course of action. If an individual member of the Kindred is acting in such a way that it threatens to damage the Kindred's Orlog, the Chieftain has an obligation to share Rede with that individual and help them understand how they can correct that behavior or action. If the matter is serious enough, he may hold a meeting that involves the individual in question, the Chieftain, the Godhi, and the Thyle so that the Rede of these trusted men can add weight to his own Rede. In addition, there are times when the entire Kindred needs to be brought together, the matter discussed, and Frithful decisions made.

The Chieftain must always be vigilant in judging the character and worth of those individuals and families that show an interest in joining the Kindred or seeking to become a part of the Folk Community that exists around the Kindred. There are those that through their actions would unintentionally, or even intentionally, damage the Kindred's Orlog if they are allowed within its Innangarth.

LORD OF THE HALL

The role of Chieftain outside of Symbel, is naturally reflected during Symbel as well. As Lord of the Hall, the Chieftain normally hosts formal Symbels and Symbels where non-Kindred members and guests are present. For small Kindred Symbels at someone's home other than the Chieftain's home, the host may sometimes lead the Symbel. But not always. This is a decision made prior to such Symbels, and is usually left to the preference of the host.

In formal Symbels and Symbels that include guests, the Chieftain works closely with the Lady of the Hall, the Thyle, the Godhi, the Valkyrie, and the Hall Wardens to ensure the Symbel goes well and brings Luck and Honor to all present. While the Valkyrie and Thyle have very specific roles during Symbel, the Lord of the Hall supports them in these roles and can and will step in if something appears to be going wrong. Since the Chieftain holds the Kindred's Luck and protects its Orlog, it is ultimately his responsibility to ensure everyone performs their responsibilities during Symbel and that everything occurs as it should.

THE FACE OF THE KINDRED

As the Kindred's Chieftain, many outside the Kindred will associate the Kindred closely with its leader. For Jotun's Bane Kindred, the Chieftain handles many of the administrative matters concerning events, gatherings, or other efforts with which the Kindred is involved. For this reason, the Chieftain often serves as the spokesperson for the Kindred. This tends to reinforce the association between the Kindred and its Chieftain.

At events and gatherings that the Kindred is hosting, ultimately the Chieftain is the host. The Chieftain usually welcomes the guests, lets them know what will be happening at the event, and guides everyone through the scheduled activities. If something goes wrong at the event, the Chieftain is always informed, and ensures the problem is quickly and quietly rectified, either by himself or at his direction. Even if a problem is immediately handled by a Kindred member, the Chieftain is normally informed what went wrong and how it was corrected.

At such an event or gathering, it is ultimately the Chieftain's responsibility that things go as smoothly as possible, that the event is meaningful and successful, and that the guests feel welcome and leave the event pleased they chose to attend. In these situations, the Chieftain should attempt to greet and talk with everyone in attendance, and get to know them. This role as host tends to reinforce the association between the Kindred and its Chieftain.

The Chieftain must never forget that without his Kindred, he is essentially nothing, and certainly not a Chieftain. Rather than reacting to the attention given him with arrogance and a sense of entitlement, a Chieftain should be generous and friendly. He should advance his men and women forward, giving them credit for their good work and accomplishments, and never forgetting that everything they achieve as a Kindred is a group-effort, accomplished through Frithful and collective effort. It is natural that the Chieftain is often seen as the Face of the Kindred, or that the Chieftain should sometimes receive praise that might be better directed at his entire Kindred. In those moments, it is important the Chieftain be generous and give credit to everyone that works to make the Kindred successful.

In turn, the Kindred must remember the enormous burden of responsibility that is often placed upon the Chieftain, and should be understanding that there will be times that outside people will closely associate a Kindred with its Chieftain, and further associate the Kindred's successes with he who bears the burden of the Kindred's oath-ring.

FACILITATOR

Every Kindred members has unique skills and specific knowledge that
no one else in the Kindred has. Over time, members of the Kindred
take on various roles of responsibility at which they are best. There
may be one or two Kindred members that are very good at organizing
a kitchen and getting a large meal prepared. There may be one of two
Kindred members that are very good at starting need-fires and tending
to campfires. There may be Kindred members that are good at
teaching, carving, keeping the bank account in order, playing music,
working with children, and this list could go on and on. One of the
most important things a Chieftain must learn to do, is to step back and
let other Kindred members do what they do best. He can support
them. He can roll up his sleeves and help them. But, as important as
the role of the Chieftain can be, it is not all about the Chieftain. What
is paramount is knowing when to step back into the crowd and simply
allow your Frithful Kindred to work like a well-oiled machine.

A Chieftain must also know when to delegate and direct others to get
things done as efficiently and effectively as possible. A Chieftain
cannot do everything himself, and must give responsibilities and tasks
to others to perform. The Chieftain must know the capabilities of his
Kindred's members, and know who he can trust to successfully
perform specific tasks. Once a Kindred member has proven their
ability to fulfill certain responsibilities successfully, the Chieftain must
rely on that member to do their job without micro-managing them or
interfering with their work.

Part of the Chieftain's role as a facilitator, is helping newer members
find their "place" or their role in the Kindred. New members to a
group must go through a process of "settling-in," and part of that
process for the new member is to figure out where they fit best into
the Kindred. Sometimes it takes some time to figure out what unique
skills or specific knowledge they bring to the table. The Chieftain can
give advice on this and help new members find their specific roles
within the Kindred.

A Frithful Kindred or Tribe is more than the sum of its parts, but the
successes of each individual member do play a role in the success,
Luck, and Gefrain of the Kindred as a whole. The concept of Frith
suggests that what one Kindred member has done, the whole Kindred
has done – and what the Kindred does as a whole, each individual
member has done. Toward this end, a Chieftain must support and
facilitate the growth and success of each individual member of his

Kindred. A Chieftain should encourage, support, and allow the individual members of his Kindred to grow and become the absolutely best and most honorable people they can be. There are times when individual members of the Kindred will get a lot of attention for their great deeds, and a Chieftain should celebrate this and even do what he can to give that individual member the spotlight they deserve.

GIVER OF REDE

Our Ancestors believed that when you asked for advice from a man of Luck, that the Rede you received contained some of that man's Luck. If you followed the Rede given by a Chieftain or the King, then the Luck of that Rede was likely to bring you success. In very practical terms, this makes complete sense. When you require advice about a business matter would you rather ask someone has built and operated a successful business or a guy who has run three businesses into bankruptcy? When you require advice about your marriage or your children would you rather ask a happy and successful family-man, or a guy who has been divorced twice and never sees his kids? When you require advice about interpersonal relationships would you rather ask someone who deals well with people and who is well-liked and respected by many friends or a guy who seems to eventually anger and drive away everyone with whom he interacts?

If the Kindred has chosen their Chieftain well, then the Kindred as a whole will benefit from his Rede on important matters and decisions that must be made. In addition, individual Kindred members may seek Rede from their Chieftain regarding matters within their own families and in their own lives. Kindred members may even ask the Chieftain about how to resolve a problem they are having with someone in the Kindred. It is possible that Heathens involved in the Folk Community surrounding the Kindred, or even Heathens from around the region, may ask for Rede from a Chieftain who is considered to be a man of great Luck.

If a Chieftain's Rede is good and leads others to success, then his Gefrain as a giver of Rede will grow.

RINGGIVER

It is said that a good Chieftain is the poorest among his men. It is a high compliment to say that a Chieftain is a "gold-hater," as it illustrates the Chieftain's generosity.

If someone in the Kindred needs money or food, the Chieftain should be the first to give what he can to help. If someone in the Kindred is facing a serious problem, the Chieftain should be the first to give advice, take action to help solve it, or to fight by their side to make things right. If someone tries something and fails, the Chieftain should be the first to pick them up, dust them off, and be available to give them Rede should they require it.

A Chieftain should be generous with is money, his skills, his time, his energy, his effort, his concern, his Rede, his Luck, and his love. He should be willing to give all that he has for his family and his Tribe. He should work tirelessly to advance his Kindred forward as a whole and to advance forward in life every individual member of his Kindred.

Often, those that deride the idea of Kindreds needing leaders, will suggest an image of the arrogant Chieftain, dictating orders, while he sits back doing nothing, and enjoying some sort of power-trip over others. This is the exact opposite of true leadership.

Some would suggest the image of the selfish Chieftain, hoarding the Kindred's assets and all the goods and money generated by the work of the Kindred. Pushing himself out in front on the backs of the Kindred's members, taking full and complete credit for all his Kindred has done. This too is the exact opposite of true leadership.

A Heathen Chieftain is the first to get to work – and the last to stop and rest. A Heathen Chieftain sees his role within the Kindred as a responsibility to those he values and cares most about in the world. A Heathen Chieftain leads by example, and not by making others do his work. A Heathen Chieftain is bound by his Kindred's Thew, not someone who can do whatever he wants, any way he wants, whenever he wants. A Heathen Chieftain is generous and sharing with both the tangible and intangible results of the Kindred's hard work.

INTERACTIONS WITH OTHER ROLES WITHIN THE KINDRED

The Chieftain works closely with everyone in the Kindred, but he must work even more closely with the other Kindred members that hold positions of responsibility within the Kindred, such as the Godhi, the Thyle, and the Valkyrie. He must be able to inherently trust the people who serve in these positions. He must communicate with them regularly, and be able to do so in a direct and straight forward manner. There are times that the responsibilities of these other roles will intersect, or even overlap, with the responsibilities of the Chieftain. So, it is important that all of their efforts are coordinated as efficiently and effectively as possible. As trusted Thanes of the Chieftain, these other leadership roles have a responsibility to support and protect their Chieftain from the actions of others that may intentionally or unintentionally hurt or diminish their Chieftain, and thus hurt or diminish the Kindred.

The Kindred's Godhi gives Rede to the Chieftain, which the Chieftain then evaluates, and decides what is to be done, what priority should be given to it, and when and how to do it. If the Godhi says that the Kindred would benefit spiritually by accomplishing A, B, and C, it is the Chieftain's role to build consensus within the Kindred regarding whether A, B, or C will be worked on, when that work should be scheduled, what will be needed to accomplish the work, etc. In the simplest terms, there are times that the Godhi may say where the Kindred needs to go, but it is the Chieftain who decides when to begin, who is going, and how to get there. The Godhi serves as an adviser to the Chieftain, and it is drastically important that the Chieftain and Godhi work together well.

The Kindred's Thyle knows and maintains the Thew of the Kindred, and plays a major role in safeguarding the Kindred's Orlog. So, there are many areas of responsibility where the Thyle and Chieftain work together. This redundancy is intentional, because these responsibilities are enormously important to the stability and strength of the Kindred. While the Thyle plays an important role in judging oaths that are made and ensuring that sufficient Shyld is offered in case there would be a failure in fulfilling the oath, it is the Chieftain in our Kindred that wears our Kindred's oath-ring. The Chieftain literally holds the oaths made on that ring, including each member's Kindred oath.

The Kindred's Thyle also serves as a safeguard, and should be free to privately challenge the Kindred's Chieftain should it appear that he is on the wrong course or making decisions that will negatively affect the Kindred's Orlog. Depending on the seriousness of the situation and the degree to which the Chieftain may be acting outside the Kindred's Thew, it may be appropriate for the Thyle to challenge the Chieftain before the Kindred, and ask him to explain and justify his actions, so the matter can be worked through and resolved.

Both inside and outside of Symbel, the Chieftain and Valkyrie must work well together. During Symbel the Valkyrie is walking among the guests, safeguarding the horn (well) and will often become aware of a problem or a potential problem long before the Chieftain, the Thyle, or the Hall Wardens are aware of it. The Chieftain and Thyle must watch the Valkyrie closely, and respond appropriately when she requires assistance from them or the Hall Wardens. Away from Symbel, the Valkyrie serves as a trusted adviser to the Chieftain, and helps to watch his back in all matters.

CONCLUSION

As the Chieftain goes, the Kindred goes. A good leader understands and accepts that he is bound by Thew more than any other member of the Kindred. He will work to be a consensus-builder and he will lead by example. He will make decisions that protect and build the collective Luck of the Kindred, and is always mindful of safeguarding the Kindred's Orlog. He must work well with everyone in his Kindred, and especially those who also hold positions of responsibility. As Lord of the Hall, he should be known for his hospitality, generosity, and honor. A Chieftain must never forget that his words, decisions, and deeds directly impact to what degree his Kindred and its members will succeed and prosper in this life. His reciprocal relationship with the members of his Kindred, is a position of responsibility bestowed upon him by his Kindred. A Chieftain with little Luck, damaged Orlog, or who does not show love and generosity toward the members of his Kindred or Tribe will not long be their Chieftain.

THE ROLE AND RESPONSIBILITIES OF A MODERN GODHI

Co-Written by Rod Landreth & Mark Ludwig Stinson

Among Heathens in Iceland, a Goði was a local Chieftain with religious and administrative duties. For modern Heathens the Old Norse word Goði, has been anglicized as Godhi for males, and the word Gyðja has been anglicized as Gythia, Gydhia or Gydhja for females in the role. The plural Old Norse word Goðar has been anglicized as Gothar or Godhar. Throughout this essay, we will use the masculine form or the plural form to keep things simple. This is not to take anything away from women being in this role, as everything written here can apply equally to both men and women. In Iceland, modern Asatruars use the term Godhi for both males and females in this role, and find our use of the term Gythia as rather odd from a linguistic standpoint.

As with most topics in modern Heathenry there is a wide range of opinions on the role of a Godhi within a modern Kindred. Some Kindred's have both a Chieftain and a Godhi, some Kindreds have either a Chieftain or a Godhi, and some Kindreds choose to have neither. Some see Gothar as a vital and important element in the growth of modern Heathenry. Others see the modern Godhi as an attempt to imitate the power structures and roles within other religions. Going even further, some see the role as playing to the delusions of grandeur of whomever claims the title.

Instead of focusing on the many controversies regarding modern Gothar, this essay will focus on the real world example of the various roles, interactions, and basic responsibilities of the Godhi of Jotun's Bane Kindred. Each Kindred will approach this role somewhat differently based on their own circumstances, experience, and needs as a Kindred.

There is not a lot of surviving information regarding Heathen priests among our Ancestors. Go to this link for a summary of some of the information we do have:

http://www.reeves-hall.org/role_of_gothi.htm

This essay is not meant to be a scholarly paper on the role and responsibilities of an Icelandic Goði or a religious-spiritual expert in ancient Heathenry. It is a practical essay regarding the role and responsibilities of a modern Godhi within our own modern Tribe.

PRIMARY FUNCTION AND ROLE

Within a Kindred, as in any group, there are many roles. In the simplest terms there are Leaders, Maintainers, and Supporters. At any one time, everyone takes on one or more of these roles. Just as the primary job of the Chieftain is to be the Leader of the Kindred, the primary job of the Godhi is to be a Maintainer of the Kindred in religious, spiritual, and personal matters. The Godhi does this by keeping actions and events on track, and concentrating everyone involved on what is important, how it is important, and why it is important.

This means that a Godhi needs to have their finger on the pulse of the emotional, spiritual, and social circumstances of the individual members, as well as the Kindred as a whole. The Godhi may have to take on different roles, acting as an arbitrator, mediator, or spiritual counselor. When serving in these roles, the Godhi calls on such skills as active listening, understanding of communication styles, and the ability to calm people down and discuss things in order to come to an amicable and satisfying solution.

In addition, the Godhi needs to fully understand the dynamics within his/her Kindred. They must know the way the Kindred interacts with itself and holds itself together, and also how to reinforce Kindred Thew or work for adjustments in Kindred Thew as needed. This requires not only intellectual understandings, but also emotional and spiritual understandings.

Being the religious-spiritual expert of the group, the Godhi must have not only knowledge of Heathen Lore, but also how to properly apply that knowledge of the Lore in various real-life situations. That means Gothar must have more than a working knowledge of Primary, and important Secondary, information and Lore; they must also be constantly striving to gain new understandings and insights into the Lore. A healthy and vigorous personal, spiritual, and intellectual regimen is necessary to balance incoming knowledge with understood spiritual "connections" to best be able to advise, guide, teach, and encourage actively-lived Heathenry.

Kindred members should be able to come to the Godhi expecting clear explanations and guidance in matters of faith, spirit, and practice. It also means the Godhi needs to be able to explain and solidly instruct the What, How, and Why of Heathenry, both ancient and modern. This is a tightrope walk, because you must temper this knowledge and wisdom with where one's Kindred is going, and its existing Thew. A Godhi guides, advises, and encourages—rather than dictating these ideas and understandings.

BASIC RESPONSIBILITIES

A Godhi needs to be able to do at least the following, and probably more:

- Get to know each new person in the Kindred to assess who they are, where they are in their Heathenry, what is important to them, how it is important, and why they are Heathen. A Godhi needs to maintain this contact and knowledge of individual Kindred members on an on-going basis.

- If there is a mentoring process for new Kindred members, the Godhi should work with the Chieftain and Thyle to properly match up mentors with applicant members.

- Serve as a resource, give Rede, guide, advise, and provide encouragement on the what, how, and why of religion, spirituality, related history, ways and modern practice of Heathenry.

- Provide guidance about understanding and honoring our Gods, Ancestors,the Vaettir, and our modern Folkway, in a manner that coincides with current Kindred Thew.

- Be an example to the rest of the Kindred in their participation, learning, appearance, goals, values, and ethics, as well as adherence to Kindred Thew, as best they can. They should also be an example to the rest of the Kindred in their interactions with greater Heathenry outside the Kindred.

- Spiritually maintain (Bless, Cleanse, and Secure) items and places of religious/spiritual significance to the Kindred.

- Conduct Fainings, both seasonal and specific rituals.

- Assist with the leadership and administration of the Kindred, as needed.

SPECIFIC INTERACTIONS WITH OTHER ROLES IN THE KINDRED

Besides the general responsibilities of the Godhi, there are also some specific interactions with various other roles within the Kindred. There is a natural overlap in responsibilities among these various roles in the Kindred. Often these areas of overlap are areas that benefit from the increased level of attention that they receive, and areas important enough to demand some level of redundancy.

In a Frithful Kindred, there is no sense of competition regarding these responsibilities. In the ancient world, there may have been some jockeying amongst the Thanes to get the Chieftain's ear, but in modern Heathen Kindred there should be more of a focus on collaboration and cooperation. The Chieftain is first among equals, and while the Godhi may be the Chieftain's right hand and may share certain leadership responsibilities, this does not mean the Godhi "outranks" any of the other titled Thanes. In Jotun's Bane Kindred, none of us has or attempts to exercise dictatorial powers. We each have our primary role and responsibilities, and we have differing areas in which we focus. The Godhi focuses on spiritual-religious issues, the Thyle on guarding the Orlog of the Kindred, the Valkyrie on protecting the layers that are put into the Well, and the Chieftain on holding and preserving the Kindred's Luck. Others in the Kindred focus on other things both mundane and sacred, based on roles they establish through their own skills, interests, and hard work.

What follows are specific descriptions of how the Godhi of Jotun's Bane Kindred interacts with the other positions of responsibility within the Kindred. The various roles mentioned here are by no means an exhaustive list, as each Kindred will develop their own positions of responsibility, based on their needs. In addition, each Kindred will likely differ somewhat in how these roles interact with one another. These examples however, will hopefully get you thinking about how things can or should work in your Kindred.

INTERACTION WITH THE CHIEFTAIN

The primary responsibility of the Godhi is to use his wisdom, knowledge, and skills to support the Kindred's Chieftain. It is immensely important that there is a mutual understanding and trust shared between the Godhi and Chieftain. A Godhi should know what his Chieftain's goals are, how he/she wants to get there, and why he/she wants to achieve those goals. Toward that end, the Godhi and Chieftain should be able to have long in-depth conversations about the direction and dynamics within the Kindred. But, the Chieftain also needs to be able to glance at the Godhi and get advice or guidance with a nod, gesture, or word.

Gothar need to *seek* connections between, within, and around. These connections may be found in what appears to be random information. Through and because of the connections and relationships with the Divine, a Godhi senses and realizes patterns in that randomness intuitively. This is where Orlog comes together. This place is where omens exist. Bringing together these connections in comprehensible ways through a spiritual-religious lens, the true meaning of gnosis, is where a Godhi is the most useful to their Chieftain.

This seeking and understanding connections is also one of those things that a Godhi has to learn "in the field." In practical terms, it means a Godhi has to be inquisitive, observant, and thoughtful. The Godhi needs to be constantly on the lookout for what is worthwhile to the Kindred, and what is not. Then, when asked, be able to advise the Chieftain with the best and most useful information one can. We joke sometimes that Rod is the "Merlin" to Mark's "Arthur." This analogy is mainly meant to communicate Rod's role as a trusted adviser. The Thyle, and other Thanes, are there to advise the Chieftain as well, but it is primarily the role of the Godhi.

A Godhi must understand their role in supporting the Chieftain. It is the Godhi's job to make sure the Chieftain is always putting his/her best face forward. A Godhi should only counter the Chieftain in public if there is an immediate need to stop the Chieftain from doing something wrong that will do the Chieftain or the Kindred harm. This is a responsibility that is primarily the Thyle's, but it is helpful to have more than one trusted person watching out for the best interests of the Chieftain and the Kindred. Remember, Heathens move from a place of strength, and it is important that the Kindred's Gefrain is protected and Honor maintained. Unless the Godhi is in the act of doing their job (meaning during ritual, or other overt religious activity as mentioned above) the Chieftain *is* the face of the Kindred and carries its Luck. By protecting the Chieftain, the Godhi ultimately safeguards the Kindred.

This is in public, of course; behind closed doors or otherwise in private, it matters less how the Godhi and Chieftain interact, but hopefully they are good and trusting friends. That trust should come about because both are there for each other, giving each other Rede, standing by one another, and earning that deep bond. While it may be the role of the Godhi to advise, "the Kindred should go to that distant mountain," it is the role of the Chieftain to trust and evaluate his Godhi's Rede and make decisions as to when and by what course the Kindred actually reaches that mountain.

This is not to say that a Godhi is subservient or lesser. A Godhi's authority spawns from a different place than the Chieftain's authority. The Godhi's authority stems from the realm of the divine, and the acknowledgment by the Kindred and Folk of those sacred connections and relationships. The Chieftain's authority comes more directly from the Kindred itself, the Folk, its Orlog, its Honor, and its Luck, usually as represented by the oath ring on the Chieftain's arm. He is the symbol of the Kindred, while the Godhi protects, encourages, and establishes the significance of the Kindred.

INTERACTION WITH THE THYLE

There are many areas where the responsibilities of the Thyle and Godhi interact. Both, for instance share a role in protecting the Kindred's Orlog. Mostly, the Godhi deals with this in indirect ways, through guidance, advice, and teaching, or by nudging and encouraging a Kindred member towards the best course. The Thyle, on the other hand, is a bit more direct and focused. Therefore, a Thyle may bluntly tell a person they are moving out of Kindred Thew, and then direct that person to speak to the Godhi on how to get back in line with Kindred Thew.

In Symbel, the Godhi may act as a "back up" to the Thyle, noting some course of action to be taken concerning Shyld, or pointing out where there may be problems for the Chieftain. During large events like Lightning Across the Plains, the Godhi may give a special blessing to the Hall Wardens under the Thyle's charge, or can step in simply to allow one of them to take a break.

In ritual, in their capacity of warder of Orlog, the Thyle may be the one that bears the flame around the ritual area, warding, and defining what is good, sacred, and holy.

In more general terms, the Thyle, Godhi, and Chieftain can act as a quick council when or if some important issue comes up. Moving from their respective spheres, they may discuss a course of action and then bring it to the Kindred's attention, covering these important bases so the Kindred can come to consensus as to the best course of action.

INTERACTION WITH THE VALKYRIE

During ritual, the Godhi and the Valkyrie interact mainly in what is called a Husal (the "round" inside a Faining where the deity or entity is toasted). Since the Valkyrie plays a role in safeguarding the horn and what is said over the horn, she takes control of the horn once the Godhi has blessed it. When the Husal is complete, the Valkyrie pours the horn into the Hlaut (blessing) bowl.

Another shared responsibility between the Valkyrie and Godhi, involves the handling of the various objects that are significant or important to the Kindred. Often after something is blessed, only the Godhi or the Valkyrie can touch the item so as not to profane the item. This is an extension of the Valkyrie's responsibility with the horn, and the well it represents.

In more mundane terms, JBK's Valkyrie tends to be more outgoing, so she is often one of the first to greet or interact with a person. The Godhi may get some first impressions, be directed to, or get other views of a person from the Valkyrie before ever meeting that person. The Valkyrie works with the Godhi to maintain awareness of what is going on within the Kindred or our region, in order to aid the Godhi in carrying out his various responsibilities and duties. The Valkyrie and Godhi both confer with the Chieftain and Thyle regularly about such matters, to ensure the proper level of awareness is maintained by the Kindred's leadership.

RITUAL SPECIALIST

You may have noticed there has not been much of a focus on rituals, rites, and Fainings in this essay thus far. While these are important works of the Godhi, all Heathens should know how to perform a basic Heathen ritual. Trú Gothar recognize that all experienced Heathens are Gothar in their own home/Hearth and no Godhi of worth would wish to interfere or impose themselves on such Heathens. It is the responsibility of Gothar to aid and guide Heathens in how to perform basic sacred functions, such as rituals, blessings, and other such spiritual practices for themselves. Those same Gothar should only do this if a householder wishes or seeks such aid. There is no requirement for an intermediary between a Heathen and their Gods, Ancestors, the Vaettir of their Home and Land, and Folkways. Most of the time Gothar are pulled in for special occasions, like Weddings, Namings, Funerals, and other significant rituals, usually because some legal aspect is required.

In JBK, Rod only performs the big public rituals at events like the Open Ostara Gathering or at Lightning Across the Plains (LATP). Even then, he tends to spread out the various parts to as many members of the Kindred as he can. In his experience, solid Kindreds spread the doing of rituals around, letting the Godhi keep track of it. It becomes more a supervisory position rather than the one who "does the ritual" every time.

There are also times when various people want to do a specific ritual, say to Ullr for a good hunt or to Eir to help guide the doctors in helping a loved one. The Godhi's role is not to write a ritual for them (though they may, occasionally) but to help the person write up fitting invocations, time the blessing rightly, and otherwise give advice on making a good rite.

ON MAGIC

Magic is not vital to Heathenry. Some Heathens perform magic at most occasionally, while others are more heavily involved. While Galdr and Seidhr are in our Lore, only a small percentage of specialized people did it, and that is a good model to follow. Magical practices are like "gravy"—magical acts can provide flavor and richness to the "meat and potatoes" of regular Heathen practice, but it is not very filling or sustaining when that's all one gets.

A Godhi should be the person that at least knows a little about the various aspects of magic within Heathenry. They do not, by any means, need to be an expert in such things, but it is possible that a Kindred's Godhi will be adept in one of these arts.

If there is a person who displays talent in Spae or Seidhr, their practice needs to be grounded firmly in the Lore, in the Kindred's Thew, and be connected with the goals of the Kindred. Too heavy an emphasis on the magical aspects within Heathenry can cause problems within any Kindred, and this is especially true for a Kindred with members that do not have much of an interest in the various magical practices within Heathenry.

Runes are less problematic, but again, too much focus on the Runes rapidly moves a Kindred away from religious practice to one more magically focused. A Godhi should know their Kindred, and what that Kindred can handle. It is part of a Godhi's responsibility to make sure the Kindred stays on track, and focused on what is truly important. If the Kindred starts careening too much towards the mere magical, it starts lacking focus on the Gods, Ancestors, Vaettir, and our Heathen Folkways. Instead of being the means of reaching a more religiously focused goal, magical practices can become the end themselves. A Godhi should work to guide his/her Kindred away from this pitfall.

CONCLUSION

A Godhi's primary responsibility is to uphold the Kindred in as many ways as they can with their skills, talents, and experience. Their role is not to wield authority over anyone, but bring information, wisdom, and guidance to those who wish support. They should work to unite, arbitrate, and encourage, always striving to assist worthy Heathens in gathering together in the best and strongest way possible. They can and do lead, but it is more by example, encouragement, guidance, and influence rather than attempting to wield some self-proclaimed divine "authority." Gothar do not get between a Heathen and their religion; instead, they do all that they can to make a Heathen's religion more deeply and richly experienced, more satisfying, and more closely suited to what will work properly for them. This makes the Gods, Ancestors, and Vaettir happy, as it brings more people closer to them and more in tune with our Heathen Folkway.

THE ROLE AND RESPONSIBILITIES OF A MODERN THYLE

Co-Written by Craig Fairhair Winkler & Mark Ludwig Stinson

Many Kindreds have designated a role of responsibility called the "Thyle" (pronounced "Thule.") Craig Winkler is the Thyle for Jotun's Bane Kindred, and he co-wrote this essay with Mark Stinson. Some of the concepts and ideas contained in this essay were outlined in a discussion held at the Midwest Thing in Minnesota (in 2010) involving Craig Winkler, Brody Derks, Mark Stinson, Rod Landreth, Gunnar Miller, and Dan B-E.

The Mead Hall by Stephen Pollington is an excellent book to read regarding how Symbel was done among our Ancestors. On page 181 he writes, "While little is known for sure of the specific duties of the feast officers, and much of our information is taken from a handful of poems, the following appear to have been the usual participants at an early English Symbel." He then goes on to to describe some of the positions of responsibility that existed in the Hall during Symbel. One of these positions is the position of Thyle which he describes on page 188.

> "The OE word thyle glosses Latin terms such as orator 'spokesman' and scurra 'satirist.' There is some confusion surrounding the proper interpretation of the word, for which our only evidence is the behavior of Unferth the Thyle at Hrodgar's court in Beowulf. In the 'courtroom' analogy of the hall, the Thyle appears as a kind of 'prosecutor' whose function is to query and question the applicant's credentials and motives, almost as a devil's advocate. This probing of the evidence presented allows the leader to reach an informed decision about the course of action to be followed."

THE THYLE DURING SYMBEL

The modern Thyle serves in the role of protecting the Wyrd and Luck of his Kindred and the assembled Folk during Symbel. At the beginning of Symbel, he announces what is acceptable and unacceptable during Symbel, and ensures that everyone present is aware of the Kindred's traditions and Thew regarding the event.

Throughout the Symbel, he is watchful for disruptive or disrespectful behaviors, and quickly addresses and stops such behaviors when they occur. The Thyle has the responsibility of ensuring that Grith is maintained during the Symbel. During High Symbel or Symbels with a fair number of people in attendance, it is helpful to assign several Hall Wardens who assist the Thyle in this task, and the Thyle directs and guides these Hall Wardens in the completion of their duties on behalf of the Chieftain. This allows the Chieftain, as Lord of the Hall, to focus on his guests and their good words spoken over the horn.

The Thyle also serves an important role in questioning and testing boasts made over the horn during Symbel. Is the boast true and stated accurately? If a boast seems a bit "off" or exaggerated, the Thyle will ask the person making the boast questions regarding the matter. While the Chieftain, Valkyrie, or anyone in the Hall can ask questions ensuring the validity of a boast made over the horn, it is specifically the Thyle's role and responsibility to do so when the need arises. If the Thyle is satisfied that a boast is true and accurate he will allow it, but a boast that continues to appear questionable after being probed and examined will not be allowed.

When an oath is made over the horn, it is the Thyle's responsibility to closely examine the oath being made, ensuring that it is clear in its meaning and intent, and a worthy oath to be made over our horn. Toward this end, he may ask questions or suggest alternative ways of wording the oath to ensure clarity in its meaning. If an oath is deemed to be silly, worthless, or inappropriate, the Thyle will not allow the oath. While the Chieftain, Valkyrie, or anyone in the Hall can raise objections or question an oath, it is specifically the Thyle's role and responsibility to safeguard against oaths unworthy of being spoken over the horn.

Every oath that is made, should include a Shyld (or obligation) that will be paid should the oath not be fulfilled. This allows the person making the oath to retain some portion of their Honor should they fail in their oath. This also protects the Luck of the Kindred, in that the Kindred can enforce the Shyld if an oath made over their horn is not completed. It is specifically the role and responsibility of the Thyle to judge the Shyld offered for an oath, and to accept it or reject it as sufficient. If the Shyld offered is insufficient or inappropriate, then the Thyle can suggest an alternative Shyld that he believes is more appropriate. If the Thyle and the person making the oath cannot agree on a proper Shyld for the oath, then the oath is not allowed.

The Chieftain, Valkyrie, and Thyle work very closely together to ensure that the Symbel goes smoothly, that good words are spoken over the horn, and that the Wyrd and Luck of the Kindred and those assembled are protected. While they each have different areas of responsibility during Symbel, there is some overlap in their duties. When an exceptionally problematic or sensitive situation arises, such as the removal of a participant for obnoxious intoxication, it is completely appropriate for the Symbel to be briefly paused, so that the Thyle can confer with the Chieftain and Valkyrie about the best way to handle the situation. But, if the problem is clear and the Thyle is confident in how it should be handled, he can take whatever actions are necessary to protect the Symbel and the Luck of the Kindred and those assembled.

THE THYLE OUTSIDE OF SYMBEL

The modern Thyle's role outside of Symbel, mirrors closely his role within Symbel. A Kindred's Thyle should be someone for which the Chieftain has immense trust. Trust that the Thyle understands how to act in a loyal and Frithful manner. Trust that the Thyle understands his position and is 100% dedicated to his responsibilities. Trust that the Thyle knows and comprehends the ways and Thew of the Kindred, and is able to communicate and preserve that Thew when necessary. For this reason, the Thyle should be someone who has been in the Kindred awhile, and has had time to get to know its history, its culture, and its ways.

The Thyle works closely with the Chieftain, warding the Luck of the Tribe. Since the Chieftain holds the Luck of the Tribe, one responsibility of the Thyle is to shield the Chieftain from harm. Shielding the Chieftain can be done in many ways. First and foremost, the Thyle acts as an adviser to the Chieftain. A frankness and openness should exist between the Chieftain and Thyle, that allows the Thyle to be enormously direct in private when he feels the Chieftain is making an unwise decision or following a course of action that will damage the Luck of the Tribe.   It is also appropriate for the Thyle to declare Grith at Heathen gatherings, and then ensure that Grith is maintained by supervising whatever security has been put in place for the event.

Publicly, when something is happening that could embarrass, undermine, or diminish the Chieftain in some way, it is the Thyle's responsibility to quickly prevent the damage that is about to occur. This can be done with a simple distraction. For instance raising a horn and making a toast, drawing all of the attention away from the negative situation. If a guest is baiting the Chieftain into an argument, and it appears the Chieftain may lose his temper inappropriately, then the Thyle should diffuse the situation with a distraction or even a joke, or simply pull the Chieftain away for an "important matter" that does not actually exist. Those Thyles that are skilled in reciting poetry or song, can also use these skills to draw attention away from or prevent a situation that could damage the Chieftain's Gefrain or Luck.

Assisting the Chieftain in warding the Luck of the Tribe can take many forms. Is a Heathen gathering hosted by the Kindred sufficiently planned for and everything prepared? Is the Kindred fully prepared for an Open Faining or Blot they are hosting? Is there something negative about a potential new member to the Kindred that the rest of the Kindred seems to be overlooking? Are the decisions being made by the Chieftain and the Kindred consistent with the Kindred's history, purposes, and Thew? Truly, the Thyle is expected to keep a close eye on things, and express concerns that may come up in an appropriate fashion most likely to lead to a successful resolution of the concerns.

A Kindred's Thyle is the protector and keeper of the Kindred's Thew, customs, and traditions. It is helpful for the Thyle to keep a book, wherein he records the history of the Kindred, events that take place, decisions that are made, and problems that are encountered and solved. This book can be somewhat general or enormously detailed, and that will probably depend on the personality of the Kindred's Thyle. But the Thyle's book, sometimes called a "Thew Book," can serve as the Kindred's memory and its Lore. Some Thyle's are skilled in verse or song, and can further fulfill this role within the Kindred, by composing and performing poems or songs that preserve the history and memory of the Kindred.

As the keeper of the Kindred's Thew, the Thyle has a responsibility to educate potential or new members to the Kindred regarding the Kindred's Thew, customs, traditions, history, and ways. He can share this information through conversations, having them read from his book, or even holding classes. This will vary depending on the needs of the Kindred and the preferences of the Thyle. A simple way to look at this though, is that the Godhi is responsible for the spiritual education and guidance of new members, while the Thyle is responsible for the Thew education and guidance of new members.

It is important that the Thyle should record in his book the oaths, promises, and obligations made by Kindred members and the Shyld they are required to pay should they fail in these commitments. Individual failure in an oath by a Kindred member, affects the entire Kindred to some degree. So, part of the Thyle's role is recording these oaths and, if necessary, prodding or reminding Kindred members that seem to be falling short on an oath. This should not be mistaken for "babysitting." Each individual is responsible for their own oaths, and ensuring that they completely fulfill whatever commitment they have made. But no one is perfect, and sometimes a firm reminder from the Thyle can turn failure into determined success. Such is the power of the Thyle.

A successful Thyle needs to be a little thick-skinned, firm, detail oriented, and able to interact well with other people. It also helps if they have equal measures of wit and wisdom. Every Kindred will approach things a little differently, and some of these differences will be dictated by the personality and skills of the person who is recognized as their Thyle. But, we wanted to share how JBK views this important role within our Tribe.

Glen and Susan Steveson - Glen is JBK's Thyle

THE ROLE AND RESPONSIBILITIES OF A MODERN VALKYRIE

Co-Written by Jamie King & Mark Ludwig Stinson

Many Kindreds have designated a role of responsibility called the "Valkyrie." Jamie King is the Valkyrie for Jotun's Bane Kindred, and she co-wrote this essay with Mark Stinson.

The Mead Hall by Stephen Pollington is an excellent book to read regarding how Symbel worked among our Ancestors. On page 181 he writes, "While little is known for sure of the specific duties of the feast officers, and much of our information is taken from a handful of poems, the following appear to have been the usual participants at an early English Symbel." He then goes on to to describe some of the positions of responsibility that existed in the Hall during Symbel. Two of those positions closely parallel the position of Valkyrie within our Kindred.

First, there is the Lady of the Hall, who serves as the hostess, "supervising the distribution of food and, especially, drink." (page 183) This was a position of great importance and nobility. On page 184, Pollington writes, "In many ways, the description of the...Valkyries...of Norse tradition, and of the Goddesses Frigg and Freyja give an indication of the ideal hostess, welcomer of guests, bearer of cups, source of hospitality." The Lady also had a duty to advise her husband to the best of her ability. (page 186) In Jotun's Bane Kindred, Mark's wife Jennifer is the Lady of the Hall. But at the beginning of High Symbel she welcomes the guests, and then passes the horn to our Valkyrie. In so doing, the Valkyrie then takes on many of the features and responsibilities of the Lady of the Hall.

Secondly, there was the Byrele, or "cup-bearer whose function was to keep the guests supplied with drink." (page 196) This position was tied to an individual's personal circle, "rather than being seen as a class of general hall-servant." There were words in Old English for a servant whose task it was to fill cups, and those terms are different than the Byrele. This was normally a role for females, but there were male cup-bearers as well. "It may be that the male 'cup-bearer' fulfilled a role more like that of a personal assistant in the hall" to the leader that they served. (page 197) The Byrele played an important role.

139

Jamie King, the Valkyrie of Jotun's Bane Kindred, describes it in this way. "When I am in the Valkyrie role during a Symbel, I look at the horn as housing for the Well. I look at it as my duty to safeguard the Well and ensure that Symbel is as powerful and positive as it should be." Throughout this essay the horn is referred to as the Well.

During High Symbel, the modern Valkyrie keeps the Well full. But she does so much more than this. She passes the Well from guest to guest, showing hospitality and ensuring Frith is maintained. She works with the Lord, Lady, Thyle, and Hall Wardens to ensure that the Symbel is good, and that the words put into the Well are appropriate and well-spoken with a positive influence. The Valkyrie can stop a toast or challenge someone making a toast, if that toast is inappropriate, lacks credibility, or is ill spoken. While this is also the role of the Thyle, the Valkyrie is in a sense the first line of defense. The Valkyrie can refuse someone the horn if they are intoxicated or it appears they will violate the Frith and integrity of the Symbel. The Valkyrie can and will indicate to the Thyle or Hall Wardens that someone needs to be quietly removed from Symbel due to their behavior.

Above all, the Valkyrie safeguards the Well that she passes from guest to guest, and thus safeguards the Luck of the Symbel. This helps ensure that the guests are able to honor our Gods, Goddesses, Ancestors and Folkway with little worry while putting their words into the Well, ensuring that our Gods and Goddesses are pleased. This is an immensely important role.

During High Symbel, the Valkyrie also performs a ladling ritual between each round of the Symbel, pouring three times from the Well into the Symbel bowl, and then ladling three times from the bowl back into the Well. This ritual symbolizes a mixing of spit – a mixing of Wyrd – between the Folk and our Gods as well as weaving each round into one collective Well. She also formally ends the High Symbel, and then libates the contents of Symbel bowl and the Well.

Outside High Symbel, our Valkyrie also has an important role. It is her responsibility to ensure that everything needed for Symbel is present. If additional Valkyries are needed, she has the main responsibility for choosing who will serve in that role and what roles they will serve in Symbel. During Symbels that are less formal than our High Symbel, the Valkyrie often ensures that the horn (Well) is full, and works with our Chieftain and Thyle to protect our Orlog and Luck, by questioning toasts or actions made during Symbel that might be inappropriate. If a male guest is present that does not wish to be passed the horn from another male, our Valkyrie will accommodate this guest to ensure they receive a Frithful horn from her own hands or the hands of another woman.

The Valkyrie of Jotun's Bane Kindred also serves as an adviser to our Kindred's Chieftain, making suggestions and helping him do his job. While the entire Kindred has each other's backs, the Valkyrie has a special responsibility for safeguarding the Chieftain's Gefrain and Luck.

Every Kindred will approach things a little differently. But, we wanted to share how JBK views this important role within our Tribe.

SECTION FOUR

REGIONAL BONDS

HEATHENS – FOCUSING ON LOCAL AND REGIONAL BONDS

There is a place for both grassroots growth and organizing, as well as a place for national organizations. This will not be an essay saying national organizations should not exist. It is an essay in favor of prioritizing our focus, efforts, and resources onto local and regional growth. To me, the formation of strong, stable, and active Kindreds and Tribes is the most important thing on which we could spend our time and money. Beyond that, it is important that Kindreds and Tribes, gather together and get to know each other on a face by face basis. This builds trust and bonds with people that are near enough to you, that you can gather with each other fairly frequently. Now, why do I think the focus should be local and regional, with national organizations as #3 or lower on the priority list? Let us look at it point by point...

I would rather have a new Heathen learning from other Heathens in his area, that he has met face to face, and can physically gather with to learn and to honor our Gods, our Ancestors, and live our way of life. It is amazingly helpful, if a new Heathen is in the same town or within easy traveling distance of an existing Kindred or Tribe.

That is vastly superior to a new Heathen learning from a website, or a message board, or a national organization.

When I work on projects or efforts that will assist our region or all Heathens, I would rather work closely with Heathens in my area or region, that I have met face to face, and with whom I can physically gather. That way, I actually KNOW them and know what to expect from them in the way of collaboration. Most importantly, those efforts can focus on what is important to our area and region, not what is important to someone living 2000 miles away.

That is vastly superior to working with people you have never met, and only know from on-line interactions or because you are both a member of the same national organization.

When I form an alliance with another Heathen or Tribe, I want to make that alliance with Heathens in my area or region, that I have met face to face, and with whom I can physically gather. That way, the alliance is based on a real relationship, and real trust. This is especially true of anyone with whom I am going to enter an oathed or committed alliance. If we can all admit that "internet-relationships and friendships" are mere shadows of face to face relationships and friendships, then this point becomes very easy to grasp.

That is vastly superior to forming alliances with people you have never met, and only know from on-line interactions or because you are both a member of the same national organization.

If my Tribe is going to expend time and resources (including money) assisting anyone, I would rather it be for Heathens in my area or region, that I have met face to face, and with whom I can physically gather. That way I know I am helping someone or a Tribe, that were the tables turned, would help me or my Tribe. Who is more likely to receive or give help when a tragedy strikes, another Kindred 300 miles away you gather with several times a year, or someone 1500 or 2000 miles away that you have never really met?

That is vastly superior to assisting people you have never met, and only know from on-line interactions or because you are both a member of the same national organization.

When I spend my money assisting someone in reaching their goals (building a Hof, buying land, etc.) I would rather it be on Heathens in my area or region, that I have met face to face, and with whom I can physically gather. That way I know my money is going to be spent wisely before I give it. Most importantly, I know that whatever the money is spent on, it is going to actually assist and advance my region and my Tribe as well.

That is vastly superior to giving your money to people you have never met, and never interacted with face to face. You may like their on-line persona, but do you really know them? Will you ever really see your gift of treasure spent on what you are hoping it will be spent on? Even if it is, will you be able to visit the Hof or tribal land 1500 or 2000 miles away? Or will you just see it in photos on the internet?

When I travel with my family and Tribe to a gathering, I would rather it be with Heathens in my area or region. Heathens I can gather with again and again, because we are close enough to gather multiple times throughout the year and form good relationships and strong bonds. Our kids can get to know each other, and perhaps form friendships that will last into adulthood – thus strengthening our Folk.

That is vastly superior to traveling across the whole country once a year, to meet Heathens you may or may not ever see again due to the vast distances between you.

For me, our priority should be on real people, forming real relationships face to face, in the real world. The future of Heathenry is tribal. It is grassroots. It is regional.

There is a place for national organizations, but we have all seen people form intense loyalties to national organizations, without ever having really met the people who operate them. We have seen people refuse to associate with other people in their region, simply because that other person belongs to a different national organization. We have all seen the politics at work. We have seen the decades old feuds. We have seen the divisiveness that seems to follow these sorts of on-line internet relationships with national organizations. I hope over time this changes.

We need strong stable Tribes, working and gathering together on a regional basis. If you have an extra $25 you want to send through the mail to your favorite national organization, so be it. But let us never lose focus on what is important and what will actually advance our Folk forward.

I know that my Tribe is willing to work and gather with any other Heathen or Tribe that is loyal to our Gods, honors their Ancestors, respects the Vaettir, who work hard and have stable productive lives. We do not care if you send $25 to the Troth, the AFA, the OR, or the AA. We do not care if you are not a member of a national organization. We are a lot more concerned about who you are and your worth, than we are about which organization you send your money to every year.

FORMING BONDS BETWEEN KINDREDS AND TRIBES

Forming strong, stable, and committed Kindreds and Tribes is the first building block of advancing our Folkway forward. These Frithful groups of families, gather regularly, work together, learn together, and build collective Luck through their efforts. They have each other's backs, their kids play together, and as committed groups they can accomplish more and withstand more, than solitary Heathens. I refer to Kindreds and Tribes as the basic building block, because they create the foundation of our Folkway.

The next level of building our Folkway, is for Kindreds and Tribes in a region to gather together, get to know one another, and begin building bonds between them. These friendships between Kindreds and Tribes, establishes a level of Grith. These Kindreds and Tribes gather regularly, work together, learn together, and strengthen each other through their collaboration. So, how and why is this done?

GATHERING REGULARLY

As in all relationships and connections, the internet is not real. It has the illusion of reality. But it is a poor way to form bonds and actually get to know people as they truly are. Regional gatherings, face to face events, and one Kindred hosting another visiting Kindred are the best ways to get to know one another and form bonds. These events allow you to look in a person's eye, talk in person, laugh and joke, honor our Gods and Ancestors together, share Heathen craft ideas, share traditions, and the children of one Tribe can get to know the children of another Tribe. The Havamal tells us not to allow the grass to grow high on the path between the homes of two friends, and this advice goes for Kindreds and Tribes as well. The grass should not grow high between two Kindreds or Tribes that wish to get along and work together.

Gifts should be given from Tribe to Tribe, and from individuals of one Tribe to individuals of the other Tribe. The exchange of gifts establishes bonds, and creates an environment of friendship that begins to grow upon itself. Gifts can be material objects, hand-made objects, resources like books and Heathen materials, lessons on how to create or craft in traditional ways, the sharing of information or traditions, or simply the gift of communication and advice asked for and given.

Hospitality should be offered, and then generously given when the offer is accepted. Hosting another Kindred or Tribe traveling to your location for an open event, a Faining, or a Symbel is an amazing way to show your generosity, and your willingness to work for and with them. The hosted Kindred, must act as good guests. Knowing how to maintain Grith and respect the Host Kindred's role as the host. The relationship and responsibilities between host and guest are reciprocal, and is a great way to build friendship between two groups.

Between gatherings, phone calls, emails, and even internet communication (through Facebook, for instance), can help solidify and maintain bonds that have been built face to face at gatherings. Phone calls are really the best form of long-distance communication, as a single quality conversation on the phone, is worth 50 emails back and forth in most cases. Phone calls can be just to catch up on what is going on, to coordinate an upcoming gathering, to ask questions about how the other Kindred approaches a problem, requests for advice, and just to joke around. But you get from any friendship, what you put into it. Not communicating yields very little, while putting an effort into maintaining communication continues to build on the bonds being created between Kindreds or Tribes when they do gather in person.

These bonds between Kindreds and Tribes, can be rather complex. Some members of one Kindred, will be closer with certain members of another Kindred. While all of the bonds created are important, it is most important that the leadership of each Kindred know and trust one another. So, the leadership of each Kindred has the most responsibility for making sure they attend gatherings, reach out to one another, form relationships, and maintain them through ongoing communication.

WORKING TOGETHER

Nothing builds bonds between people, like working together. The harder you work alongside someone else, the stronger the bond that is built. Two Kindreds or Tribes working together can take many forms.

First, gatherings with two or more Kindreds present always take work. The event must be planned, the resources gathered, the location prepared, and then there are the events at the gathering that must be organized, the food must be prepared, Fainings or Symbel areas set up, and the location must be cleaned up afterward. To form strong bonds with the hosting Kindred, offer to help them with whatever they need and then follow through when they ask for assistance. Two or more Kindreds working side-by-side on an event, will just naturally form bonds.

When another Kindred is going through a bad situation generously offer your help. Perhaps the Kindred is going though a sad situation, or a tornado has affected their community and homes, or there is some crisis afoot. If you learn of this situation, offer your help and then ensure you follow through on what they need. This action is a reciprocal action on your part. You can rest assured that the help, comfort, or advice you offer in a time of need is a gift the other Kindred will offer in return when your Kindred is in need.

There are other ways that Kindreds and Tribes can work together. Collaboration and a willingness to work together, by its very nature, builds bonds and establishes Grith between the two groups.

LEARNING TOGETHER

Kindreds that remain isolated, tend to stagnate in their development of Traditions and Thew. During our reconstruction, nothing adds to the depth of understanding of our Folkways, than visiting other Kindreds and Tribes and seeing how they do things. You will see approaches, ideas, beliefs, and other spiritual and practical approaches that you have not thought of yet. Ask about these things. Learn why they do them. You will find approaches that you may want to adopt, or alter to fit your Kindred or Tribe.

When a Kindred or Tribe visits you, share with them why you do things the way you do. If they ask questions, answer them well. They will take away approaches, traditions, and practices that they like as well. This is not an insult to you – it is quite the opposite. It validates the strength and cleverness of your own ways, that another Kindred would find them wise enough to emulate.

When one Kindred finds a great book or resource, they share this with the Kindreds with which they share Grith. When one Kindred finds a solution to a common problem, they share this solution with the Kindreds with which they share Grith. When one Kindred runs into a problem, for instance a problem-Heathen that attempts to cause discord within their group, they share this with the Kindreds with which they share Grith.

There is an aspect of learning that takes place when you gather with other Kindreds that is often overlooked. Going to gathering and meeting with other Kindreds, can also teach you what NOT to do. When you see a Kindred hosting an event, you not only learn great things you might want to emulate, but you also learn what does not work. When you see a bit of chaos going on within another Kindred, you make note of the source of that chaos, and strive to avoid the source of that problem within your own Kindred.

This exchange of information and ways is a reciprocal one. Two Tribes that gather frequently and establish Grith, will over time borrow many ideas from each other. This makes both Tribes stronger. When ten Kindreds in a region, are gathering regularly and sharing ideas the effect of this strengthening is multiplied exponentially. The goal is not that the ten Kindreds become identical. That is very unlikely, due them being located in different locations, and being made up of different people, with different ways of looking at things. The goal is to move all ten Kindreds towards traditions, Thew, and practices that are tested and true.

STRENGTHEN EACH OTHER

Two Kindreds or Tribes, gathering regularly, working together, and learning together are in fact strengthening one another. When ten or more Kindreds in a region are gathering regularly, working together, and learning together, the strengthening effect is that much more powerful.

It is very similar to a committed Kindred, working together in a state of Frith, and building collective Luck. Kindreds and Tribes working together, in a state of Grith, build collective Strength. Every Kindred in the regional alliance becomes individually stronger, and the regional alliance itself is stronger than the sum of its parts.

Baldr

HEATHEN TRIBES – FOCUS ON YOUR COMMONALITIES

Asatru, and Heathenry in general, has no central dogma. No central authority. So, beliefs and practices tend to vary from Heathen to Heathen, and ultimately from Kindred to Kindred, or Tribe to Tribe. Jotun's Bane Kindred believes in a grassroots approach to Heathenry.

Individuals and families band together into local Kindreds, or Tribes. They develop trust and an accepted way of doing things at the local level. These accepted ways become Thew within that Tribe. No two Tribes have the same Thew. Thew develops from how situations are reacted to or handled in the past. Tribe members see these past reactions or actions, and that shapes and forms their expectations and decisions the next time that same or similar situation comes up. Over time, as conditions change, Thew can also change and evolve. As never-before-encountered situations develop, Thew is added to and grows with the experience of the Tribe. All members of a Tribe, including its leadership or those in positions of responsibility, are bound by Thew.

Based on the fact that every Tribe has its own Thew – its own beliefs – its own ways, how should Tribes react to one another when they gather together? This can be a challenge for everyone involved.

When Tribes gather in Frith, it is important we look to what we have in common rather than focusing on our differences. We are all loyal to the same Gods. We all honor our Ancestors. We respect and give gifts to the Vaettir. Perhaps the way we do these things vary, but at the heart of things we share these commonalities.

Heathens understand the importance of gifts. We know what an oath means, and we realize a man's word and honor matter. We all guard our Wyrd and our Luck. We all attempt to differentiate between those that are Innangarth and those that are Utangarth, and we know the value of Hospitality. We know the role of a host and the role of a guest. Perhaps the way we do these things vary, but at the heart of things we share these commonalities.

We all care dearly about our families, and understand the importance of passing good Orlog to our children. We know that after death, all we will have left on Midgard is our descendants and our Gefrain. What have we done for our children, our family, our Tribe, and the greater Heathen community – and what will people remember? We know this matters. Perhaps the way we seek to meet these goals vary, but at the heart of things we share these commonalities.

So, when your Tribe gathers with another Tribe in Frith, know and understand that there will be differences in how each Tribe sees things and how they do things. Approach this situation with patience and understanding. If you are the Host, be generous and make a reasonable attempt to accommodate the ways of your guests. If you are the Guest, understand your role as a good and reasonable guest and do not expect the host to completely throw out their own Thew in favor of yours.

If you come to that gathering in Frith, and focus on the friendship and fellowship of the other Tribe without expecting them to agree with you on every point, your experience will be much more rewarding and worthwhile. You can build bonds on your commonalities, rather than causing drama and discord by harping on your differences.

We do not need a central dogma. We do not need a central authority. That only weakens us. We need strong Tribes with established Thew, who are secure enough to allow other Tribes their own Thew.

The concepts expressed in this essay are behind the success of Lightning Across the Plains, a regional gathering held here in the Midwest every year. Heathen individuals, Kindreds, and Tribes attend the gathering in large numbers despite differences in their view-points, their religious practices, and their Thew. Lightning Across the Plains is a very positive and productive gathering, and in both 2010 and 2011 it was the largest heathen gathering in the world. That success is directly tied to the fact that the heathens that attend focus more on their commonalities than they do their differences.

RESPECTING THE AUTONOMY OF OTHER TRIBES

We have all watched or heard the "internet debates" regarding roathnicity, and what role blood and ancestry play in our Heathen culture and world view. The debates have raged for decades on the internet. national organizations fight over it. People name-call over it. It is a divisive issue, and a major distraction from what we should be doing and where we should be headed.

This debate essentially disappears with a tribal or grassroots approach to Heathenry. When Heathens gather face-to-face, they are more likely to talk about their lives, their families, their Kindreds or Tribes, their Gods, their Ancestors, or about 100 other topics before they talk about the "Folkish/Universalist" debate. That debate and others, are almost entirely internet phenomenon. Having attended at least twenty Heathen gatherings at this point, I can honestly say I cannot remember anyone at one of these gatherings debating this issue. It is always on the internet that this issue takes on a life of its own.

Honestly, the homosexual issue has a similar "internet" life. It is just not something people debate and argue about in-person. When we gather face-to-face as Heathens, we have more important and pressing things to discuss than the "homosexuals in Heathenry" debate. Again, it is primarily an internet phenomenon.

There are other topics that seem to "live" on the internet, but quite simply evaporate away when people gather together face-to-face.

This brings us to the topic I wanted to discuss. A tribal approach to Heathenry requires that we respect the autonomy of other Kindreds and Tribes with whom we gather. If we are to move beyond these distractions – these topics that hold us back – we must begin to understand Innangarth and Utangarth, and the fact that we have no business telling other Tribes what they should do.

For instance, you might be a enormously Folkish Kindred. As a group, you have certain beliefs about ethnicity that influence or even dictate who you allow into your Kindred or Tribe. This is your Innangarth, you control it, and it is completely your decision how you run your Kindred or Tribe.

It also follows, that if you are a non-Folkish Kindred, and believe as a group that ethnicity and ancestry plays absolutely no role in Heathenry – this will influence or dictate who you allow into your Kindred or Tribe. This is your Innangarth, you control it, and it is completely your decision how you run your Kindred or Tribe.

I think it is important to note that the the Folkish-issue is not a dichotomy, but instead a sliding scale that encompasses a wide range and degree of beliefs. Here, I have described the two extremes in order to illustrate my point.

Here is the real heart of the matter. When at a regional gathering, it is overstepping boundaries to tell other Tribes how they should manage and run their Tribe.

The Folkish Kindred should respect the autonomy of the non-Folkish Kindred. It is not the Folkish Kindred's business who the non-Folkish Kindred accepts or does not accept into their Tribe. It is not your Tribe!

The non-Folkish Kindred should respect the autonomy of the Folkish Kindred. It is not the non-Folkish Kindred's business who the Folkish Kindred accepts or does not accept into their Tribe. It is not your Tribe!

If we are approaching Heathenry from a tribal standpoint, then we need to understand that insisting that other Tribes must believe exactly as you do, is overstepping tribal boundaries. You have your Thew and ways, and the other Tribe has their Thew and ways.

Understanding this, and respecting the autonomy of other Kindreds and Tribes, allows Kindreds from across a region to gather in Grith, and honor our Gods and Ancestors together. It allows Heathens with a wide variety of beliefs, to gather together for collective efforts, without getting into distracting and divisive fights over tired old issues, that get us no where.

This goes far beyond just the Folkish debate. It goes to every issue, where one Tribe is tempted to push its own Thew and ways upon other Tribes – Tribes that have no obligation to follow another Tribe's Thew and ways. It is rude, it is divisive, and it shows a lack of respect for the other Tribes involved.

When you are gathered at home with your own Tribe, then your Thew – your ways – guide everything that happens within your Kindred or Tribe. When you are at a large Heathen gathering with many other Tribes, then Grith dictates that no one Tribe insists that all other Tribes must agree with their specific Thew and ways.

Our Ancestors understood this, and I believe those of us who come at Heathenry from a tribal standpoint understand this.

A tribal approach allows our Tribes to move forward as a people, as a culture, and as a way of life in a more unified fashion, without forcing or artificially applying a unifying orthodoxy.

HEATHEN ROAD-TRIPS AND TRAVELING

Absolutely nothing builds bonds like a good road-trip or traveling together as a Kindred. Your family and Kindred pack themselves into a car, or perhaps a convoy of several cars, for hours on end. You munch on crappy snacks or whatever caught your eye at the last fuel or bathroom stop. You often have 2 hours, or 4 hours, or 8 hours together to talk, debate, give each other shit, joke around, and just have a good time. We have often joked that for getting to know someone, one weekend road-trip with another Kindred member equals ten regular events with them back home.

Jotun's Bane Kindred goes on road-trips throughout the Summer, with one or two in the Spring and Fall and one big trip up to Minnesota to visit Volkshof Kindred every Yule. We have been on short trips to Kindreds half a state away and we travel 16 hours up to Michigan every year for a gathering. We look forward to our road-trips. They can be exhausting and uncomfortable at times, but they are always fun. This essay will cover the reasons your family or Kindred should be taking road-trips and traveling to visit other Heathen families and Kindreds, and it will address some things to keep in mind if you are planning a road-trip.

GETTING TO KNOW HEATHEN KINDREDS IN YOUR REGION

First off, internet Heathenry, message boards, Facebook interactions, and everything you may do on the internet are no substitute for actual face-to-face gatherings. Getting to know the other Kindreds in your State or Region by traveling to their gatherings helps your Kindred and their Kindred, and the face-to-face relationship that you build will help prevent future problems or discord between you. Plus, it is both rewarding and fun to travel to visit other Kindreds and get to know them better.

Another thing that happens when you travel to the gatherings of other Kindreds, is that they are now more likely to want to come visit your Kindred at one of your events or gatherings. Both friendship and Heathenry are reciprocal, and when you jump in your car and visit someone, they are much more likely to be willing to jump in a car and visit you. If you hit it off, this process continues and the friendship between your Kindreds deepens and grows.

There is also an exchange of information and traditions that takes place, whether you mean for it to or not. If your Kindred sees things the other Kindred is doing that they like, your Kindred will try these things out and see if they work for your Kindred. The other Kindred is doing the same learning and borrowing from you. Perhaps it is something as simple as how they welcome you or how they organized the cooking at the visit or gathering, but it could be as complex or as meaningful as something they do during their Fainings or Symbels. This back and forth of information and traditions, enriches everyone involved. Ideas, techniques, and traditions that work in one location, begin to spread to other locations. If they work well in multiple places, these good ideas, techniques, and traditions become widespread.

A Kindred that does not visit other Kindreds or does not encourage visits to them from other Kindreds, tends to stagnate. The only place they are exposed to new ideas is possibly the internet, and that is really a poor medium for seeing if a new idea actually works in practice. Visiting other Kindreds or attending a gathering is exactly how one sees what other Heathens and Kindreds do in practice.

PUTTING HEATHENRY IN CONTEXT FOR YOUR CHILDREN

At the time of this writing, most Heathen families and Kindreds are fairly small, when held up in comparison with today's Christian Churches, let alone the mega-Churches. Heathen children watch television, attend school, and go out into the world – and rarely see any other Heathens or Heathen children, other than the 5, or 10, 20, or maybe even as many as 40 people involved in their Kindred. When have you seen a Heathen child or a Heathen family portrayed on television? Besides children involved in your Kindred, how many Heathen children attend your child's school? At some point, it is likely a Heathen child will begin to wonder if they are alone in all this.

Visiting other Heathen families and Kindred, or attending Heathen gatherings where there are other Heathen children lets your Heathen child know that he or she is not alone. That there really are Heathens in the next town, and the next state, and the next state after that.

There were around 70 Heathen children at Lightning Across the Plains in both 2010 and 2011, and it was amazing to watch them learning, and playing, and running together for that entire weekend. They learned names. They made connections. They talked with each other about seeing each other at the next year's LATP. It is impossible to overestimate how strongly this affects and motivates our children.

I mentioned at the beginning of this essay that JBK travels up to Minnesota every Yule to visit Volkshof Kindred. We are close friends with them, and closely aligned with them. With our trips up there and their trips down here, we gather with them 4 to 5 times a year. The children of our two Tribes know each other by name, look forward to seeing each other, and are forming friendships that we hope will create lasting bonds between our two Tribes. Bonds that last beyond our current generation. Some may say that is too much to hope for, but we would say, "Let us do the work, lay the foundation, and pass to our descendants a chance for something we did not have."

BONDING AND GETTING TO KNOW ONE ANOTHER WITHIN YOUR KINDRED

As I have already stated, nothing brings a Kindred together like traveling together, overcoming hardships, camping, cooking over a fire, and visiting another group of Heathens or a Heathen event as a united Kindred. Just the fact you are showing up together, and representing your group together has a positive impact on how you view each other and the group.

Now, as promised, here are some things to keep in mind if you are going on a road-trip or traveling with your Kindred.

MIX UP THE SEAT AND CAR ASSIGNMENTS

I know, I know. You want to ride with your spouse, and people who know each other a little better all want to ride together in one car. But resist the comfort of this. Mix it up a little. Purposely end up in a car with someone in the Kindred you are feeling a little distant from, or have not talked to in depth for awhile. If there is someone new to the Kindred or someone who is in the process of joining the Kindred, make sure you end up in a car with him or her.

After all, you see and talk with those you are closest to all the time. So, a road-trip gives you the opportunity to spend perhaps multiple hours in a car with someone, talking, joking around, and getting to know each other. Plus, it is just a lot more fun riding and talking with different people now and again.

If you have been arguing with someone, or there seems to be some tension between you, work it out so you end up in the same car together. You will either quickly blow up and talk through the problem, or you will both decide there was not that much of a problem after all.

SNACKS, EATING ON THE WAY, AND PICNICS

If the trip is 4 or more hours, you are likely going to want to eat. We have had great luck in packing a lunch in the car, and stopping at a rest stop on the way and having a big sandwich and chips meal on a picnic table. It gives everyone a chance to get out of the cars for a bit. If there are multiple cars in the convoy, you can compare notes about what sort of things are being discussed and joked about in the other cars. If you have kids along on the road-trip, the picnic stop gives them a chance to run in the grass and work out some energy.

It is also sometimes fun to try a local restaurant along the way. A German Restaurant that has a good reputation, or just a sit-down restaurant that gets you all out of your cars and talking as a larger group. Sometimes, when we are pressed for time, we just hit a drive-through window on the way, in order to put some food in our bellies and keep moving.

Regardless of what meals you plan, bring snacks. Something to drink, something to munch on, something to keep people happy. Multiple hours in a car can be uncomfortable, but for some reason, snacks make it all better.

SMOKERS

In most groups of people, there may be some smokers. It is very difficult for most smokers to go hours and hours without a cigarette, but most non-smokers do not like people smoking cigarettes in their car. Smoking on the fuel-stops and bathroom breaks can be an answer, but it can also slow down the trip. Regardless of what answer you come up with, it is necessary to plan for your smokers.

SHARING THE EXPENSES OF THE TRIP

Each Kindred has their own way of working this out, I am sure. There are times when some Kindred members are a little more flush with cash, and are willing to take other Kindred members in their car without asking them to contribute gas-money. But more often than not, it is a very nice thing to offer gas-money or to jump out and pay for gas at a fuel stop. It can be easy to take for granted those that seem to bring their cars on every road-trip, and the money they end up paying not only in fuel, but also in maintenance for the many added miles they put on their car. Regardless, always offer gas-money and leave it to the driver to decline you if he or she would rather just take care of everything themselves.

Even if someone is a little more flush with cash and willing to pay all the fuel costs, find an appropriate way to return their gift. Bring along their favorite snack on the trip, treat them to a meal, help them set up their tent at your destination, whatever is may be. But, let them know you appreciate the ride.

DO NOT BE AFRAID TO STOP AND HAVE FUN

The highways and roadways of the United States are just full of interesting things designed to make you stop and buy things. There is a truck stop and hotel on the way up to Minnesota with giant viking statues inside the store. We almost always stop there for a photo, a bathroom break, and perhaps a candy bar or some chips. In Wisconsin, they have the Hodag, which I am certain we will visit every time we travel up to the Upper Peninsula of Michigan to visit Winterhof Kindred. We have stopped at giant evil looking rabbit statues, I have photos of my wife riding a giant fiberglass moose outside an out-of-business restaurant. We have stopped to take photos at a water-tower painted like an black 8-ball and a giant concrete mushroom.

Road-trips are about having a good time, so do not be afraid to get side-tracked now and again, and have a good laugh exploring some of the odd landmarks that dot our countryside.

INSIDE JOKES

One of the things I really enjoy about road-trips, is the number of inside jokes that develop within the Kindred. Road and business signs that are seen, things that are said, jokes that are told, and strange events that take place can all lead to little inside jokes that only those on the trip really understand.

We have gotten to the point, that when we get home from a road-trip, those who went attempt to inform those who could not on exactly what inside jokes developed. Otherwise everyone who could not go feels a little left out.

KIDS AND DOGS

Kids and dogs almost always cause some extra stress on a road-trip. Things with both kids and dogs rarely seem to go according to plan, and their presence requires some extra thought and care.

Splitting up the kids into different cars can be a great way of dealing with the situation. Two or three kids piled on each other in a car will start acting up, or fighting, or irritating one another without fail. If you can get one kid per car, they are vastly outnumbered by adults and just naturally behave better. It is also a great way for the adults and kids in the Kindred to get to know one another better. At Kindred events, often the kids will spend at least some of the time off on their own doing kid-things while the adults are gathered doing adult-things. But, hours in a car will definitely familiarize you with a child in your Kindred.

One trick we have used on the kids, is leaving on road-trips very late at night or very early in the morning, so that the kids sleep through several hours or more of the trip. It is a little hard on the driver, driving the car at odd hours of the night or morning, but driving a car of sleeping kids makes it worth it.

Another common trick, is having a portable DVD player and plenty of movies along for the trip. You can have movies running from start to finish of the actual road-trip, or you can reserve the movie-option for emergencies when the kids are critically bored during the drive. There are also silly games you can play in the car during the trip to keep everyone at least mildly entertained.

Dogs need a comfortable place in the car to lay down. They will be all excited at first, but eventually they just want to lay down. They need stops now and again to go to the bathroom, and you have to make sure you have a way of stopping and giving them food and water along the road-trip.

All children and all dogs are going to misbehave a little, and everyone knows and accepts that. They are going to misbehave now and again, both on the road-trip and at the Heathen gathering at the end of that drive. But, it is important to correct that behavior and know when and how to discipline and care for either your children or your pets. I know kids and pets are different, but in one way they are very much the same. **They are your responsibility.** Heathens tend to respect those who know how to take care of their responsibilities, and they tend to scoff at those who have no control over those for whom they are responsible.

COMMUNICATIONS AND TECHNOLOGY

If you have several cars in a convoy for the road-trip, it is important you have ways to communicate with one another. You need to be able to tell each other when you are running short on gas, need to stop for food or a bathroom break, and you need to be able to find each other if you get separated.

Cell phones and texting are excellent ways of staying in easy communication, but there are places where cell coverage is nonexistent and if there are three or more cars, cell phones really only facilitate quick communication between two people in two different cars.

JBK uses walkie-talkies. Each car in the convoy has one, and while they do not always work perfectly, they do allow us to communicate with all the cars in the convoy at once. Sometimes we use them only for telling each other when we need to stop. But we have also held quizzing contests on the Lore from car to car by walkie-talkie, and exchanged jokes and other odd communications to pass the time on a long trip.

GPS devices have made road-trips so much easier and more fun. The thing sits on your dashboard and does everything it can to keep you from getting lost. It gets pissy and scolds you when you make a wrong turn or miss a turn. It keeps track of your arrival time, and you can watch as you lose time or gain time along your trip. In addition, there are the various voices, and even languages, you can set the GPS device to use. Anyhow, if you are going on a big road-trip and no one in the Kindred has a GPS device, it might be time for someone in the Kindred to bite the bullet and buy one.

THE GATHERING ITSELF

Keep in mind when you arrive at a gathering, that the other Heathens, Heathen families, and Kindreds there are trying to learn about you and to get to know you. They are watching you and your Kindred's actions, just as much as you are watching their Kindred's actions. You want to make sure that you do not isolate yourself from the rest of the gathering, and that you get out there and talk to people. Speak well

and honestly. Be generous with your food, your mead, and with gifts.
Participate in the events the hosting family or Kindred has planned. A
whole essay could be written about how to present yourselves as a
Kindred at a Heathen gathering, but I think the main thing to keep in
mind is that you have a limited amount of time around these other
Heathens. Use that time fully and wisely to get to know them, and let
them get to know you as well as possible. Someday, I will write that
essay about attending gatherings.

TALK A BIT ABOUT THE EVENT, THERE AND BACK

One of the things I enjoy most about road-trips, is the anticipation on
the the way up to the visit or gathering, and then the debriefing that
takes place on the way home. Hours in the car on the way up let you
catch up on things you have heard about the gathering you are headed
toward.   Things you hope to see and do there. People you cannot
wait to see again. Things you want to learn at the gathering.

On the way home, you have hours in the car to rehash the funny
things that happened or were said at the event. You can talk about
what went very well at the event, and what did not go as well. You
can compare notes on ideas, techniques, and traditions you saw during
your visit that you think your Kindred should try out. You get to sort
of relive and relish the time you spent at the gathering, with those
people you care most about in the world. You cannot beat that.

THE HEALTHY EVOLUTION
OF TRADITIONS AND THEW

We often speak of "the ways of our Ancestors" or "our ancestral Folkway" as if there was over-arching tradition, one uniform belief system, and one set of traditions and practice that was the "correct" one. The traditions and religious practice of our Heathen Ancestors varied from geographic area to geographic area, and even from town to town, and Hearth to Hearth to some degree. Besides geography, the ways of our Ancestors also varied based on socio-economic status and one's standing within the community.

The ways of our Ancestors were also evolving constantly over time. They had no written alphabet to codify religious practice, and nothing approaching the modern "church" or organizational structure to set, teach, and enforce dogma. They lived in a culture based on oral tradition and passing religious beliefs and traditions down generation to generation. For this reason, there would be small changes that would occur from decade to decade, and larger changes that would take place century to century. Some of these would be mistakes, omissions, or misunderstandings as information about traditions was passed verbally from generation to generation. But some of these evolutions were a result of the extreme practicality of our Ancestors. If they found a way of doing something that worked better, they would adopt it. Some of the changes would be environmental in nature. Moving from place to place may bring them in contact with different animals, plants, weather patterns, advantages, hardships, social structures, etc., and this could result in the modification of a tradition to better fit the new environment in which they were living.

Reconstructionists acknowledge these differences and variations in tradition, by often choosing a certain Tribe, and often a specific time-period, to study and emulate.

Now, in saying all this, I am not trying to deconstruct or diminish the idea that we as modern Heathens are part of one larger Folkway. We are loyal to the Aesir Tribe and the Vanir among them. We honor our Ancestors. We respect the Vaettir of the land. There are cultural values and concepts that were important to our Ancestors and also important to us, such as Honor, Luck, Gefrain, Courage, Loyalty, and Frith. We understand that a man or woman is his/her deeds, and that if one has done wrong, he/she must fix what they broke – not just ask for forgiveness. We understand Innangarth and Utangarth, and the impact this has on how we interact with our kin and kith, and the outside world. We are living lives guided by our ancestral Folkway.

But the variations in detail that existed among our Ancestors, also exist among us. The process of evolution is alive and well among modern Heathens as well. While we share some very important over-arching beliefs and values, our individual Kindreds and Tribes vary greatly sometimes in how we apply these beliefs and values to our own traditions, practice, and Thew. That is natural, and I would argue it is also enormously healthy.

When a local Kindred or Tribe forms, it usually begins with some very basic traditions and ways. Traditions and ways that it has learned either from books, the internet, or another existing Kindred. That new Kindred is of course unique in many ways, and there are many factors that will guide and shape the new Kindred's traditions as it grows and matures. Each member's personality, experience, dedication level, socio-economic status, geographic location, age, marital status, and other factors will all have an influence on the evolution of that Kindred's development of traditions and ways. The overall Kindred dynamic, and how all the individual members work together will have an impact, as will the events, successes, and failures that this specific Kindred encounters over time.

One of the strengths of agreeing on the over-arching beliefs and values while differing on the details, is the fact that the specific traditions and ways that work for one specific Kindred of Heathens, may not work as well or at all for another specific Kindred. By acknowledging and accepting that we will all develop our own local traditions and Thew, we allow each Kindred and Tribe to develop exactly the tradition and Thew that works best for them. I have heard some Heathens say that their way is "the way that pleases the Gods," and that saying that we can vary in our beliefs means everyone that varies from what they do is displeasing the Gods. But, it seems to me that our Gods care about good men and women, living with honor, and showing their loyalty to our Gods and our Ancestors. I have never seen our Gods as caught up in the details of dogma set by one man – or one group – that believes his way is the "right way."

Over time, each Kindred then encounters new situations and factors, that cause them to make their traditions and Thew more complex, and this adds depth to that Kindred's traditions. Over time, they fix little problems, make adjustments, and improve on what they do. When they try these fixes, adjustments, and improvements some work really well, some sort of work, and some do not work at all. Each Kindred tends to keep trying, changing, and evolving. Now let me draw a distinction. Modern Heathens are a practical people as well. They do not usually like to change things, just for the sake of change. When modern Heathens make adjustments to their traditions and Thew, it is almost always for a specific purpose, and it is almost always to fix a problem or fill in a blank they have never had to deal with before.

What is interesting to watch, is what happens with Kindreds gather with other Kindreds. Kindreds tend to watch each other very closely, to ask questions, and to evaluate the traditions and Thew of the other Kindred. This is very much a back and forth reciprocal process that takes place when two Kindreds gather together in fellowship. When one Kindred sees the other Kindred doing something they have never thought of before, and it is working rather well, they will try it out themselves. If it works, they will keep doing it. By this process, ideas that work spread. Ideas that are not working, are rarely borrowed or emulated, because only the unwisest among us seeks to emulate a tradition or Thew that does not work.

This exchange of ideas is one of the most important results of Heathen gatherings. On the internet, you never really see what another Kindred does. You can read about it, but you cannot see it in action or properly evaluate if it is working well. But face-to-face encounters between multiple Kindreds at a gathering, gives everyone a chance to watch, to ask questions, and to truly evaluate ideas another Kindred has put into practice. This is rarely a one-sided exchange. If two Kindreds are present, they both walk away with borrowed ideas they would like to try out. If many Kindreds are there, the exchange of ideas is even more complex.

This evolution of tradition and Thew, and the ongoing exchange and implementation of borrowed ideas that are proven to work, is constantly ongoing. It is an ever-shifting process within Greater Heathenry, with 100's or 1000's of little fixes and solutions being tried out, passed on, tested, adopted, abandoned and tweaked all at once throughout Heathenry. Each solution or fix is at a different step in the process at any given time. As more Kindreds meet and exchange ideas within a region, there are general trends or movements that take place within that region over time. These regional trends can eventually cause an evolution or influence across all of Heathenry, if the tradition or Thew in question is one that works enormously well in practice.

This evolution and migration of tradition and Thew that takes place among modern Heathens, also took place among our Ancestors.

So, the next time someone tells you that their traditions and Thew are the "one true way," realize that this is a somewhat odd thing for a Heathen to say. The next time you hear someone calling for a unified orthodoxy or orthopraxy across Heathenry, realize that this may be an even odder thing for a Heathen to say.

The real future of Heathenry lies in local Kindreds and Tribes developing and evolving their own traditions and Thew in a very practical way, to fit who they are and what works for them. The real future of Heathenry lies with these Kindreds and Tribes gathering together at face-to-face events, where they can get to know each other, build bonds, and exchange ideas that may work better for them. The real future of Heathenry lies with us passing these fully developed and vetted traditions and Thew to our children, so they can continue what we have worked so hard to build.

TIPS FOR HOSTING A SUCCESSFUL HEATHEN GATHERING

Lightning Across the Plains 2009 was attended by 120 Heathens from around the Midwest. Lightning Across the Plains 2010 and 2010 were attended by 240 and 225 Heathens, respectively. Kindreds. Hearths. Families. Individuals. As the hosting Kindred, we feel that all of the Lightning Across the Plains events have gone very well, and met all of our goals and expectations. The feedback we receive from our guests has been enormously positive, and we are very much looking forward to Lightning Across the Plains gatherings in the years to come.

Hosting a weekend Heathen gathering is not as simple as picking a time, date, location and then posting that information on the web and hoping for the best. There is a lot of thought and planning that goes into it. The hosting Kindred is very busy both prior to and during the event ensuring it goes well. This essay shares some tips on how to hold your own successful Heathen gathering.

1. Sit down as a Kindred, and fully discuss the pro's and con's of holding a gathering. Ensure that everyone is on-board. If one or more people in the Kindred are hesitant about hosting a gathering, find out what their concerns are, and fully discuss them. Hosting a

gathering can be a lot of work, and it will take your entire Kindred to really pull it off well.

2. Consider whether there is a need for another Heathen gathering in your region. In most regions, there is still a need for additional gatherings. Take the time to really research the existing gatherings in your region. Talk to the other Kindreds in your region, and really do your homework. Where are the other gatherings and what time of year are they held? You do not want to make Heathens choose between your event and another event scheduled at the same time. You certainly do not want them choosing between your event and one they they already regularly attend. There is a limited number of Heathens. When we split our efforts and schedule competing events, everyone loses.

3. Give yourself plenty of time to promote the event. Do not sit down and schedule an gathering for 2 or 3 months from now. You will not have time to plan it and prepare properly, nor will you have time to promote it properly. Plus, your guests need time to get your gathering on their calendar, make their own preparations for it, schedule time off from work, etc. Jotun's Bane Kindred usually plans out our travel plans a year in advance. It can be difficult for us to attend a gathering that is announced just a few months before it is held. If this is a new gathering, set the date at least a year out, if you can.

4. Once you find a date that works and does not conflict with other gatherings in your region, reserve a location for the event. You need to take into consideration the level of comfort your guests will expect and the cost of the location you are reserving. Some gatherings involve camping in tents, and these events usually cost less to attend. Some gatherings involve cabins, and can cost quite a bit more to attend. When choosing a location, keep in mind the weather that time of year, the need for bathrooms, etc.

5. Organize your gathering well. Plan it, make a schedule of activities, and really think through what you want to happen at the gathering. People do not want to travel to something that is disorganized, or has very few activities planned. When you have a rough schedule made, go through every single activity on the schedule and thoroughly examine what you will need for each one. Make sure that you can realistically accomplish everything you have put on the schedule.

6. If you have Heathen workshops on your schedule, make sure the subject matter and the tone of the workshops are something that will appeal to Heathens in your region. Workshops that might be a big hit in one region, might not work in another region. While you can

certainly have members of your Kindred give workshops, it is always nice if some of the workshops are given by knowledgeable guests in attendance. It takes more pre-planning to have people outside your Kindred give workshops, but it can definitely be worth the extra work.

7. Plan the event so that it will work whether it is well-attended or sparsely-attended. This is especially true if it is your first time hosting the event. You have plan the event so that it will be a success, spiritually and financially, if there are 20 people there or 100 people there. That means choosing a location for the gathering that is not immensely expensive. If you set up a gathering that only financially breaks even if 60 people are there and only 30 show up, it is unlikely you will have a second gathering. If your Godhi prepares a Blot or Faining that works well for 30 people, and 100 people show up, the Blot or Faining can go really badly.

8. Do not make the gathering about YOU and YOUR Kindred. For instance, if you are Folkish, do not make it just a Folkish gathering. If you are AFA, Troth, or OR, do not make it just an AFA, Troth, or Odinic Rite gathering. Make it about Heathens in your region gathering in mutual respect, and focus on your similarities with other Heathens – not your differences. A Heathen gathering should be about our Folk gathering to honor their Gods, their Ancestors, the Vaettir, and to get to know one another face-to-face. If you focus on this goal in all that you do in hosting the gathering, then you are more likely to keep on-course, and have a meaningful gathering that people really enjoy.

9. Personally, I believe that a Heathen gathering that focuses on being a regional event will draw together Kindreds, Hearths, families, and individuals from that region that are likely to get to know each other, and that will be likely to want to continue gathering. A gathering that focuses on being a national event, will have a different feel to it. I have written extensively on the importance of regional face-to-face relationships between Kindreds and Heathen individuals. Your regional gathering will spark other regional gatherings, and over a relatively short number of years, bonds can be built between Heathens in a region – bonds that strengthen and enliven all that are involved.

10. Heathenry is about families and communities. There is nothing more disturbing, than the idea of a Heathen gathering with very few children and no activities planned for children. Our children are the future of Heathenry. So, if you are planning a gathering, put your money where your mouth is. Do not just talk the talk, walk the walk. Set up your registration fees in a way that encourages families to attend. Plan activities for children, and communicate these activities are part of your promotions for the event. Lightning Across the Plains

2010 and 2011 were both attended by around 70 Heathen children, nearly a third of those in attendance. We are enormously happy with this ratio of children at our events.

11. Keep the price to attend the gathering as affordable as possible. Heathens tend to be middle class, lower-middle class, and working-class people. Especially the Heathens with children. They are not made of money and you want your gathering to be affordable for them to attend.

12. Some gatherings do not provide any food for their guests. Some gatherings provide one or two feasts, and ask guests to provide their own breakfasts and lunches. Some gatherings provide all of the food, throughout the entire weekend. If you do provide food, you need to make sure everyone walks away satisfied from any meals you do provide. Running out of food is absolutely not acceptable.

13. Make the gathering both fun and spiritually meaningful. Plan for one or more Blots or Fainings, one or more Symbels, and ensure that the event is as "Heathen" as possible. But, also plan activities that are purely for fun and enjoyment. If you know the Heathens in your region fairly well, then you will have a better idea of what they will consider to be fun. Viking games, poetry and song contests, and a lore game-show are all activities that can be really enjoyable, if planned well.

14. Once you have a location reserved for the date of your gathering and a thorough plan for the gathering, announce the gathering as widely as possible. Find ways to clearly communicate the details about your event. Share everything about it you can. The schedule, the plan, the details. People do not like the unknown, and will not travel to something that is sort of nebulous and mysterious. Traveling to a gathering is a big commitment of time and money, and the more they know about your gathering, the more likely they are to attend.

15. Heathenry is about reciprocal relationships. Gift for a Gift. You need to get to know and forge bonds with other Kindreds and Heathens in your region. Communicate with them. Get to know them. Travel to the open events and gatherings they are hosting. People are more likely to travel to something you are hosting, if you have already traveled to visit them. This seems like common sense, but a lot of people just completely miss this whole concept. In the year 2010, Jotun's Bane Kindred traveled 2843 miles to gatherings with other Heathens. It is likely we will travel just as many miles, if not more, in the years to come.

THE ENORMOUSLY LIMITED ROLE OF MODERN OUTLAWRY

Outlawry among Heathens in Viking Age Iceland provided a way of dealing with serious trouble-makers. It provided a way for Icelandic society to remove those that "could not or would not abide by its rules." "Once outlawed, a person could be killed with impunity, that is with no vengeance expected...." There was lesser outlawry and full outlawry, both of which resulted in the outlaw losing all of his property. Lesser outlawry involved a three year exile from Iceland, while full outlawry meant that you could receive no assistance in Iceland nor help leaving Iceland. This was essentially a death sentence. "Because of the seriousness of the penalty and because it often resulted from arbitrated settlement, an outlawry judgment required substantial consensus." (Quotes are from pages 231 and 232 of Viking Age Iceland by Jesse Byock.)

Outlawry was something imposed by an established legal body, acting under set laws and rules, regarding specific serious crimes. It was not something imposed by a single family or group. It was not imposed over minor conflicts or disappointments between people. It was a measure put in place to put limits on and mitigate vengeance and blood feuds between individuals and their families.

This begs the question of whether Outlawry has a place in modern Heathenry, and in what circumstances and by what methods should Outlawry be applied?

INDIVIDUAL KINDREDS AND "OUTLAWRY"

Well, I am a tribalist, and if a Kindred wants to apply some form of limited "outlawry" on someone that has done some serious harm to them, then they can do what they want. Obviously, this is more of a "shunning" or an official "driving them off" action by the Kindred. Since it is done by the Kindred, it is often done at a Kindred meeting rather than an actual Thing of any sort. The person outlawed is rarely present at the meeting where this is done, and the action is taken unilaterally by the Kindred in question. For this reason, the effect of this sort of "Kindred-Outlawry" is limited to the actions of that Kindred and perhaps other Kindreds they are aligned with toward the "outlaw." Those outside the situation have very little ability to judge whether the action taken was done fairly, or was even necessary.

169

I think the more accurate and appropriate terminology for such an action by an individual Kindred would be a "shunning" or "declaring someone an enemy," rather than calling this "Outlawry." It is not done at an established legal body involving parties outside of the conflict, and the action is normally done exclusively by those that believe they were injured, against the person they believe injured them. As such, the action taken by the Kindred will be acknowledged by some, and not acknowledged by others – making it much more limited and less effective than true Outlawry.

MODERN THINGS AND OUTLAWRY

The purpose of modern Things, usually on a regional basis, is to bring a region of Heathens together in some common goals and purposes, and move that region and all the participating Kindreds forward. Toward this end, it is best if the time and attention of the Thing is focused on positive efforts. Communication, collaboration, and a certain unity of purpose in the region.

Small conflicts, disagreements, and issues between Heathens and Kindreds in that region, are best resolved between the adult parties concerned, and these resolutions work best when arrived at in private. If a mediator is needed, then one can be agreed to by both parties involved, and the matter resolved. Most conflicts among Viking-Age Heathens in Iceland were resolved in just this way. Once a matter was taken to Thing, it fell outside the direct control of both parties involved in the conflict. For this reason, there was a certain amount of pressure on both parties to negotiate and mediate the problem prior to Thing. What was true then, works well today.

Of course, in modern Heathenry, if the matter cannot be resolved privately and without assistance, then the Chieftains, Godhi, and Elders of the Thing can be asked in private to help mediate the matter. Even in these cases, it is best that the matter be mediated by a mediator appointed by the Lawspeaker, and agreed to by both parties involved in the conflict. If at all possible, the matter should still be handled privately. Only in cases where mediation has completely failed, should a matter be brought to Thing. Even then, if at all possible it should be decided by the participating Chieftains, Godhi, and Elders in private.

In all but the most serious crimes (as I describe in the "Real Modern Outlawry" section below), it is not the purpose of a modern Thing to solve everyone's little conflicts and issues. We are all adults, so we should be adults and figure out ways to handle your own problems without making it everyone's problem.

OUTLAWING IRRITATING, DISRUPTIVE FOLKS?

We have all seen it. A Kindred "outlawing" someone who has caused them problems. These are usually irritating people, who enjoy causing low level discord and chaos where ever they go. They do this mostly on-line, but they also attempt to do so between real people in their region, at gatherings and between gatherings. They tell little lies, stir up trouble, and seek some level of importance by tearing down others. They are troublemakers, but do these people need to be brought to Thing and officially outlawed?

I would argue that there are several good reasons not to bother with actually outlawing them. First, they would like nothing better! The idea of being the center of everyone's attention is usually exactly what they want, whether it is negative attention or positive attention, they do not really care. They would delight in the moment their name is announced as being called to Thing. They would grouse, and fume, and rant on-line and love every minute of it. Then at the Heathen gathering where the Thing was being held, they would make the entire event all about them. Whether they are officially outlawed at Thing or not, they will not cease to be a problem. In our modern world, they cannot truly be silenced. So, if "outlawed," they will live on in their joyous outlawry, continuing to stir up the trouble that got them in that position in the first place.

The real solution to people of this sort – the shit-disturbers and disruptive worthless folks – is simply to ignore them. It is amazing how over time, they eventually piss off and drive away everyone they come in contact with and essentially become ostracized by their very own actions and negative reputation. Nothing is more painful to this sort of person, than to not be the center of attention. But it is the natural and inevitable result of their worthlessness. They either catch a clue and change their ways, or they become irrelevant all on their own.

BUT IF WE DO NOT OUTLAW DISRUPTIVE PEOPLE WILL THEY NOT ALWAYS BE AROUND?

Nope. People do not have a "right" to come to gatherings. At events Jotun's Bane Kindred hosts, if we choose to not allow someone to come to the event, then that is our choice. We do not make the decision lightly, and we only exclude the most disruptive of people who have proven themselves unable to exist in Grith with other Heathens at a gathering. But that is our choice. We are host. Excluding

171

consistently disruptive people is actually part of our job as host. Outlawry is not required to keep dishonorable people from coming to one of our gatherings.

You will hear people insisting that unless a person is "formally outlawed" you must welcome them to your gathering. This is absolutely false. Usually the people insisting this, are the disruptive people themselves – insisting that no matter how bad a guest they have been in the past, they have a "right" to attend an event. In fact they do not.

If the person in question is disruptive enough, eventually there will be 2 or 3 different gatherings where they are not welcome. Eventually, by their very nature, these people will piss off enough people to not be welcome at any gatherings. They bring this Shame upon themselves, by their own hand and their own deeds. No outlawry is needed to make that happen.

OUTLAWING PEOPLE WE GET IN CONFLICTS WITH?

One modern use of Outlawry, that can be enormously over-used and appear somewhat silly, is a Kindred that outlaws everyone with whom they get in a disagreement or a conflict. Among our Ancestors, outlawry was a big deal. A very big deal. Outlawry was reserved for serious crimes that would spark vengeance of blood feuds. Not simple conflicts and disagreements.

The point of outlawry is not to publicly humiliate every person who ever causes you problems. Life and interactions with other people is just full of problems, by its very nature. So, to some degree, you need to just chalk it up sometimes when you or your Kindred has a problem with someone. It is going to happen, and should never come as a surprise. Earlier in this essay, we covered the idea that a unilateral "shunning" or "declaring someone an enemy" by a Kindred is not the same as Outlawing someone.

Then there is the dirty-laundry issues. People do not like hearing about your dirty laundry, and they find it ridiculous when people air their dirty laundry over issues that do not rate as all that important. So, someone owes you $20. No one cares to hear about it. So, someone called you a name at a Pubmoot once. No one cares to hear about it. So, someone was not a good fit for your Kindred, and left on somewhat bad terms. No one cares to hear about it. That is between you and the person in question. If your Kindred wants to exclude them from your events and consider them an "enemy" of the Kindred – then you certainly can do that. But, making a big dramatic public announcement about it is simply drama-inducing, divisive, and somewhat pointless. It is a local issue, and a private one at that.

Then there is the situation where a Kindred or group seems to outlaw quite a few people. At some point, it lessens the impact of bothering to "outlaw" people. Moving a bit further down the line, it becomes suspicious that perhaps the Kindred itself is the problem. If they seem to be getting in all these conflicts, and outlawing all these people, and making all these "outlawry" or "this person is our enemy" announcements – then maybe they are doing something wrong to be having all these problems and conflicts.

There is also the the misuse of "outlawry" that takes place, such as outlawing every ex-boyfriend of a female member of the Kindred or group. At the point where 3 ex-boyfriends are outlawed, it sort of becomes clear that this is not "real" outlawry, but simply an attempt to get revenge on or humiliate guys when relationships do not work out.

REAL MODERN OUTLAWRY

Modern Outlawry works best, when it mirrors fairly closely the use and purpose of Outlawry among our Ancestors.

A modern example would be a child-molester that has committed a crime against a member of a Heathen Kindred. Real criminal charges should be brought of course, and upon conviction, it would be utterly and completely appropriate for that Kindred to share this information publicly and widely to the rest of Greater Heathenry. Doing so, makes it very clear what was done, what was done about it, the conviction that took place, and it serves to warn and protect all other Heathens that this shit-bag is a convicted child molester. If the Kindred has bonds with Kindreds in their region or an actual regional Thing in place, then bringing this situation and the conviction to the attention of the other Kindreds in the region or the Thing, would be completely appropriate. In my view, this would be real Outlawry.

Another modern example would be if a Kindred's Godhi, Chieftain, or Treasurer were to steal $10,000 from the Kindred's bank accounts and skip town. I think criminal charges should be brought, and the matter resolved in court. Then a similar announcement could made to the one I described in the child-molester example above. The situation and conviction could be brought to other Kindreds in the region or the Thing in that region. This serves to let other Kindreds know, that this person is not to be trusted around their Folk. In my view, this would be real Outlawry.

There is a spectrum here, and there may be a place for Outlawry in lesser cases. It is very much a case by case issue, and it is not the purpose of this essay to set up a comprehensive system of law for the purposes of Outlawry.

OUTLAWRY LEADING TO DEATH?

Often, outlawry in Viking Age Iceland could lead to the death of the person outlawed, as in some cases they were basically made "free-game" to those who wanted to kill them. Obviously, we live in a different sort of world. We have a law of the land and an established legal system in our country, and it does not allow for the sorts of punishments that we see among our Ancestors.

So, outlawry within modern Heathenry is more of a warning to other Heathens about a Heathen that has committed a serious crime. In my opinion, it should be used only in cases involving the most serious of crimes or threats against other Heathens, and not as a public tool for humiliating or ostracizing people with whom individual Kindreds get into conflicts.

THE FIRST FIVE LAWS OF THE MIDWEST THING

At the Lightning Across the Plains Heathen gathering in September of 2010, Chieftains, Gothar, and Elders from 23 different Kindreds met in Thing. The following laws were discussed, and received unanimous approval of everyone present.

1) Every Kindred and Tribe will be autonomous. Every Kindred and Tribe will have its own leadership and the Thing will not interfere with the internal matters of any Kindred or Tribe.

2) The activities and efforts of each autonomous Kindred and Tribe will remain their own. The Thing serves only to coordinate efforts and allow Tribes to work together more effectively. The Thing itself will not run or control any of these efforts.

3) At each Midwest Thing, the Lawspeaker will be elected for the upcoming year and the next Midwest Thing. The Lawspeaker is a

facilitator of the Thing and not the leader. Leadership of the Thing lies with the Chieftains, Godhi's, and Elders of the involved Midwest Kindreds and Tribes.

4) Individual Heathens, Kindreds, and Tribes are responsible for resolving their own conflicts and problems whenever possible. The resolution of problems brought before the Thing shall primarily be done by third party mediation by someone both parties agree too, whenever possible.

5) The Thing will be held annually at Lightning Across the Plains, in order to provide a centralized and inexpensive venue for Heathens, Kindreds, and Tribes to most easily attend.

These laws are not private, and can be shared and discussed publicly. They will form the basis of how Tribes in the Midwest will work together in the coming years.

SECTION FIVE

HEATHEN FAMILIES

WHAT TO CONSIDER BEFORE MARRYING A NON-HEATHEN

The spouse we choose to spend our lives with, to have children with, and to face all of life's challenges with is one of the most important decisions we make in our life. The oath of marriage is one of the most serious oaths we will take as Asatruars or Heathens. Maintaining that oath in a healthy way, affects our life, our spouse's life, our children's lives, the lives of our families, our Kindreds, and our friends.

The optimal situation within a family, is when both parents share the same religion. This avoids conflict, confusion, misunderstandings, and all manner of problems. When two spouses have two different religions, there are differences in world-view, priorities, goals, how to raise one's children, how to live one's life, the seriousness of the marriage oath, and all areas of your life together. That is not to say it cannot work, but if one had to generally define the optimal situation for stability and workability, it would involve both parents sharing the same religion.

For single Heathens, meeting another Heathen that you want to marry can be difficult at this time of Reconstruction for our Folkway. There are not a lot of Heathens to choose from. The single Heathens you do meet, may not fit the bill, so to speak. When two single Heathens in a Kindred begin dating, it can lead to all sorts of drama and hurt feelings if it does not work out. There are many factors at work that make it difficult for single Heathens to find a Heathen spouse.

So, many single Heathens end up dating and considering marriage with atheists, agnostics, Christians, Buddhists, Wiccans, etc. There are some serious issues to consider when you begin dating non-Heathens, that should ultimately have a huge impact on whether the marriage with the non-Heathen is right for you.

How many times have we read on Heathen message boards the post from the Heathen father whose Christian wife will not let him teach their children about his Gods and their Ancestors? The post from the Heathen wife, complaining that her indifferent agnostic husband is frustrated with the time she wants to spend with the kids at Kindred events? The post from the Heathen father, who does not want his children baptized in a Christian church, but his Christian wife's family is insisting on it? I have read posts like this innumerable times.

So here are some questions to ask your self about a non-Heathen you are considering marrying. These are questions that should be 100% considered, discussed, and asked about before marriage.

What non-Heathen religious activities are you willing to participate in?

What Heathen activities is the non-Heathen willing to participate in?

What non-Heathen religious activities are you willing to let the non-Heathen go to on his/her own?

What Heathen religious activities is the non-Heathen willing to let you go to on your own?

What Heathen knowledge and practices will you be allowed to teach your kids?

What non-Heathen knowledge and practices will you allow the non-Heathen to teach your kids?

Where will you be allowed to take your kids?

Where will you allow the non-Heathen to take your kids?

Will you have to hide your Heathen beliefs from the non-Heathen's Family?

Will the kids be Baptized and Confirmed in a Christian Church, or some other non-Heathen tradition?

Will the kids be named, blessed, and made men or made women in a Heathen fashion?

Will you be able to have a location in your home and yard to honor your Gods and Ancestors?

Will you be able to have a location in your home to honor and gift your house wight?

Will the non-Heathen be able to have statues of saints, Jesus, or other non-Heathen religious symbols/statues?

Will your marriage ceremony be completely non-Heathen (i.e., Christian)? Will your marriage ceremony be completely Heathen? Will your marriage ceremony be a mixture of the two?

Will the kids know only Christianity or the non-Heathen religion? Will the kids know only Heathenry? Will the kids be brought up to know both?

Will the kids attend only Church or non-Heathen events? Will the kids participate only in Heathen Fainings and Symbel? Will the kids participate in events from both religions?

These are some pretty basic questions. But they dramatically affect your life, your beliefs, and your dignity as a spouse and a parent. To not be able to teach your own children about your heart-felt beliefs and faith, is a smothering feeling. It feels like a lie. Imagine not being able to pass on your ancestral Folkway to your own children. Ultimately, if your freedom to express and practice your religion is limited within your own domestic situation, then you are forced to choose between your family and your own beliefs.

Carefully discussing these sorts of questions with the potential non-Heathen spouse, prevents a lot of fighting, heartache, and broken marriages. Sometimes in the heat of a new relationship or the moment of attraction, considerations regarding compatible religious views, are not always at the forefront of your mind. But, there is a point where you have to take a hard look at the person you want to date or are already dating, and you have to begin asking the questions that need to be asked.

One thing that can certainly help, is to welcome the non-Heathen to come to some Heathen events. Let them get to know good stable Heathens, and see what Heathenry is all about. There is nothing like actually attending a Heathen event, to strip away all the fear, apprehension, and disgust that other religions teach their followers about any religion that is not the same as theirs.

Ultimately though, if the non-Heathen is close-minded, or wants you to hide who you are and what you believe, what sort of marriage is that? If the non-Heathen wants to shield the children you have together, from your world-view and way of life, then what sort of marriage is that? If you are not allowed to participate in Heathen gatherings, or are not allowed to take your children with you, what sort of marriage is that? If you spouse tells you everyday that you are going to flaming Hell for your beliefs, then what sort of marriage is that?

If you cannot find a good Heathen spouse, then focus on finding a good stable non-Heathen willing to respect your faith and willing to support the practice of your religion. A non-Heathen willing to get to know the members of your Kindred (or future Kindred), and be on friendly terms with them. A non-Heathen willing to allow (or even help with) teaching your children about your Gods, your Ancestors, and your Ways.

Sometimes we fall in love with the wrong people, and when we do, we need to be strong enough to identify and address that problem before it has a negative impact on our life. The time and emotion we spend on a relationship that cannot work, is precious time and emotion we will never get back.

INVOLVING NON-HEATHEN SPOUSES IN OUR KINDREDS

The optimal situation would be for our Kindreds and Tribes to involve our entire family, including our spouses and our children. This would be the most natural state, with the entire family involved in our Folkway, our way of life, our religion, and everything that Asatru or Heathenry means to us. But some of us are married to non-Heathen spouses. Many of us came to Heathenry after we were already married and already have children. So, how do we involve our non-Heathen spouses in our Kindreds and Tribes?

First, this essay is not about "How to Convert your Spouse." We each return to our native Folkway in our own way, and for our own reasons. So, the idea of writing an essay about "how to convert your spouse," just feels wrong. This essay focuses purely on how to get your non-Heathen spouse involved in your Kindred and your Kindred's activities. Nearly everything in this essay would also apply to dedicated girlfriends or boyfriends, but I will use the term "spouse" throughout.

When you are attempting to convince your non-Heathen spouse to attend a Kindred event, keep in mind that for them it probably feels a lot like you are trying to take them to your "church." That is the main cultural example they have to work from, and so they may feel like you are trying to "convert" them. The more you pressure them, the more you make demands, the more you try to "force" the issue – the more they are likely to resist it, and resent both you and your Kindred.

Your own actions and the tone you set with your spouse, is probably the most important part of making them feel comfortable with becoming involved.

Another part of this equation that you control is the example you set. It helps if your non-Heathen spouse sees that your religion and your Kindred encourage you to be a better spouse. A better father or mother. A better employee. If they see that your religion and your Kindred encourages you to be hard-working, honest, honorable, loyal, successful, and strong – they will see the value of your beliefs and your involvement in the Kindred. As in all things, we are our deeds, and the rightness of our actions and decisions will encourage a non-Heathen spouse to see the Kindred as a positive in his/her life, marriage, and family – rather than a negative.

A Kindred is not a "church." Your Kindred is not something you just do on Sunday. It is not purely religious. A Kindred is about loyalty. It is about being involved in each other's lives. It is about sharing trust and Frith. Is about supporting one another's families and our children playing and learning together. It is about sharing good times and laughter, but it is also about helping each other during times of need. These are all values and activities that a non-Heathen spouse can support and get behind, even if they do not personally hold to Heathen beliefs.

But if your Kindred is much like a "church" or a "club," that meets and gathers only for religious events. If you do not share loyalty and Frith, and are not involved in one another's lives, then a non-Heathen spouse really will not have any motivation for becoming involved. If the Heathen members of your Kindred, do not see the benefit of having non-Heathen spouses involved, then you will run into a whole host of other problems. So if you think this may be a problem, you will need to talk to your Kindred about how important it is to involve your non-Heathen spouse, and why it is important.

All of this points very clearly to the fact, that the sort of activities and events that your Kindred plans, has a direct impact on your chances of convincing your non-Heathen spouse to become involved. Below are some events your Kindred can hold, that would surely help.

DINNERS - You can invite another couple or an individual from the Kindred over to your home for dinner. A simple dinner. Do not make you non-Heathen spouse cook, unless he/she loves to cook. Do the work for him/her. Or go out to dinner with another couple or an individual from the Kindred. You could have the whole Kindred over for dinner, or meet the whole Kindred at a restaurant for dinner, but if you are just starting out, start slow.

There is nothing like eating together, having good conversation, and laughing a bit to build friendships and a comfort level with other people. A simple dinner is non-threatening, not "religious" in nature, and will allow you non-Heathen spouse to grow in appreciation for your friends within the Kindred.

Do not spend the whole dinner talking about Heathenry! Make sure the conversation at dinner covers topics of interest to your non-Heathen spouse, and allows him/her to get to know your friends in the Kindred better.

MOVIE-NIGHTS - Movie-nights are also good. Plan a movie night with the Kindred and encourage everyone to bring their non-Heathen spouses. Choose some great movies. Have lots of great snacks available. Talk before, between, and after the movies. Joke around and have fun. When Jotun's Bane Kindred has movie nights, we will usually pick one movie that involves Vikings and one that does not. We feel you have to have at least one Viking movie in the mix.

SOCIALIZING IN GENERAL - Parties, social get-togethers, fires in the backyard, trips to a museum, going to a concert, amusement parks, camping, and other social gatherings are another way to involve non-Heathen spouses, and encourage them to form friendships and bonds with the members of your Kindred. The more fun the event you plan, the more tempting it will be to your non-Heathen spouse. These sorts of activities are non-religious in nature, and thus non-threatening to your non-Heathen spouse.

CRAFTING - Learning crafts and crafting really brings people together. Many non-Heathen spouses have crafting skills (knitting, crocheting, weaving, sewing, woodworking, metal working, etc.) that the rest of your Kindred may also be interested in, or may want to learn. Bringing them all together for that purpose is a great way to involve your non-Heathen spouse. Activities like mead-making can also bring together an entire Kindred with the non-Heathens spouses.

ROAD-TRIPS - Jotun's Bane Kindred travels frequently to visit other Kindreds in our region. Sometimes it is for the day and sometimes is a multiple day camping trip. Road-trips are the best way to get to know people. Hours in a car. Fun crazy breaks at truck-stops and convenience stores in the middle of no where. Just being together like that all day or for days at a time, can build friendships that will never fade. If you can convince your non-Heathen spouse to go along, they will almost always have a good time and bond with your Kindred.

ONCE THEY ARE INVOLVED - Once a non-Heathen spouse is comfortable with your Kindred and shares friendships with some or all of your Kindred members, you will find they will be much more comfortable attending Kindred events that are more religious in nature. They will be more likely to come to a Faining or Blot. They may even participate, just out of respect for your Kindred and your beliefs. They will be more likely to sit in Symbel, and enjoy the friendship and fellowship of the Hall. They will be more likely to come to a study group session, out of interest in learning more about your beliefs. Ultimately, they are even more likely to return to their native Folkway, but that is not really the goal. Sometimes that just happens as the natural course of things.

Now, nothing is guaranteed. Some non-Heathen spouses are just not going to want to be involved, no matter how much effort you put into making them feel welcome. You cannot force people to do something they do not want to do. It is important to keep in mind that you share a marriage oath with your non-Heathen spouse, so a balance will need to be struck and there will be problems that will come up that you will need to address. But following some of the above steps should help in most cases, and the potential pay-off is well worth making the effort.

FAMILY IS FAMILY

For our Ancestors nothing was more important than their families. They shared Frith within their family, which translated to complete and utter loyalty. They shared honor within their family, and took vengeance if that honor was threatened or damaged in any way. They had a deep and sincere connection with their own Ancestors, and knew that the most important way they could live on was in the memory and tales of their descendants.

For modern Heathens, nothing is more important than our immediate families. Our spouses and children. One of the most important oaths we take in our lifetime, is our marriage oath. It serves as the foundation of our families, and provides our children with a stable and unshakeable framework in which to grow up, in a world where almost nothing is stable or unshakeable anymore. One's home or Hearth is at the core of one's Heathenry.

Modern Heathens focus a lot of time and energy on forming and developing Kindreds and Tribes, where they bring together families into a social and religious grouping that learns to share loyalty and Frith much like an extended family would have among our Ancestors. Forming Kindreds and Tribes and making them work allows modern Heathens to accomplish more in their lives, both within Heathenry and outside of it. These strong bonds formed between our individual Hearths or homes is an important part of our very community-oriented religion and way of life.

Regardless of the time, effort, and energy that you put into your Kindred or Tribe, you must never lose site of the core of Heathenry, and the basic building block of our Heathen communities – your home. Your family, your spouse, and your children. Family is family, and family comes first. In a healthy and balanced Kindred, it is completely expected that your family comes first.

Nothing your Kindred does should be contrary to or threaten your family in any way. No oath you are asked to take should be contrary to or threaten your family in any way. No activity, religious practice, relationship, or responsibility within the Kindred should be contrary to or threaten your family in any way. If at any point your Kindred is asking you to make a choice between Kindred and family, then really stop and look closely at what is happening. Because something has gone drastically wrong with you or your Kindred.

THE FLIP SIDE OF THIS IS ALSO TRUE

Of course the mirror of these statements should be true as well. Nothing your family does should be contrary to or threaten your Kindred in any way. If at any point your family is asking you to make a choice between family and Kindred, then really stop and look closely at what is happening. Because something has gone drastically wrong with you or your family.

Now, some Heathens will choose or have chosen to marry non-Heathens. Some Heathens were already married to non-Heathens prior to becoming Heathen. In this circumstance, there can be difficulties if the non-Heathen spouse strongly disagrees with your Heathen beliefs, and seeks to subvert your participation in anything Heathen or Kindred related. Suddenly, your non-Heathen spouse is not letting you go to Kindred events, or is at the very least, making it very difficult for you to attend. Perhaps punishing your for attending, by starting arguments and expressing a lot of anger toward you. This is a sticky situation, because you share an important oath with the non-Heathen spouse and may even have children with this spouse.

But, marriage is about compromise and working together. Marriage is not about controlling every thought, belief, or action of your spouse. So a non-Heathen spouse that never allows you to attend Heathen or Kindred events, is wrong. A non-Heathen spouse that will not allow you to talk to your own children about your Heathen ways, is wrong. A non-Heathen spouse that tries to make you hide who you are and what you believe, is wrong.

So, if you find yourself in this situation, you have a lot of work to do. It is our responsibility to work through these issues in our marriages, through conversations and honest communication with your non-Heathen spouse. A healthy balance must be struck, where you give some ground to gain some ground. You may have to stand your ground and firmly set some boundaries as to what they can and cannot make you do. There may be some heated debates, and likely some anger. But, you have to do the work to reach an understanding that allows Family and Kindred to work together and coexist in your life.

Allowing a non-Heathen spouse nearly complete control of your interactions with a Kindred or other Heathens, will actually hurt you both, your marriage, and your family in the long run. It is a slow burn, but that level of control over what you do and cannot do breeds resentment, and resentment eats away at a marriage from the inside.

185

FAMILY IS FAMILY

It takes a lot of dedication and work to keep one's family strong, stable, and healthy. Living Heathen values and ways, and building bonds between your home and the homes of other Heathens, can help in this endeavor. Good families reinforce and improve the Kindreds they belong to, and good Kindreds reinforce and improve the families they contain.

WHAT IF YOU CANNOT PUT DOWN ROOTS?

Recently, a young couple wrote me and asked for some advice. They said they saw the great value in belonging to an existing Kindred or starting a new Kindred, but they were in the military and were going to be moving every couple years for the foreseeable future. They did not want to start a Kindred or oath to a Kindred, only to leave a year later, so they wondered what they could do.

I wrote back the following ideas. If you have additional ideas, feel free to post them in this discussion string.

1. If there is a Kindred in your area, then become friends with them. Almost all Kindreds welcome a chance to meet additional Heathens, and if they know your situation, they will not expect you to oath. They would just be happy to meet two Trú Heathens and to have an opportunity to get to know you better. Some Kindreds do not even have oaths, and operate more as "clubs" (I do not mean that in a negative way, though that is not my cup of tea). If a Kindred in your area is more of a club-model, then joining up with them for awhile would be very simple. Just be up-front about the fact you will likely be leaving in a year or so.

2. If you are in the military and having trouble finding a Kindred or other Heathens in your area, find the "Open Halls Project" on Facebook. Or you can contact them by email at openhallsproject@yahoo.com.

3. If there is no Kindred in your area, you could start a Heathen study group. Even if you only found one or two other people of worth to

gather and study with, it would still be beneficial. You could also eventually Fain and Symbel with the study group. It is entirely possible that the seed you plant there may turn into a Kindred even after you are gone. Sometimes it just takes a spark to get something started, and you might be that spark.

4. You can also find Kindreds within driving distance, and visit them. Almost all Kindreds would show you hospitality if you introduced yourself and expressed an interest in visiting them. Though you may see them only once or infrequently, I think you would get a lot out of meeting a Kindred and gathering with them.

5. There are regional gatherings in many areas of the country, so if there is one in your area, you can make plans to go to the gathering. Many of these are immensely fun and rewarding to attend. There is nothing like gathering with other like-minded Heathens.

I told the young couple, that these ideas could travel with them. Each place that they move, they could follow any or all of these ideas, and they would likely serve them well. Even without the ability to plant roots, it is possible to enjoy getting together with other Heathens, and amazing benefits to doing so. By the time they do plant roots, they will have Heathen friends in many places and a lot of experience gained towards starting a Tribe to which they can fully dedicate themselves.

REASONS HEATHENS SHOULD REJECT CIRCUMCISION

The topic of circumcision might be seen by some as too personal or too intimate to discuss. But, when you consider the impact of the topic and the fact it deals with our beloved children, I think it is well worth discussing. Especially among Heathen parents.

Our Heathen Ancestors in Europe did not circumcise their male children. Actually, a little reading suggests circumcision was something done to adults in Egypt, then spread into the Semitic peoples as something they performed on their children, and has had varying popularity among Christians. I think a Germanic Heathen of old – one who honored the Aesir and the Vanir – would have either laughed his ass off or killed someone over the suggestion that a part of his son's penis be sliced off shortly after birth. On the day of the son's birth, or nine days later, I do not think it would have mattered much. Even the suggestion to circumcise would probably have ended in someone dead.

I have real trouble picturing the Heathen women of old suggesting or allowing this be done to their male children. It does not seem to fit with my understanding of the history of paganism at all. Druids cutting skin off their son's penises? Mass penis-trimmings as part of Sabbat celebrations? I mean, it is hard to even consider, is it not? Just the suggested symbolism of removing part of a male child's penis is sort of striking, if one things about it a bit. Can we all agree that Odin, Thor, and Freyr are intact? Seems like a safe bet.

I was circumcised as a baby. The vast majority of male children in my age-group were circumcised. I do not feel victimized or anything of that nature. My parents made the decision 40 years ago, at a time before the internet, when all the doctors pushed for the procedure, and back then people tended to treat what their doctors said as absolute truth. So, my parents decision to have me circumcised is what it is. It is unfortunate, but it cannot be changed.

But, it would have been nice to make that choice for myself. I think people should make choices about alterations to their own natural body. Especially when those alterations have nothing to do with health, or risk of health, or life-saving necessity.

188

Parents today have enormously easy access to information. We have a healthy skepticism of what the medical establishment pushes on us and the rest of the Western World (everywhere except the United States) knows exactly how pointless and possibly destructive circumcision really is. I feel comfortable saying that parents should know better today, and should learn everything they can about circumcision before letting this be done to their male children. While I am not upset with my parents for the decision they made (nearly every kid of my generation in the U.S. was circumcised), I am very happy to have made a different decision for my kids

My wife and I chose not to circumcise our boys. It just seemed incredibly unnatural to have a doctor alter our sons' bodies with a sharp blade a few days after each were born. When they are 18, if they want to get circumcised, then more power to them, I guess. Given the choice of what to do with their own bodies, I am guessing they will not choose to be circumcised!

I cannot imagine a grown man that was left uncircumcised being angry about not being circumcised. I mean, try to picture an adult male yelling angrily, "I cannot believe my parents left my genitals intact!" In the off chance someone was upset about being intact, I suppose that anger would be easy to fix. The uncircumcised man can go get it done. But it is much easier to imagine a grown man that was circumcised being upset or disappointed about it. There is no easy fix once what is done is done. It is important to understand, if you make the decision to have your male child circumcised, what is done truly is done.

After doing our research, we were determined to NOT circumcise our boys. But, there was a lot of pressure from the doctors and nurses to go ahead and circumcise them. For each boy, we had to tell nurses and doctors "no" multiple times. We had both doctors and nurses attempt to talk us into it. They seemed dead-set to circumcise our boys, and I was surprised at the amount of time they spent trying to convince us.

It is funny, because I know people who would not dare get their cats declawed, but do not even blink at having their male children circumcised. People who talk about eating and living natural, but are willing to let a doctor cut the foreskin from their son's penis. I think because none of us have memories of being circumcised, we tend to think it is not a big deal. But they have to hold the male babies down during the procedure, and the baby is awake without the benefit of pain-killers. The alteration to their body is not an insignificant change.

189

Photographs of the circumcision procedure are almost too terrible at which to look. The practice is both barbaric and unnatural.

You will hear some people in the United States argue it is "normal" to have your children circumcised. The fact that something is the "norm" does not make it "right." Otherwise, all of us that call ourselves Heathen would be Christians I suppose.

You will hear some people say the procedure is necessary for hygiene purposes. But, worries over whether my teenage son will keeping the area under his foreskin clean, does not seem like a legitimate reason to cut the skin off his penis when he is a baby. It think it is a bit simpler to buy him some soap and a washcloth.

People hold rallies and throw a fit over the mutilation of the genitalia of females in Africa, but the mutilation of the genitalia of our male children right here in the United States continues. It is a strange world.

I think people at least owe it to their children to read just a little bit about it before they choose to circumcise their male children. I would think Heathens especially would be a little suspicious of a practice with origins outside of our traditional culture and Folkway and promoted by the big-three Middle Eastern religions throughout history. A procedure which is unnatural, and has no parallel in our pre-conversion way of life. A procedure which unnecessarily injures and alters our male children. As a final thought, think about these eight points about circumcision:

1. Circumcision is a Jewish and Muslim Religious Tradition
2. Circumcision has no parallel in Northern European culture among Heathens
3. Circumcision removes a natural part of a male's penis
4. Circumcision is essentially irreversible
5. Circumcision is normally performed on child within days of birth
6. Medical reasons for Circumcision are not compelling
7. Circumcision is rarely done elsewhere in the world, except by Jews and Muslims
8. If an intact adult male really wants circumcision, he can make that decision as an adult

RAISIПG UP STROПG HEATHEП CHILDREП

I do think it is a parent's responsibility to teach their child about their religion. I think the idea that a parent will not share their religion with their child and will instead "let them figure it out on their own" is somewhat harmful. Children need to be taught spiritual beliefs in the same way they are taught how to behave in public.

If you do not teach your children about spirituality, the Gods, their Ancestors, and the way to live their lives in relation to the divine – then someone else most certainly will. If you do not teach your children your belief system as the basis for which they live good and honorable lives – then someone else most certainly will.

It might be their classmate, their Uncle Bob, their first girlfriend or boyfriend, or even some television show. But, when we leave a spiritual hole or emptiness in our children, they will find someone willing to fill that hole. When that happens, you will have very little input or control regarding how they fill that emptiness.

Some will say that teaching your child about your spirituality or belief system, is somehow "forcing them into a religion." I believe that much of this reaction is based on negative experiences with being forced to go to Christian church or being forced to pray as a child. It is not about "forcing" your children to do or believe anything. It is about communicating, sharing, explaining, and letting them know what you believe.

I know that if I do not teach my kids about Heathenry, no one will. I reached the age of 37 or so, without even HEARING of Heathenry. I had no idea Heathenry even existed.

Heathens describe being drawn back to our Folksoul.
Soul. Heathen talk about the Gods calling us back to our native Folkway. But, our Ancestors taught their children our Folkway from the day they were born. They did not remain mute about their Gods and Ancestors, and just let the Gods call their children when it was time. Our Ancestors shared their culture directly with their children all through their lives. It should be no different for us as modern Heathen parents.

We live in a world and culture with an immense amount of Christian pressures and indoctrination. There is also all this pressure from

Science, which in many ways encourages a strong agnostic or atheist point of view. If we do not teach and share Heathenry with our children, there is an immensely high chance that they will end up Christian or Agnostic. Having been Agnostic for 25-plus years, I can attest that it gave me a very empty and cold feeling about the world. I do not want that for my children.

If you are a parent and you are new to Heathenry, take your time. Work your comfort level up, while also improving your own understanding of our native Folkway. When the time is right, share with your children the wonders of the world that you now know. Our Gods are amazingly inspiring, and your children deserve to have that inspiration in their lives. Our Ancestors are an amazing foundation, and your children deserved to have that foundation in their lives. The Vaettir are a wonder all about us, and your children deserve to have that wonder in their lives.

THE TRANSITION FROM CHILDHOOD TO ADULTHOOD

In our modern American culture, at what point do we mark the transition to adulthood? At 16 when a teenager gets a driver license? At 18 when a teenager can vote, or when young men must register for the draft? Is it at 21, when the legal drinking age is reached? The truth is, in our modern American culture, there is not clear point where childhood ends and adulthood is reached. No dividing line. No rite of passage. No signal to everyone that this human being is now considered a full-adult, and must meet the responsibilities of a full-adult.

Our definition of when adulthood begins is blurry, at best. Even this blurry line keeps getting moved further and further along into the lives of young people. We are at the point, where we have "children" living at home at the age of 22, 26, 30, and many of these children have never really taken responsibility for themselves. They do not hold steady jobs, have their own place to live, pay all their own bills, or make decisions in the way that an adult can and should. I think at times, the transition to adulthood can be enormously confusing, and a methodical well-thought out transition can ease some or most of the confusion involved.

THE TRANSITION TO ADULTHOOD WTIHIN OUR KINDREDS

Our Kindreds and Tribes are an excellent place and mechanism for providing this guided transition to adulthood. A healthy Kindred that includes families, is likely already organizing activities and learning opportunities for the children involved in the Kindred. By purposefully shaping these children's activities and learn opportunities into a process of learning and action, we can provide our children with a guided process that logically and inevitably leads to their roles and responsibilities as adults. This process and the rite of passage at the end of such a process, make it very clear to a child that it is time to take on the role of adult. The process itself is a proving time, with the rite of passage as the final test that communicates to them that they have learned, they are capable, and that their relationship and participation in the Kindred or Tribe will be different from this point forward.

The rite of passage also clearly marks for all the adults of a Tribe, that a child has made the transition to adult. It makes it clear what the expectations of this new adult in the Tribe will be. It marks the point in time, that the Thew for adults now applies to this young adult, and that they have proved themselves ready for those responsibilities.

The rite of passage is not something that you can throw together over a weekend, and think it will have much of an impact on the anyone. The rite of passage itself should be the culmination and completion of years of learning from and interacting with the Tribe. It should incorporate the things the boy or girl has learned, and it should incorporate things that will be expected of them as adults. It should reinforce the Thew of the Tribe, and set the young adult on the right course within the Tribe. But it takes time, resources, and effort on everyone's part to make this happen properly.

THE ACTUAL PROCESS OF MAKING AN ADULT

So, how should this process work? What should be included in it? That is going to vary greatly from Kindred to Kindred. Every Kindred is different – sometimes enormously different. Thew varies from Kindred to Kindred. The responsibilities, activities, and deeds expected from adults in each Kindred are different. There is no cookie-cutter way to do this.

This process and the rite of passage that marks the point of transition is not simply for the boy or girl in question. It is something that serves a purpose for the entire Tribe. Jotun's Bane Kindred is in a position, where we need to seriously start looking at this. We have two boys and two girls who are at a point, where we need to begin a process of transitioning them to adulthood within the Tribe. We have been trying some things, to see what works, and really examining what we hope to accomplish in this process.

What follows are some of our thoughts on the matter.

1. Whatever method we choose, it should have a male and female path. Boys growing into men, need different knowledge, responsibilities, and experiences than girls growing into women. To some degree, there will be variations in the process, based on the needs and personality of the child who is going through it as well. Just as some adults are more spiritual, or intellectual, or physical, or crafty – so do our children differ in their skills and strengths.

2. There has to be a methodical build up to the rite of passage. It cannot just "happen one day" out of the blue. I think years of methodical preparation are needed, with the last year or so featuring an increase in the rate of learning and activities. There are skill sets to be taught and learned. Mental conditioning applied and learned. Lore, Thew, and the expectation of the Tribe to internalize and understand.

3. The rite of passage itself should be over a weekend. Perhaps a long weekend, but it should be a weekend. The rite of passage should include the application and of skills and mental conditioning that the boy or girl has learned up to that point. This is a test to ensure they have learned and can apply what they have learned, and a way of showing the boy or girl in very concrete terms exactly how much they have learned and the extent of their capabilities.

4. There should be symbolism and a certain level of drama involved. It should mean something, and truly communicate to all involved exactly how important that moment in time is. A child has become an adult within the Tribe.

5. There should be a clear understanding and expectation of behavior put in place, that EVERYONE understands and agrees to follow from that point forward. The new adult's responsibilities and privileges should be spelled out, and everyone should clearly understand them.

6. The new adult, should from that point forward be welcomed into adult activities. After the right of passage, the new adult should sit in Symbel with the other adults from that point forward. They should participate in the Fainings. Participate in the Study Groups, the Kindred meetings, etc. If we train a child to be an adult, and then

194

ritually transition them to adulthood, then they need to fulfill the adult role and responsibilities from that point forward. They should also enjoy certain privileges and trust in return for fulfilling these responsibilities.

7. This should be done at a fairly early age, by today's standards. 13, 14, or 15. Males and females are capable of exercising adult responsibilities within a Kindred at these ages. A 13 or 14 year old at a Heathen gathering, should be participating with the adults, rather than running about the whole time with the little ones.

IT REALLY COMES DOWN TO RESPONSIBILTIES AND PRIVELGES

The whole process really comes down to preparing our children to fulfill their adult responsibilities, and to be mature enough to enjoy adult privileges without abusing them.

When I have talked about this in the past, there are some that like to point out that among our Ancestors, it was often the norm for children to grow up and remain living at home at the age of 30 and beyond. You might live on the same land and the same grouping of homes until your parents died, and then you would take over as the patriarch or matriarch of the family and land.

But even in these situations, the grown children were working the land and fulfilling enormous responsibilities. They were expected to act as adults, provide as adults, and contribute as adults. They would often build an addition to the homestead for their family (wife and kids), or a separate building nearby.

They were not underachieving. They were not sponging off their parents. They were not in a perpetual state of childhood, wifeless, childless, and without adult responsibility. In our modern world, there is a stigma on adults living at home with their parents, because in a majority of cases, 30-year-old children still living at home are not great examples of success, responsibility, and achievement. Certainly there are exceptions to this rule. There are adult children who temporarily stay at home, working and saving up for a house. Some adult children move home temporarily while recovering from some crisis, after getting laid off, etc. But, beyond these exceptions there are a lot of people not acting their age.

195

THE CHILDREN OF JOTUN'S BANE KINDRED

Jotun's Bane Kindred has reached a point, where we need to make some decisions about this issue and plot a course. Obviously we cannot just wait for our oldest children to be 13, and then start worrying about it. We need to start forming our plans on this, and putting them into action. We already take our children camping throughout the year, and teach them skills we feel adults should know. We involve them in Fainings and Symbel. We read lore to them, and now that they are getting older, we are giving them materials to read on their own. We are already preparing them for adulthood.

But we need to create a more organized and systematic way of preparing them so that we do not miss anything. So that our training of our children is a little more complete and consistent, and that we do the best job for them that we can. I envision that this is going to take a lot of time and effort on our part, but like all things worth working for, the results should be well worth it.

By Saga Erickson - For Prints Contact Her at starkravenstudios@yahoo.com

HONORING ONE'S
ANCESTORS

A large part Heathen practice involves honoring our Ancestors. While living, our Ancestors were living breathing people, with hopes and dreams, families and friends they loved, successes and hardships, and if not for their hard work, dedication, and sacrifices we would not be here. A part of our Heathen soul, our Orlog, is passed to us by our Ancestors. We work hard all through our lives to pass good Orlog to our own children, and thus our descendents. We share blood and culture with our Ancestors, and it is through our Ancestors that we find connection with our Gods.

In death, we as Heathens have various ideas about where they might be. Perhaps a part of their Heathen soul is in our Ancestor's Halls in Hel or perhaps they rest in the mound. There are other concepts of the afterlife among modern Heathens, but these are probably the most common. Regardless of where they are, there is a belief that our Ancestors are aware of us and watch us throughout our lives. That our Alfar and Disir are able to bestow advice and a bit of needed Luck to a deserving descendant. That our Ancestors take an interest in us and may look out for us during a trying time. Regardless, we owe our Ancestors our lives, and they deserve to be honored and remembered.

ENCOURAGING NEW HEATHENS

Many newcomers to Asatru or Heathenry focus first on our Gods, and only later develop a true interest in honoring their Ancestors. This is probably a vestige of the mainstream religions within which they were raised. To your average person in our Western Culture, religion is all about honoring a God or Gods. For the majority religion, Christianity, the entire focus of the religion is on worshiping their god. So, it makes sense why new Heathens first focus on our Gods, and do not usually come to fully understand the importance of honoring their Ancestors until they have been around Heathenry a little while.

But our Ancestors have a direct and vested interest in us, and how we live our lives. They share the Frith of kinship with us, and properly honoring them and making them proud is of great importance. So, when new Heathens approach you or your Kindred looking for guidance, share with them the importance of their Ancestor. Teach them how to honor and value their Ancestors at least as much as they honor and value our Gods.

Sometimes new Heathens will ask, "But what about all my Christian Ancestors, how am I supposed to honor them?" Quite frankly, I do not believe that there should be any difference in how we honor our Heathen Ancestors from our Christian Ancestors. We honor them by knowing them, remembering them, gifting them, leading worthwhile lives, and raising strong responsible children. All Ancestors, regardless of what religion they held in life, would appreciate all that we do for our Ancestors.

WAYS TO HONOR ONE'S ANCESTORS - KNOW THEM

There are many ways to know one's Ancestors. One of the best ways to get started is to talk with your living relatives, and find out all they know about your grandparents, great-grandparents, and as far back as any one of your living relatives can go back. Take notes. Write down names, dates, where they lived, and their occupations. If they remember little details from their lives, make note of those as well. What where their interests and hobbies? What were their greatest hardships and accomplishments? What was their favorite foods or treats? What stories are known or have been passed down about these Ancestors.

While your parents, grandparents and great-grandparents are still alive ask them to tell you stories from their lives. This may take some convincing with some of your quieter or more modest relatives. But some living relatives will tell you all sorts of stories from their lives. Ask them how they felt about or reacted to important historical moments that took place during their lives. Ask them about the jobs they held, the homes they lived in, the schools they went to, the adventures and misadventures they lived. Once these living relatives are gone, their stories will go with them if you do not ask and listen. Take careful notes and keep them all in one place you will not lose them. Details are easy to forget or mix up, so keeping notes will keep the information clear and accurate in your memory, and give you something to refresh your memory. Notes also make it easier for you to preserve and pass on the information you collect.

Genealogy can also be enormously interesting and enlightening about one's own background. You are in luck if you already have a relative that has done a lot of the genealogical footwork for you. Usually they will be very happy to copy of the information and families trees information they have gathered. Sometimes it will be so complete, that you do not have to really do much more with it than read it and learn from it. But, with genealogy you can always strive to go further back with the research, and existing genealogical information given to you by another relative can give you an amazing starting place for further research.

Whether you are starting nearly from scratch in researching your family tree or if you are given a head-start on the information by a relative, there are a variety of on-line sources of genealogical information. One such site is http://www.ancestry.com. You can do some very basic searching for information for free at ancestry.com, but you will get much further along and more quickly, if you go ahead and pay the $20 a month fees to register with their website. Ancestry.com has searchable census documents going back to the 1700's. They also have all manner of birth records, death records, service records, marriage license records, immigration records, ship passenger lists, and the list goes on and on. All of this is searchable, and with a little practice you can start piecing together your families history from home on the internet.

With today's technology, you also have the option of having your DNA tested and analyzed. There are a wide variety of services and pricing methods based on this technology, but if you do your research and have some money to spend you can learn a lot about where your Ancestors come from, who you are currently related to in the world, and many other helpful areas of information about your Ancestors.

If you have managed to do some or all of this work to learn more about your Ancestors, then it is definitely worth bringing all that information together in one place, and putting it in a format that can be shared with other relatives and your descendants. This can be as simple as photo-copying and stapling together packets of information to share and pass down. Some families bring the information together into a book format, and print off a number of actual books to share and pass down. The book creation option is enormously easy using today's print-on-demand book services available on-line. http://www.createspace.com and http://www.lulu.com are both excellent options in this area. With today's technology, it is even possible to use family-tree software to enter all of your information into a professionally designed computer interface that makes the information searchable, easily browsable and, when copied to a disk, enormously easy to share and pass down.

I have been asked before, "What if I am adopted and do not know who my Ancestors are?" Or, "I never knew who my father was, so I do not any of my Ancestors from that side of the family?" We cannot help it if circumstances make it impossible for us to know or learn more about our Ancestors in all or some of our family. But regardless of whether you know your Ancestors or not, 100% of us do have Ancestors. Even if we do not know them, you can be assured that your Ancestors DO

KNOW YOU. Though you know nothing of your Ancestors, they are still worthy of being honored and gifted.

The act of knowing one's Ancestors and all the time and sacrifice that can go into such an on-going process, is a great gift to one's Ancestors. In addition, the knowledge you gain about them, makes your connection with them and your ability to honor them just that much stronger.

WAYS TO HONOR ONE'S ANCESTORS - REMEMBER THEM

Remembering an Ancestors gives them the respect and recognition they deserve. It allows them to live on in this world, in the form of memories, stories, and the lessons that their lives can teach us. Everyone wants to be remembered, and there is no reason to believe that our Ancestors would be any different. There are many ways to remember one's Ancestors, and the following are just some of them.

Talk with your children about your Ancestors. Tell them the interesting, funny, and moving stories that you know. Show them photos and home movies if you have them. Share what you know about who they were, what they cared about, and what they were like to be around. Explain to your children why their Ancestors are important and why it is good to honor them. In essence, make these people "real" for your children and give them the tools they need to connect with them and to feel like they have a relationship with who they were (are).

Use whatever creativity you have, and create art that memorializes your Ancestors. If you carve stone, carve a rune stone in honor of a specific Ancestor. If write songs, poetry, or prose, write something that memorializes a specific Ancestors, and expresses who they really were and why they are important to you. If they had a specific craft that they were good at or enjoyed, then it may be beneficial to learn and practice that craft yourself. If they had a favorite food or dish that they liked to prepare or are known for within your family, then prepare that food or dish keeping that Ancestor in mind. If you take the food or dish to a family dinner or wider gathering, tell those present about the food and the Ancestor that inspired you to prepare it.

During meals at special occasions prepare an Ancestor's plate and set an empty seat at the table. At the beginning of the meal, invite Ancestors or a specific Ancestor to dine with you. During the meal, tell stories of that Ancestor and share why they were so important to you.

During Symbel, speaking good and true words of your Ancestors or a specific Ancestor is a wonderful way to remember them and to share with those you care about something special about that Ancestor. When making such a toast, say who the Ancestor was by name, and then share from your heart something meaningful about them. These words and the honor you give them go into the well, and everyone participating benefits from them.

Photos are an amazing way to remember people, and having a large wall of your house dedicated to photos of your Ancestors reminds you of them daily. If you have certain belongings or artifacts passed down to you that belonged to Ancestors, care for these objects and keep them safe. Find ways to preserve and display these items in your home, to show their importance to you and to also serve as a reminder of your relationship with that Ancestor.

In taking steps to remember and memorialize one's Ancestors, it is the act of doing something that shows them your respect and admiration. It is one thing to say, "I honor my Ancestors," but there is something so much more significant to actively do something that honors them.

WAYS TO HONOR ONE'S ANCESTORS - ALTARS AND GIFTS

One traditional way of honoring one's Ancestors is to establish an area in your home specifically for honoring and gifting your Ancestors. Many call this an Ancestors' altar, but the name or shape of it is not nearly as important as what you do with it. The altar could take the form on one set of bookshelves in your home dedicated to this purpose. Perhaps the altar is an old table or piece of furniture that belonged to an Ancestors that was particularly special to you. Perhaps it is simply a wide window sill overlooking a beautiful view outside. Really, it depends on how much space you have and what you have at your disposal to create this holy space.

Once you have a spot picked out and prepared, place things in the area that remind you of your Ancestors and represent who they were. This can include photographs, objects that belonged to them, and objects that they would have liked based on their interests in life. Establishing this holy space is a deed that you have performed, that in a concrete way shows your Ancestors how important they are to you and that they are not forgotten. This holy space in your home also serves as a constant reminder to you and your family, so that everyday as you pass the alter, thoughts and memories of your Ancestors are brought to mind.

This altar also serves as a place for gifting your Ancestors, and these gifts can take many forms. Placing an offering bowl on the altar with some of their favorite drink, food, candy, or other object will actively show them the honor you are showing them. It is a gift you are giving them in return for the many gifts they have given you. Gifting is a powerful way to build bonds and friendships among the living, and gifting has the similar affect of maintaining our connection and relationships with our honored dead.

WAYS TO HONOR ONE'S ANCESTORS - MAKE THEM PROUD

This particular method of honoring one's Ancestors is not often discussed Or at the very least, it is not discussed enough. One of the greatest gifts you can give your Ancestors, is to live a life of which they are proud. What better way to honor your Ancestors than to lead the sort of responsible, eventful, and accomplished life that would make them proud of who you are and what you accomplished with your time on earth? When making a choice in life, it is worth considering what would Grandmother Hattie think of what I am about to do? When deciding whether to watch 6 hours of television or actually accomplish something, it is worth considering what Great Uncle John would want you to do with your life.

We all wish the best for our children and our descendants, and will do nearly anything to give them the nudge they need to lead responsible and productive lives. When our children and grandchildren do grow up to be strong accomplished adults, we feel great pride in them. It should be no different for the dead. By living a life of which they would be proud, we show them that we have not squandered or taken lightly the gift of life and Orlog they have passed to us. Many of our Ancestors struggled and sacrificed greatly to give their descendant's a better life than they had, and when we recognize this and lead our lives with this in mind, we show them in a concrete way that we acknowledge and appreciate them and what they did for us.

WAYS TO HONOR ONE'S ANCESTORS - YOUR CHILDREN

Another way of honoring our Ancestors that does not get spoken of enough, involves the children we bring into this world. What better gift to our Ancestors than raising, to the best of our ability, healthy and well-adjusted children? We see in the faces of our living parents, grandparents, and great-grandparents the pride they feel in those children that are descended from them. It should be no different for the dead. What pride they must feel to see those that are descended from them, growing and prospering in the world.

Even a tree with deep roots but no limbs will eventually die.

Continuing our families, and strengthening and improving the lives of those that come after us brings great joy and honor to our Ancestors.

IT IS A PROCESS...

It is unreasonable to expect that a new Heathen would hit the ground running, and attempt to do everything talked about in this essay from day one. Just like forming and maintaining relationships with the living is a process and takes time, so does building and maintaining our relationships with our Ancestors. So, if you read this essay and find that you are doing nothing that is listed here, or very little of it, then pick one or two things and work toward making them happen. When those are in place in your life and working well, choose a few more things to add and bring into your Heathen practice. Over time, you will establish a connection and a bond with your Ancestors that will serve you, your family, and your Kindred well.

SO, YOU DO NOT KNOW YOUR ANCESTORS

Sometimes people post on our board about their inability to connect with their Ancestors because they do not know anything about them (for instance someone who is adopted and does not know anything about their birth family, or someone who does not know who their dad is, causing them to know nothing about their dad's side of the family.) Sometimes they worry about connecting, because a grandfather or grandmother died before they were born.

It is important to remember that while you may not know your Ancestors – or anything about them – **that does not mean they do not know you.**

Think about it. After your death, if you are able, will not you want to check on your descendants and see how they are doing? If you are able to help them in some small way, will not you want to help them? The way we love our children and grandchildren, will not you check in on them and help them regardless of whether they know you or not?

Granted, a gift for a gift does have an impact. Honoring your Ancestors and gifting them, does facilitate a better relationship and connection with them. But there is a blood connection – a soul connection – that exists regardless of how little you may know of your Ancestors.

So, do everything you can to learn about them. If you do everything you can, and learn nothing, so be it. Gift your Ancestors. Raise a horn to them. Honor them. Set up a shrine to them in your house. Talk to them every day, and let them know how thankful you are for the hardships, sacrifices, and hard work they performed to ensure that you are here on this earth and have a life to live to its fullest. Live a life of which any Ancestor would be proud. If you do these things, you will see their influence in your life.

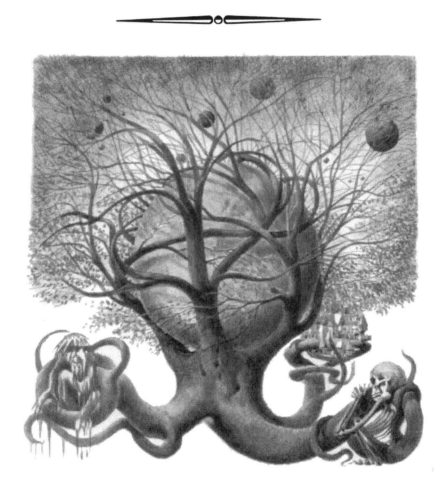

SECTION SIX

MISCELLANEOUS ESSAYS

HOW HEATHENS CORRECT A WRONG

In the Christian culture, you ask for forgiveness and you receive it. Admitting fault and saying "sorry" puts the wrong in the past. The Christian god just wants his followers to ask forgiveness, and he gives it. Christians are also told to grant forgiveness to other people, in much the same way.

Heathens have a set process for correcting a wrong, and gaining what Christians would call "forgiveness." Our Ancestors believed that if you do something wrong, you should fix what you broke. You should pay for the wrong you have done. When you have fixed the wrong or paid for it, then (and only then) the matter is put behind you.

So, if a Heathen tells a friend that he will help him do something important, but something comes up, and the Heathen fails to help his friend, he does not just say "sorry." He should go to the friend and say, "I know I was supposed to help you, but I did not. That was wrong." Then the Heathen should offer to help the friend with something even more important and follow through. Or perhaps the Heathen would give the friend something that would make up for letting the friend down.

If a Heathen breaks something that belongs to someone, he replaces what was broken or pays for it. If a Heathen unintentionally says something that causes unintended problems for someone else, he does what he can to correct the problem or make up for it. If a Heathen says he will do something or be somewhere, and he fails to follow through, he goes to the person he made the failed commitment to and compensates them in some way for the failure.

When correcting or paying for a wrong you have done, sometimes it is sufficient to decide how to fix it or make up for the wrong and just do it. But often, especially in important matters, it is better to go to the person who was wronged, and ask them exactly how you can fix it or how you can make up for it. If the person wronged names a reasonable action or payment they wish you to make, then you accept the Shyld (payment or obligation) that they set and follow through on it.

When a wrong is done, the intentions of the wrong-doer are not of paramount concern. The primary focus is on the actual wrong – the actual injury – that was done. Whether that wrong was intentional or accidental, it was still wrong-doing and still needs to be fixed or payment made. The injured or wronged party may look at the intentions of the wrong-doer when setting Shyld, or when considering whether the wrong-doer will repeat the injury in the future. But accidental wrong-doing still demands the wrong be corrected or payment made.

In very small matters between friends or Kindred members, things that really are not a big deal, we give each other a "pass" sometimes. A simple acknowledgment of the small wrong that was done and a statement of regret will usually suffice in small matters. But, even in these small matters, it strengthens a friendship when you actually care enough to take steps to make up for a small wrong you have done.

The problem with the concept that a simple "sorry" fixes all wrongs, is that in practice it does not actually work. The wrong is not actually addressed, and even if the wronged person accepts the apology, it is just human nature to continue to be upset about the wrong because it has not been fixed or the debt paid. Only by actually addressing the wrong and showing through one's deeds that you recognize your own accountability for what you did, is the matter actually repaired and properly set aside.

In not giving forgiveness easily, it is not that Heathens are mean, or pointlessly vengeful, or hold endless grudges. They just expect that when someone wrongs them or hurts them, that they should make up for it in some way. It restores the balance, the reciprocity in the relationship, and honor is restored.

Honor is really at the heart of this Heathen process of correcting a wrong you have done. This process restores the honor of both parties involved. Among our Ancestors, the wronged party would take vengeance upon a wrong-doer in order to restore their honor and the honor of their family. In addition, a wrong-doer, in correcting or paying for a wrong, shows his own sense of honor in trying to fix what they have broken.

SELFISHNESS, INTENTIONS, AND EMOTIONS

As Heathens, "we are our deeds." When we do something, we are judged by the nature of our action and its results, rather than on our intentions, or our state of mind, or our emotional state. In the simplest terms, Good is defined as what helps your family and loyal loved ones, while Bad is defined as what hurts your family and loyal loved ones.

Our Ancestors did not spend a lot of time looking at intentions, or emotions, or state of mind. Why? Because they realized that what is REAL and what REALLY MATTERS are our actions and the impact those actions have on the real world.

This can be difficult for modern people raised in our modern culture to grasp. We are raised with this whole need to understand "why" someone did something. What were the root causes? What was he thinking? Did he mean for that to happen? How does he feel about what he has done? Add to this, a modern aversion to actually taking full responsibility for one's actions, and it can be difficult to understand that for Heathens, "we are our deeds."

This comes into play in many situations, and the mistakes people make in this area come in many forms.

SELFISHNESS IS A HARD HABIT TO UNLEARN

Our Ancestors had a rugged individuality, but they also understood that a man without kith and kin, was nothing. Literally nothing. There was no one to help him, no one to stand up for him or speak for him, and no one to take vengeance on his behalf. A man without kith and kin was alone, unprotected, and nothing.

So, one's Innangarth was enormously important. At the center of this was a man's family, and then his friends, and then his community. If a man's actions helped this Innangarth, then the actions were Good. If a man's actions hurt this Innangarth, then the actions were Bad.

But, as modern people, these bonds and connections with those around us have decayed quite a bit. Marriages do not last. Extended family bonds are rare and getting rarer. Friends are temporary and often based on shallow bonds. We do not know our neighbors, let alone anyone else in our community. Modern culture actually seems to encourage us to seek individual pleasure, fulfillment, and satisfaction over concerns for those for whom we are most responsible.

This can of course result in selfish behavior. Breaking that modern habit, and learning to live with true consideration for one's family, one's Tribe, and those closest to us is part of the culture reeducation that nearly all Heathens must go through when come home to Heathenry. Some learn it and live it, while others are not so successful at it.

HAVING GOOD INTENTIONS
DOES NOT FIX THE HARM YOU CAUSE

One reason that intentions just did not matter to our Ancestors, was their close attention and need for Honor. If someone's actions hurt or injured you or yours in some way, then your Honor had been taken from you. That was an intolerable situation that had to be resolved. When one's honor was taken, even in bits and pieces, it was not something with which you could just live. You either took vengeance or the person that injured you must pay something to restore your Honor. The fact someone "did not intend" to hurt you or insult you, does not completely mitigate what they did or its affect on you.

Our modern world has forgotten Honor. People hurt or insult people accidentally, and then just shrug and say, "Oh well, I did not mean to do that." The fact remains that they hurt or insulted you, and that hurt or insult may have lasting effect. Accidents do not matter. Intentions do not matter. If you hurt or insult someone, and wish to make things good between you again, you must "fix what you broke." It does not matter if you meant to break it, you have to fix it.

It is only by fixing what you broke, that you can truly put the matter to rest. Have you ever hurt or insulted someone, apologized for it, and then a month or a year later had the event brought up again? That is because apologies are just words. They are simply a statement of regret, without any real action or steps taken to correct what you have done. Our Ancestors understood, that it is deeds that matter, and not words.

So, as Heathens, we need to understand that intentions just do not matter a whole lot. It is the actual actions you take, the results of your actions, and how those actions affect others that actually matters. When we do something bad, claiming we had "good intentions" just does not make it all better.

EMOTIONS ARE NOT AN EXCUSE FOR BAD BEHAVIOR

Modern culture is enormously tied up in emotion. Emotions, must like intentions, just do not matter a lot when it comes to the things we do and how they affect other people.

For instance, let us say a man has a wife and kids, but emotionally he is detached from the relationship. He is bored with his relationship, he is feeling constrained and stagnant within his family, and he is looking around at other women and thinking about leaving his wife.

From a Heathen perspective, these emotions just do not matter that much. If the man has emotional needs that are not being met, and decides to leave his family, that is a Bad act. Our Ancestors would not have judged his act based on his emotional needs. They would have looked at what he did, and how that affects his Innangarth.

I have a friend come to me, in this exact circumstance. He tried to make the case to me that he was entirely justified in leaving his wife and kids, because he "was not in love anymore." I told him, that from a Heathen perspective, that was not a good enough reason to leave his wife and kids, and disrupt his family. His oath and his responsibilities came first. Rather than making emotional and selfish decisions, he should be spending all of his time and energy working on his marriage, and finding that spark that he lost. Even if he never found that spark, he needed to fulfill his oath and fulfill his responsibilities to his kids to make his family work.

Emotions bring color to our lives. They are a part of life, and I am not saying emotions should be suppressed or ignored in our lives. I am saying, that emotions are no excuse for Bad behavior, or that behavior that hurts our Innangarth. When you do something selfish, and hurt one's own family, emotions do not give you a free pass.

IT ALL COMES DOWN TO OUR DEEDS

It is your actions and deeds that matter. This is true in all things. Your actions and deeds are judged by how they affect your Innangarth. Your family, your close friends, and your Kindred or Tribe. While emotions are an important part of who we are as humans, they are never a license to shirk one's obligations and responsibilities, or an excuse for bad behavior.

Intentions are internal. You can intend to start a Kindred, but until you do so, your intentions just do not matter much in the real world. You can have the best of intentions, but if you actions hurt someone, then your intentions do not fix or mitigate the damage you have done. You can intend to get around to teaching your kids about Heathenry, but intending to do something accomplishes nothing. It is the action leading from intention that actually affects and shapes the world.

Emotions are internal. You can love your daughter, but what she will really remember when you are gone are your actions. She will remember the times you read to her at bedtime, the hugs, the conversations you have with her, the advice you give, the assistance and protection you actively provide, the holding her hand in a scary movie, the time you spend comforting her when she has had a nightmare, and everything else you DO for her as a father or mother.

Even within our practice of Heathenry, it is our deeds that matter. You can have all the Faith in the world for our Gods, but what are you DOING? Do you honor them and gift them? Do you live openly as a Heathen, explaining what Heathenry is to those that would ask? Do you teach your children about our Ways? Do you meet and gather with other like minded Heathens? Do you study and learn what you can, and help new Heathens learn what you have learned? Do you lead a life, of which our Gods would be proud?

THOSE THAT DISRUPT OR DESTROY

My dad was a wise old man. He said "if something is not working, do it differently." He was a man who did not like "change, for the sake of change." Old sayings are old sayings for a reason, and Dad certainly believed, "If it ain't broke, do not fix it."

Now you would think this would mean my dad liked the status quo. But you would be wrong. He loved to fix things. Build things. To create. He started businesses, would build them into something profitable, and then sell them. He started and ran charitable organizations. He improved everything he touched. He questioned everything that was not working, and was always willing to look at better ways of doing things. He was willing to "rock the boat," when it was needed. He was no friend of the status quo. But he was also not a friend of chaos and disruption.

See, there are people who "rock the boat" to make things better, healthier, more efficient, stronger, and more ordered. My dad was one of these people. Something's broke, then you fix it. Something's stagnant, then you help liven it up in a way that does not destroy what you hope to enliven. Something stands in the way of progress, you move it aside and keep moving right on past it.

Then there are those that "rock the boat" to make things worse, corrupted, messier, weaker, and more chaotic. These "boat-rockers" do not do it to make things better. They usually do it out of a selfish need to destroy that which they cannot have for themselves. If they cannot build something, then they get some satisfaction out of tearing it down. Defying it. Causing disruption and trying to destroy it. It validates them in some way. Makes them feel important.

Sometimes this latter sort of "boat rocker" – the destructive kind – does not even have a clue how destructive they are being. Other times, they literally delight in their destructive efforts. They will speak of chaos, and strife, and fighting as some sort of holy calling; as if they are doing a favor to everyone by going around disrupting things. They will say they are weeding out the "weak." They will say they are making systems, groups, and movements "stronger" by causing problems within them. They will describe themselves as if they have been given some special role as a destructive force, and we should accept them and be happy to have them around, doing what they do.

212

It is clear to me that that those that honor the Aesir, should strive to build things – not just tear things down. It is clear that our Ancestors did not tolerate or thank those that caused disruption, discord, and chaos among their families or their communities. They had very clear ways of dealing with such people. While we do not have the same means at our disposal, we have an obligation as Kindred-builders and Folk-builders to protect our families and loyal friends from such disruptive efforts.

Odin went by the name "Bolverk" (trouble) among his enemies. But not among his own Folk. Let us try to never forget that.

HEATHEN INTERNET DRAMA AND HOW TO AVOID IT

To avoid drama, I am not going to use any names in this essay. I will also leave out enough details, that I can talk about this topic generally without directly insulting anyone.

Internet drama. There are some Heathens that have been around Heathenry for years and years, that just will not even get on the internet anymore. They have fully withdrawn from discussions of Heathenry on the internet. They have gotten tired of being attacked, and maligned, and insulted by people they have never met, and people they will never meet. I used to wonder at their withdrawal from all things "internet," and I could not understand it. But, as time goes on, I can see why they have withdrawn. It all comes down to internet drama, trolls, personal attacks, and keyboard cowboys and cowgirls, who never do anything in the real world, but find all the time in the world to be enormously negative and destructive on the internet.

Do not get me wrong. 99% of the comments and discussion on the essays I write and my status posts is constructive, whether it agrees with me or not. I do not expect people to agree with me. I am usually writing from the perspective of "what MY Kindred does," not the perspective of "this is what YOUR Kindred must do. So, of course we will differ in approaches and methods and opinions. We are Heathens! It is just natural.

Constructive disagreement and discussion are helpful to me, and to other people reading the discussion. I learn from it, they learn from it, and the person disagreeing with me is likely to learn from it too. I sometimes even change my mind or viewpoint, or at the very least, come to understand someone else's approach. I could write essays all day, and stick them in a drawer – but what does that accomplish? I post my essays because I want to spark a varied discussion, and get people thinking about a topic, and how THEY might approach it in their own life and their own Kindred.

So, what is this internet drama I am talking about?

THREATS - Physically threatening someone, or suggesting that you would like to kick their ass, because of an argument on the internet is pretty silly. It is easy to type a threat on the keyboard to someone you have never met, will never meet, and who is likely a 1000 miles away from you. It does not make you look tough, but instead has the opposite effect.

NAME-CALLING - Just because someone disagrees with you, does not make them a racist, evil, stupid, uneducated, ill-informed, etc. Everyone has different ways of looking at the world and different life experiences, and two intelligent, sane, and reasonable people can hold opposite viewpoints on the same issue. Name-calling is not a discussion, and often shows that the name-caller cannot legitimately back up what he/she is saying. In Heathenry, the most subtle form of this is when someone writes, "Well I can understand how a newbie like you would think that," or "I think you will have a different opinion once you have been Heathen as long as I have."

PLAYING GAMES - You know that boyfriend or girlfriend that was always testing you? Stupid little tests that caused both of you stress, but somehow gave your girlfriend or boyfriend power, or reassurance, or love by testing you? Well, putting people through meaningless "tests" in a discussion is equally jacked up on the internet. Game playing can go further of course, when people suggesting nefarious things, or suggest that they represent some larger (but invisible) group that will now crush, or turn against whomever disagrees with them or whomever failed their test.

ENDLESS NITPICKING - I know I am having a discussion with a troll, when during the discussion I post a long response with lots of well thought out opinions and points in it (at least in my opinion), and then will pick one word or phrase from my entire post and tear it to pieces, completely ignoring the context of that word or point. The extreme example of this happens on message boards, when someone quotes you, and then posts line by line everything that is wrong with you and what you said. You get the feeling you could type, "The sky is blue," and they would find 100 reasons you were wrong.

OBSESSIVE DISAGREEMENT - A somewhat silly example of this, would be if you wrote an essay about the right sort of rain gear to wear in a storm, and someone engaged you in an argument about whether you used the word "sleet" correctly. No matter how you respond to them, they just keep posting about how badly you used the word "sleet" and all the other words you could have used. Twenty posts later they are still stuck obsessively on this little detail, and everyone has forgotten that the essay was really about the best sort of rain gear to wear.

ILLUSION OF FAMILIARITY - I get this one a lot, and I am always amazed by it. People who I have never met, who I have never spoken with, people that have never even posted a comment on my essays before, will just occasionally go off on me in the most incredibly nasty ways. Usually they are accusing me of something, the intersperse it with extremely negative suggestions about me, including name-calling, and then they will tell me they are "only telling me this because they are my friend." Then will sometime even go further, suggesting that "real friends are willing to tell you the ugly truth," when in fact the person writing this is not my friend, not someone I have even ever met or heard from before.

CASTING YOU IN A SCRIPT - Garman Lord in Way of the Heathen talked about this one. He said it much better than I will, but allow me to summarize. This is when someone has some sort of baggage, and this baggage forces them to come into a situation with a preconceived notion of who you are or what you are saying, even when you are not really that person and you really are not saying what they think you are saying. Usually this is an "anti-authority" thing, where they cast you in a script as "bossing them around," and some sort of villain. As they read your essay or any comments you make, they color their understanding with this preconceived script. No matter what you write or how you respond, they will interpret everything you say according to that script. With these people, you will never convince them you are anything other than what they have already decided you are.

ALL ABOUT THEM - Somehow, everything these trolls read is actually about them. If I write, "I lost 20 pounds over the last 2 months," they think you are suggesting they are fat. If you boast about getting a new job, then you are somehow being insensitive to them because they are still looking for a job. If you say that all things being equal, it is better for children to grow up in a home with two parents, they think you are insulting the single-mother that raised them. When you enter discussions with them, based on their "all about them" viewpoint, everything you say usually just reinforces how offended they are.

I could go on and on, and I am sure everyone reading this could add to the list.

There is a few things to keep in mind when dealing with on-line discussions, when you disagree with someone. First of all, try to keep the tone of your comments and responses reasonable and free from anger. Of course not everyone agrees with you. How boring would the world be if we all agreed on everything? Keep in mind, that just because someone does not agree with you, does not mean they are evil, stupid, out-to-get-you, or uneducated. They are likely just coming at if from a different perspective, and a different set of life experiences. Learn to enjoy discussions with people you do not agree with, and not to get into pissing matches every time you do not agree with someone.

Also keep in mind, that if you really want to share constructive criticism with someone on a personal level, you will do it in a private message. Publicly calling someone "offensive," "insensitive," "unreasonable," and other negative things is not the best way to have your message heard. If you really care about the person, and are really trying to communicate a heartfelt concern you have about them, the last thing you would do is post it publicly so that 50, or 100, or a 1000 people will read the negative things you are saying about them or to them..

If you are engaged in a discussion, and it is beginning to get unreasonable or even a little irrational, write them a private message. Tell them what they are doing, and how that makes you feel. They will either get what you are saying, and you will have a fairly decent private discussion with them. Or they will continue the internet drama with you privately, and at least you will know with what you are dealing. But, the quicker you take a bad situation or discussion private, the more likely you are to resolve it successfully.

Anyhow, it seems to me as Heathens, that we have a lot of work to do for our families and our Folk. That work takes a lot of thought, a lot of time, a lot of energy, and a lot of resources. Let us use our time and our resources wisely, in doing things that actually move our Faith forward. We may disagree and there may be times we do not even like each other very much. But internet drama, trollish attacks, and keyboard cowboy antics never got us anywhere. Never.

In the end, the only thing in this world I can really focus on and care about is me, my family, Kindred, my close friends, and Heathens we know and like in our region. Communicating on the internet has its benefits, but it clearly has its pitfalls. As long as I keep what is important to me up front and center, all the internet drama really does not matter much.

THE LACK OF EMOTIONAL BOUNDARIES ONLINE

Rod Landreth, a member of Jotun's Bane Kindred, wrote an essay about Faux Brotherhood. It was an interesting rant about people he has never really met and does not know who call him "brother" just because he is also Asatru, or because they liked something he posted on-line. In his note, he strongly suggested (paraphrasing) that this flippant use of the term "brother" cheapens and makes a mockery of his relationship with his real brother by blood, and those Kindred-brothers with whom he has taken the time and effort to build brotherly relationships.

I think the over-use of the terms "brother" and "sister" on-line is just one of many overly-sentimental, overly-emotional, overly-familiar, and completely boundary-less behavior that we all see on the internet, and especially Facebook. My parents taught me to have boundaries, and decades of experience have reinforced the value and personal dignity of having boundaries. In Heathen terms, we recognize these boundaries as our Innangarth and Utangarth, those that are within our trusted inner circle and then everyone else.

Now, there are certainly people I like, respect, and enjoy interacting with on the internet. There are people on the internet, that I hope to meet in-person in the future. But, I also realize that I do not know these people enormously well. There are people on-line that I will write and thank or congratulate for what they have done. That is not what I am talking about in this essay. I am talking very specifically about people who express strong emotions or emotional bonds toward someone they only know on-line.

For instance, someone I have only interacted with on-line is not my "brother," my "sister," my "BFF", my "close friend," or any other closely bonded relationship. I also do not "love" people I have never met, or only really met once or twice. I do not gush emotion onto other people on the internet, and certainly not publicly on the internet. I do not list people I only know on-line, among my "closest friends" or "confidants."

I have never had one of my purely on-line "friends" bring me food when I was hungry. Loan me money when I was a little short. Mow my lawn or watch my kids when I was injured, having a medical procedure, or just needing a little quiet time with my wife. I have never had one of my purely on-line "friends" drop in on me and hang out for hours at a time, eat a meal with me, honor my Gods with me, or sit in Symbel with me. But I have had my real-life friends do all these things for me – and I have done these things for my real-life friends.

Since we do not know people on-line very well, it is very easy to be mislead about who they are. But in real-life, there are many indicators and clues you can use to know someone better, that just are not available on-line. Their body language. Their voice. Their laugh. Their reactions. The look in their eye. Meeting their friends or spouse in person. Watching them interact with their children. Watching them interact with your children. Visiting their home and seeing what sort of host they are. Having them visit your home and seeing what sort of guest they are. I mean, you can go on an on with examples like these.

If I have met a Heathen in-person once or twice, I have a much better idea of who they are. I have shook their hand, looked in their eye, had conversations with them, shared some laughs, and perhaps met their family. But, even in these situations, can we truly gush on-line that we are "best friends" after meeting once or twice in-person? Even in these situations, we should not confuse being on the path to friendship, with an actual close friendship.

I do not think the people who gush emotionally on-line to people they hardly know, realize how it looks to the rest of us. It is obvious that there are plenty of people who fall right in line with it, and seem deeply moved while being gushed over by someone they barely know. But, for those of us that do not do this, it raises questions in our mind about those that do. Especially when you consider the likely causes for this behavior...

1. Perhaps they do not really have any boundaries. Perhaps they do develop strong (but fleeting) emotions for a wide variety of people, sporadically, and without much cause. This makes them sort of an emotional loose cannon, bonding with people based on minimal contact or knowledge about the person, and then bonding with the next person they have minimal contact with, and so on. This would

suggest a real difficulty in knowing the reality and value of a real relationship.

2. Perhaps there life is so empty of real relationships, that this is the reason for their not knowing the difference. They have very few true friends, causing them to mistake even the slightest emotional connection as something much more. Or perhaps they have people in their life that are real friends, but they take these emotional connections completely for granted.

3. Perhaps emotional bonds with people they barely know, and will likely never really know, are easier. After all, all interaction over the internet is "easier." It is easier to insult someone on the internet, because you are not face to face. Easier to be sarcastic, pick fights, and even to threaten people. So, it could be that for some people the internet is a safe place for them to have emotional bonds with people. That does not make it real. On the contrary, it makes it a little like a video game where you sit at your keyboard and pretend you have close relationships with people you do not really even know.

4. Perhaps it is a method of manipulation. After all, there is no shortage of people who enjoy and seem to seek out flattery. You give them a little emotional flattery, and you have them on your hook. In return for your strongly expressed on-line emotions, you are able to get things from them. Maybe they make you feel important. Perhaps they send you things, or do you favors.

5. Perhaps it is some sort of reciprocal role-playing. There is a sick little dynamic that happens, where you tell someone that they are your BFF, and then they say it back. With very little investment, you both feel greatly gratified that someone really likes you. Nevermind the fact that you do not really know each other. Admitting that just gets in the way of your mutual beneficial on-line emotional masturbation.

6. Perhaps the person expressing emotion without boundaries, is simply imitating what he/she has seen other people do. They see it seemingly work for other people, and they conform to the on-line culture that does this, thinking that this is what people do on-line. I think this is especially likely to happen when someone it trying to fit into an on-line subculture, like on-line Heathenry.

I am sure it could be asked what real harm any of this really does? Personally, I think it leads to unhealthy situations where emotional ties with people on-line become too important, and emotional ties with people in real life suffer. The people we barely know on-line do nothing wrong. They portray themselves however they like, and we co-exist with them in an electronic pixel world without real problems, concerns, or difficulties. The internet, and specifically Facebook, is an escape. The on-line faux relationships we form there, are also a form of illusory escape.

Real relationships with real people take work, and effort, and compromise. Real relationships take real trust, and they exist in a messy world with problems, concerns, and difficulties. They have up's and down's. They also represent "risk." When we tend properly to our relationships in the real world, they become the strong foundation of a meaningful life.

What does all of this say to me? It says we need to never mistake a warm feeling or agreement with someone on the internet, as something more than a warm feeling or agreement with someone's on-line persona. It says that we all need to focus on the real relationships in our lives. We need put ourselves out there in real life, and make and maintain real friends, real love interests, and real emotional bonds with real people we actually know. As Heathens, we need to seek out other Heathens and other Heathen families, make the efforts to form bonds and get to know each other well, and thus build up our Innangarth with people we know, and respect, and with which we can form legitimate emotional bonds. We need to travel when we can, and gather with Heathens in surrounding communities and in our region.

We need to avoid blurring the lines between our true Innangarth and the on-line Utangarth, the same way we must avoid blurring the lines between real friends and people we barely know in real-life.

FAILED ATTEMPTS AT HEATHEN GLORY!

We are our deeds. As Heathens, our reputations and accomplishments matter. Have we had an impact on this world? Have we advanced our Folkway forward? Have we lived a life of which our Gods and Ancestors would be proud? Are we a man or woman that will be fondly remembered by our Family and our Folk?

Contrary to what you might see on the internet, being a great Heathen man or a great Heathen woman is all about living a responsible life. Taking good care of one's family and standing by one's friends.

Working hard, maintaining a stable life, providing for those that depend on us, and getting things done. There are many ways of meeting these obligations, and many different sorts of lives that can be lived well. But, the real meat-and-potatoes of being a good and respected Heathen, is fairly simple and straight forward.

But on the internet, you will see people seeking to impress other Heathens in some fairly strange ways. I see it as glory-seeking. The other night, some of our Kindred sat around discussing some of the odd things we have seen people do on the internet. In an attempt to appear more important, more relevant, or more powerful, people will say and do the strangest things. Now, this essay has two purposes. First, it will likely make you chuckle a bit because it is very likely you will think of examples you have seen yourself for each of the categories that follow. But the second purpose of the essay is to perhaps to clue-in these people to the fact the rest of us just are not buying any of this.

UNVERIFIED PERSONAL TOUGHNESS (UPT) - This is actually one of my favorites. Since it is the internet, people can portray themselves however they want. So it is UPT when someone posts on a message board how they are the expert in 6 different martial arts and a master of sword fighting, when for all we know they are 5'5", 98 pounds, and the only fight they have ever been in is on their X-box.

There is also the claims of incredible stare-down powers. Something like, "I was in a bar the other night and these three guys were picking on my friend, so I gave them a hard look that let them know their time on this earth was short, and they fled the bar. I think one even wet himself." This one cracks me up, because it just seems straight from a Hollywood movie or something.

Then there is the feats of strength. Claiming one can bench 500 lbs. Claiming one fist-fought a grizzly bear to death. Claiming one ripped a car door straight off its hinges in a fit of rage. This one also ties in with people's claims that they go into berserker rages, like our Ancestors of old, and perform great and epic deeds during these rages.

UNVERIFIED PERSONAL ANCESTRY (UPA) - I ran into an example of this at the very first Heathen event I attended. UPA is when someone claims that have traced their ancestry back to Frey, or Thor, or perhaps the King of Norway. I have seen some Heathens claim to be descendents of heroes in the Icelandic Sagas, or other important people. Nevermind that the person claiming this great ancestry has been fired from 10 jobs in the last year, or is living a life that is a complete mess. They boldly proclaim incredible ancestry, and rarely do they do so credibly or with anything to back it up.

Occasionally, I have seen Heathens claim to be descendents of some great Heathen that killed many Christians during the Conversion period. They will usually put this in their message board signature line, somewhat literally: "John Smith, blood descendent of Rollo the Butcher, who slaughtered 1000's of the White Christ's followers."

I have met Heathens that claimed to have "troll-blood" or "jotun-blood." I have seen some Heathens claim to have more Neanderthal DNA than your average Northern European. UPA of this sort, often ties in with amazing claims of toughness and strength (UPT), so UPA and UPT sometimes go hand in hand.

THE DOCTOR DOOLITTLE OF FETCHES - Some Heathens like to write huge stories of their face-to-face encounters with real bears. The story is always embellished with details of the Heathen and the bear circling each other, eye to eye, until there was a clear feeling of mutual respect and admiration, and then they wandered off their separate ways. Clearly the bear recognized the fact the Heathen's fetch was a bear, and that he was a Kindred spirit. Right?

I have seen someone post about being covered with hundreds of bees, but that that not a single bee stung them, which made it clear to them that their fetch is some sort of bee.

I do not think anyone has a problem with a Heathen believing or expressing that they have a Fetch. I think the ones that reach Doctor Doolittle status clearly separate themselves from the crowd with the amazing and epic nature of their stories. Their tales often sound like a cross between a fairy tale and an action movie, with them facing down some incredibly dangerous creature, in absolute fearlessness – and the wild beast walking away with an appreciation of the "Doctor Doolittle" Heathen's strength, resolve, and spirit.

PHONE CALLS TO THE GODS - "Odin talked to me when I was a little boy (girl) all the time. He told me when I was five that I would be a great Heathen leader, and bring our Folkway back into the mainstream with my leadership and strength. He said, you are mind." I think we have all seen examples of this posted on message boards and other internet venues.

Honestly, if a God or Goddess ever did appear to me here on Midgard or spoke to me directly (a booming voice from the sky), I do not think I would go posting about it on the internet. I would share that with my family and my Kindred, and I would pass on whatever message I felt had been conveyed to me. But posting on the internet to essentially strangers about one's direct and frequent communication with the Gods and Goddesses just seems to cheapen it, and call it into question.

"Freyja told me this." "Thor taught me this." "Frey told me I would do great things." This seems like something left over from Christianity, in a sense. I mean, even in the Sagas, our Ancestors looked to signs from the Gods. They threw their Thor poles in the water, to see where they would land, and thus where they would build a settlement. They did not phone up Thor so he could give them exact coordinates in-person. I know we have stories of Odin walking the earth, and interacting with humans. But this was rare.

An odd variation on this theme, is the women who claim to be married to Odin. If they wish to believe they are married to Odin, then more power to them. But do not expect me to drop what I am doing and be impressed with such a claim.

GRAND POO BAH SYNDROME - We see this fairly often. You will see a Heathen that is not particularly well-read or knowledgeable, with a life that is a complete mess – a Heathen that has no Kindred and does not gather with other Heathens, and yet – this Heathen wishes to be seen and respected as some sort of Asa-Pope. You will see them starting up-start national organizations, that never quite get started, and never last. You will see them starting large national efforts at something (prison ministry, a Heathen magazine, a scholarship fund, a lobbying group), that never quite get started, and never last.

Over time, I have begun to see some ways to spot these seekers of Heathen "glory." They have accomplished very little in the past, and yet are biting off some incredible task, and expect us to believe that contrary to type they will be able to pull this off. Their ideas always seem like schemes, with other people expected to carry the heavy water and do the work, or donate the money. They always seem to be good at coming up with a catchy name for their effort and designing a cool logo for it, but it never goes very far beyond that. They usually get frustrated with their own efforts very quickly, for they expect to accomplish great things while doing very little work, and thus abandon their own effort right as they have fooled 50 to 150 people to go along with them.

An subgroup of this category are those with the pretty titles, that you are never quite sure how they earned. A 17-year-old kid living in a town of 50,000 souls who has never met another Heathen in-person, and yet he calls himself a "Godhi." A 27-year-old man who is friends with 5 Wiccans, and calls himself a "Chieftain" of a Kindred that does not even exist. Titles of responsibility are earned, not in a school or an on-line course, but they are earned from the people who support you in that role. You really are not a Godhi, unless other Heathens know you, and respect and acknowledge you as a modern Godhi. You really are not a Chieftain, unless there are strong Heathen men and women that look to you for leadership, and respect and acknowledge you as their Chieftain.

ELITE (SHUT-IN) SCHOLARS - I greatly respect good scholarship, and those that spend their time learning and sharing what they have learned. Where would we be as a Folkway without scholars, after all? So, I am not talking about scholars or scholarship in general.

What this category of glory-seeking actually refers to, is the Heathen man or woman who is fairly smart, and can write a good essay or a good book, but cannot seem to apply anything in those essays or books to their own life. What good are essays about Kindred, if you have never been in a successful one? What good are essays about honor, if your life reflects that you have no honor? There is this sub-group of scholars within Heathenry, that do not walk the walk. But on the internet, you do not have to walk the walk. Talking the talk is enough for everyone to think you are amazing. We may say, "We are our deeds," but there are those that people read and listen to, who in "real-life" are a complete and utter mess – and have always been a complete and utter mess.

If you are reading this essay, and think I am talking about you, or someone you know, just drop it. I am speaking very generally here, and if you insist on believing I am talking directly about you, then I am fairly certain I will not convince you otherwise. I would just quickly remind you, that it is not all about you and this essay does not name anyone specifically, and very deliberately does not give enough detail to even hint at anyone specifically. I am talking about a tendency – a tendency that we have all seen at some point or another. I think these are tendencies we should be able to recognize, and even avoid. But this essay is not aimed at anyone specific, nor does it name or hint at anyone specific.

All that being said, a little boasting never hurt anyone. But would it not be nice to hear more of the boasting focused on what is actually important to us as Heathens. Our Families. How we treat our Friends. Our Hospitality. How hard we work. Living up to one's responsibilities. A life well lived in these areas is the real road to Heathen "glory." Not what we see passing for "glory" on the internet.

I need to give credit where credit is due. Monty Maxwell a good friend to our Kindred originally coined the term "Unverified Personal Toughness," and hearing that inspired the rest of this essay.

MY GRANDMOTHER ELIZABETH SHOOP

Elizabeth Schweiger was the daughter of Ludwig Schweiger, my great-grandfather, and his wife Rose. Ludwig was German, and immigrated to America from Hungary. His daughters, Elizabeth and her sister Rose were first generation Americans.

Elizabeth was a beautiful young woman and a dancer. She married Richard Shoop, my grandfather, and they had a son (my Uncle Rick) and a daughter (my Mother Carol). Elizabeth was known by most that knew her as "Betty," a once common nickname for "Elizabeth," that is not so common anymore.

Shortly after I was born, my parents moved onto a 35 acre farm in the Northland of Kansas City, Missouri. My mother and I traveled the 30 to 40 minutes to Mission, KS 4 or 5 times a week to go shopping with Grandma Betty, or just to hang out at her house. My mother and grandmother were very close, and so I was around Elizabeth Shoop constantly.

She would baby sit me all the time, take me shopping, and just hang out with me. She was the sort of adult, that never got tired of playing games with me. Never got tired of telling me crazy made-up stories. Never got tired of just being a fun, engaged, friend to me. Some fun stories from my time with Grandma Shoop...

1. Elizabeth Shoop would drag-race with me in the car. She had an Olds Delta 88, and she would pull up next to teenage boys in their fast cars, and signal that she wanted to drag race them from the red stop light. They would look at her like she was crazy, but she would goad them into it. That Oldsmobile really had some pick up and go. I just remember the force of the acceleration pushing me back into my seat, as she would destroy these teenage boys when the light turned green.

2. Elizabeth Shoop insisted that mannequins at department stores were alive, and that when the store closed they would come alive, and dance, and talk, and have a good time. So, when we were shopping, she would take me up to the mannequins, and introduce them to me by name. She had names for all of them, and at stores where we went often, she always used the same names. Any suggestion that she was fooling around in this regard, was always met with a certain amount of hurt and anger that anyone could doubt her regarding the secret life of department store mannequins.

3. Elizabeth Shoop would run up and down the grocery store aisles with me in the shopping cart. Speed was the name of the game, and she was a mad-woman when sprinting down the aisles. We were confronted by many a grocery store manager, and asked to leave at least once that I can remember. i always thought that was a great time.

4. Elizabeth Shoop would call me on the phone, and pretend she was a girl named "Laura" that liked me. I grew up on that 35-acre farm, and from the age of 1-5, I really did not have any kids around. Even after my brother started to get older, when I was away from school, there was only one friend within walking distance of our farm. So, getting these calls from my friend "Laura" was a pretty big deal. I seem to remember knowing it was Elizabeth pretending to be this little girl named "Laura," but like so many of our games, even though I knew it was silly, it had a sense of reality to it that made it real.

5. In the department stores, Elizabeth would play hide and seek with me. Both of us would hide in the center of clothes racks, and we would often get in trouble with my mother. She would get frustrated with us, and get a bit loud about having to deal with "two children" when shopping.

6. Elizabeth fed Racoons in her backyard. She was the "Racoon Lady". The racoons were so used to her, that she could sit on the back patio with the food bowls sat all around her, and the raccoons would come right up out of the woods with their babies and everything, and just gather around her to eat. She would talk to them, and they were completely used to her being there. We would watch all this through a large picture window at the back of the house, and it was amazing.

7. Elizabeth loved to cuddle with me. She was very thin, and would have me sit beside her in her big chair. She would even say, "Aren't you glad you can sit beside me here. Your other grandmother is too big to sit beside you in a chair, isn't she?" LOL. That sounds horrible, but as a kid, we would both just laugh and giggle about this.

8. Elizabeth Shoop as a night-owl. She would sleep all day, and stay up all night. She would call all-night radio shows produced here locally, and was well known on those shows as the "Racoon Lady." When she would baby-sit me, she would let me stay up as late as I wanted. To keep out of trouble with my parents she tried to teach me how to fake being asleep, so that when they came to pick me up after a night out, I could pretend I was sound asleep. Despite 20 to 30 minutes of training, she just could not get me to stop squinting my eyes hard (I

was only 4 years old!), and when my parents came to pick me up, they immediately figured out I was faking and scolded Grandma for letting me stay up late. After that, we worked on it more, but I could never figure out how to fake being asleep and kept her out of trouble. It is funny, because Grandma Betty was a night owl, my mom was a night owl, I am a night owl, and I have noticed my children tend to be night owls as well.

Those are just some of the stories. She was incredibly imaginative, generous, and fun when it came to me, her grandchild.

I do not want to go into too much detail on this next part, but let us just say that Elizabeth Shoop was not a happy woman. Her marriage to my Grandfather had been damaged decades before, and they slept in separate bedrooms, and really did not get along well. I did not really realize all this until much later, looking back. In finally realizing it, I came to understand that my Grandmother Elizabeth Shoop had been so sweet, and funny, and childlike with me – at the same time the rest of her life was fairly dark and unhappy.

We lost Elizabeth Shoop to cancer when I was only 10. She had breast cancer, and even surgery did not save her. She was in immense pain, both physically and emotionally during her fight with cancer, and it really hurts to think all that she went through. She died in her middle-60's, which was just much too early.

Losing her was a big big deal to me. A life-changing scenario for a 10-year-old. Here was a woman that had been so incredibly important in my life, constantly there, constantly sweet and nurturing, fun, imaginative, and positively crazy in her pursuit of laughter and joy – and suddenly she was very ill, declined horribly, and then died. She was gone.

We moved to a new house and a new school just a year later, and I can pretty much mark my real childhood as being when my Grandmother Elizabeth Shoop was alive and we lived on that 35 acre farm. My post-childhood is began with her death and our move away from that wonderful farm.

I had never written at length about My Grandmother Elizabeth Shoop, and I have wanted to for awhile. She is a big part of who I am. How she interacted with me, guides a lot of my interactions with my own children. It goes without saying that I want my grandchildren to have memories of me, similar to the happy memories I have of Grandma Betty. She was an amazing woman, who went though a lot of emotional hardship, and came out of it intact and able to be an amazing Grandmother to me.

My daughter Elizabeth is 8-years-old, and is named after Elizabeth Shoop. When I put Elizabeth to sleep, I call her Betty. There is a song I sing her when she is going to sleep, where I call her Betty – and I have made sure that she knows exactly why I do that. If I mess up or forget and use a different name in the song, she quickly corrects me.

I hope to someday see Elizabeth Shoop again, and I hope her name lives long in my family....

A FINAL NOTE ON CHRISTIANITY

To my way of thinking, the Christian god is a Middle-Eastern God. My Northern European Ancestors honored Northern European Gods for thousands of years, until Rome pushed Christianity northward by every means at their disposal. The conversions from the Gods of our People (Folk), were sometimes peaceful, but there are many many instances of forced conversions, using economic pressures and outright violence to suppress the native religion and replace it with a foreign one.

Now, it is 2010, and a growing number of people are returning to the religion of their Folk. The Gods of their Ancestors. Our efforts at returning to our native Folkway, should focus on honoring our Gods and Ancestors. We should not be anti-Christian. We should be beyond Christianity. We need to shed Christian baggage and beliefs, and move forward into the future. Not dwell on the past. Towards this end, I wanted to write a Final Note on Christianity, as I do not intend to talk much about Christianity in the future. They get enough attention as it is.

These past two weeks, I have been dealing with the issue of a teacher at my kids' public school teaching them Christian songs. Songs-of-Worship that talk about people not getting into heaven and "Obeying the Lord." We have been in this school district for 5 years, and this has never been done with our children before. So, I wrote emails to the teacher and Principal, and eventually met with the Principal, and he agreed with me. He felt there should be a policy against this, and he is working to ensure Christian songs-of-worship are not taught to my children again. Everything turned out well.

But during this past two weeks, I have had Christians writing me and telling me that Christianity is not trying to indoctrinate my children. Telling me that I sound paranoid. One said I sounded like a "lunatic." Telling me that my wishes to not have my children taught Christianity in school, is somehow ruining their education and education of their Christian classmates. Telling me that I sound like some sort of fanatic. Telling me that Christians are very respectful of other religions, and that Christians trying to convert others is "very, very rare." Let me tell you my story over the past three years.

AT WORK - I was being looked at for a new position at work. A Christian co-worker called my future boss, and told her that they should not bring me down to that position, because I was into "Devil Worship." My future boss knew me well enough, and liked my work ethic enough, that she disregarded this attempt to destroy my job opportunity and possibly my career, based on my religion.

"GOING TO HELL" - My wife and children have been told they are going to Hell, more than once by Christians. Every single person in Jotun's Bane Kindred has been told at some point that they are going to Hell by Christians. The children of the other families in Jotun's Bane Kindred have all been told they are going to Hell by Christian classmates.

NEIGHBORHOOD - The Christian members of my neighborhood association actually held a meeting, to decide "what to do about my family," as they saw our religion as a threat to their neighborhood. A neighbor that knows and likes me, stood up and told them they were idiots for even discussing it, and helped stop whatever efforts they were thinking of initiating against us.

And the list goes on.

Let us be clear. Christianity is made up of individuals, and I have no problem with those individuals. I have family, friends, neighbors, and co-workers that are Christian that I respect, like, and love. In saying these things, I am not trying to insult or destroy these good people, who are Christian.

But, the religion itself teaches that the Christian god is the "one true god." It teaches that all other Gods are false or outright tricks of the Christian "devil." It teaches that those that do not accept Christ are going to the Christian hell. It teaches and encourages its followers to actively recruit and convert people, using fear and whatever else might work.

These Christian teachings encourage people to disown their own family members that are not Christian. It encourages job discrimination. It encourages harassment. It encourages abuse and bullying at school. It encourages fear-mongering. It encourages a lot of behaviors on the part of its followers that are absolutely harmful to non-Christians. Would your Jesus have wanted things that way? I doubt it. But that is the way things are with a fairly large intolerant segment of Christianity.

So people can call me paranoid or a fanatic. But for me, this is the reality of living in our culture. Are all Christians like that? Nope. But there are plenty that are. Am I being a fanatic when I insist Christians do not try to convert my 4, 7, and 9 year old children using fear-mongering? Am I a fanatic when I insist my public school does not attempt to indoctrinate my children? Am I a fanatic if I take steps to ensure I do not end up losing my job or career based on my religion? Am I a fanatic when I defend myself as peacefully and calmly as possible from Christians treading on my family? Well, if those things make me a fanatic – then I will wear the title proudly.

So, to my Christian friends, family, and co-workers, there is really not a thing in the world you can say that will somehow magically erase the things that have happened, are happening, and will likely continue to happen because my family is not Christian. It is just something with which we have to live. There will be other attempts to hurt my career. My wife and kids will have to hear "You are going to Hell" falling from the lips of Christians many more times. These things are just reality.

Am I a victim in all this? Nope. I am proud of who I am, and what my family believes. I am more than willing to defend my family and our beliefs. We live a good life, live in a good house, and we are happy. To me, living among a Christian majority is simply another challenge to overcome. Life is full of challenges, so what is one more challenge?

I just want Christians to know, the pretty picture you paint of how tolerant and non-judgmental Christianity is as a religion, is not the reality we have experienced. You can insist it is, but that does not make it so. Non-Christians know better.

It is why I am thankful for the Constitution and the Freedom of Religion. I wonder how bad it would be without these protections in place.

PRISON KINDREDS VS. KINDREDS OUTSIDE OF PRISON

I have never been incarcerated and so my knowledge of prison Kindreds comes entirely from what I have read, what I have been told by friends and acquaintances who have belonged to prison Kindreds, and from one visit I made to a prison Kindred a couple of years ago. So, I fully admit that my own first hand knowledge of prison Kindreds is limited. This essay is written from the point of view of someone in a Kindred outside of prison, and will attempt to discuss some of the issues that can come up when a Heathen is released from prison and approaches Kindreds that are outside of prison.

Obviously every prison Kindred is different from every other prison Kindred. It follows, that every Kindred outside of prison is different from every other Kindred outside of prison. But, in order to discuss some of the issues a certain amount of generalization is required. I realize that not everything expressed here will fit every situation or group.

MOST KINDREDS OUTSIDE OF PRISON ARE NOT WARBANDS

By circumstance and necessity, nearly all prison Kindreds are all male, and are usually organized in what we might call a "warband" model. There are some all female prison Kindreds, but they are not nearly as common as the all male prison Kindred. The potential violence one might experience in prison tends to form prison Kindreds into something that focuses on the defense of the individual members by the group. Besides the religious activities (study groups, group Blot, etc.) that each prison Kindred organizes, there are sometimes prison-related illegal activities with which the Kindred becomes involved. So, within prison Kindreds things are oriented very strongly toward a male-perspective and a martial approach to most situations.

Most Kindreds outside of prison are not built upon the warband model. Usually Kindreds outside of prison are family oriented, and very often include spouses and children in the equation. There is not the constant potential for violence. So Kindreds outside of prison tend away from a completely male-perspective and martial approach to most situations. Kindreds outside of prison are very often organized in more of a tribal fashion. Whether the Kindred has a strong leadership structure or not, more attention tends to be given to each member's

232

opinion and to building consensus within the Kindred.

So, it is important to keep in mind that the difference in organizational structure of a Kindred can bring up issues for a Heathen transitioning to life outside of prison.

INTENSITY AND SERIOUSNESS OF BLOTS

I have heard from a number of Heathens that have been incarcerated, that the Blots with their prison Kindreds "felt more intense" than the Blots they experience with Heathens once they are out of prison. This can translate to a misinterpretation that Kindreds outside of prison are less serious about our Folkway, our Gods, and our Ancestors than those inside of prison.

But this misinterpretation does not take into consideration the reality of the situation. At most Blots outside of prison, that are many more distractions present. They are often held in someone's home, or yard, or some other location that lacks completely freedom from distraction. Those in attendance often include children and parents having to care for these children. There are pets, phones, neighbors, car traffic, and we could go on and on regarding the distractions that can come into place during a Blot outside of prison. While we try to eliminate or mitigate as many of these distractions as possible, as a practical matter we cannot eliminate them all.

One also has to look to one's own situation and mind-set at the time of the Blot. Heathens outside of prison have to worry about their jobs, their bills, their home or apartment, their spouses or romantic interests, their kids, their pets, and a 100 other details of living life outside of prison. Yes, there are worries and distractions inside of prison, but they are different than those worries outside of prison, and not nearly so numerous or varied.

Finally, the feelings that exist between the members of a warband and the members of a Tribe can be quite different. That is not to say that one is better or stronger than the other. But the emotions and connections involved are different, and may take some adjustment. I am of the opinion that the emotions and loyalties in a warband may be more intense than in a tribal Kindred, but that the emotions and loyalties within a tribal Kindred run deeper than in a warband.

LEVEL OF DEDICATION AND CONSISTENCY

I have seen some of the hand-written notes that a close friend of mine brought with him out of prison. He hand-copied whole chapters of books that he had borrowed and needed to return. He had notebooks and notebooks full of information and notes that he had the time in prison to just sit and write. He has told me stories about their prison-Kindred's study group sessions, where answering a certain number of questions wrong earned you a rib-punch from everyone in the Kindred. A Heathen inmate really does not have a lot of options beyond the prison Kindred they have joined. There is no real point to leaving a prison Kindred, and no where to go if you did.

Life outside of prison is obviously different. When you factor in my job, my wife and three kids, and my responsibilities at home, I really do not have a lot of spare time on my hands. I have to maximize what spare time I do have, in order to get things done for our Kindred that I need to get done. I never get to just sit and read or take notes for hours at a time. My life is really one big multitasking juggling act. Now, do not get me wrong. I enjoy staying busy and I would not really have it any other way. It helps me get things done. But, life on the outside for many of us does not facilitate hours and hours of quiet reading, note-taking, and contemplation.

While learning and studying are important to members of a Kindred outside of prison, you will not find members trading mandatory rib-punches for wrong answers to quizzing. More often, you will find men and women discussing issues in the Lore together as a group, and possibly involving their teenage children in the discussions. While a greater percentage of a Heathen's time outside of prison is spent on matters not directly relating to Heathenry or their Kindred, this is just a natural feature of real life, not a statement on their level of dedication or commitment.

Unfortunately many Kindreds outside of prison suffer from the many many social and entertainment options and distractions available to Heathens outside of prison. Whether it is reality television, movies, video games, a softball league, watching sports, role-playing games, chasing members of the opposite sex, or whatever it is – there are many options for socializing and entertainment other than being actively involved in a Heathen Kindred. So, there are some Heathens who walk away from their Kindred when they get a little frustrated with their Kindred, or when they realize being in a Kindred takes dedication and work. This is just a sad side-effect of our current culture, and reflects more on the individuals that do this, than it does on Heathens outside of prison in general. Most Heathens are enormously dedicated to their Kindred, and would face nearly any consequence or do any amount of work necessary, rather than even consider leaving their Kindred.

THE TIME IT TAKES TO JOIN

Outside of prison, it can take awhile for a Kindred to get to know you and be willing to consider making you one of their members. First of all, most Kindreds outside of prison have numerous closed events open only to Kindred members and then a handful of public events. Since a new person approaching the Kindred can only attend the handful of public events, this means a new person may only be able to gather with the Kindred once every month or two months.

Since Kindreds outside of prison involve spouses and children, and often enter every part of its member's lives, these Kindreds tend to be very careful about who they allow to join their Kindred. Many of them have a Kindred oath, and they do not want to risk sharing an oath with someone they do not know at least fairly well. They also judge new members in a wide array of areas. They look at the new person's character, history, stability, temperament, loyalty, honesty, and even social compatibility. So, it takes time to get to know someone this well, and size them up based on nearly every aspect of who they are.

We have experienced people that think that our Kindred should just immediately let them into our Kindred, as if they are doing us a favor by wanting to join and like we are sitting around desperate for new members. Some of these impatient people were recently released from prison and some of them have never been in prison. So, I am not saying this is a problem only among those Heathens that have been in prison. But I do think that sometimes Heathens that are coming from prison Kindreds, expect our Kindred to meet them once and then just sign them up as a member. That is not how we work at all.

PAID YOUR DEBT?

There are some Heathens that do not want to deal with Heathens that have been in prison. They see them as outlaw, and do not want them around their families or their Kindreds at all. There are other Heathens that feel that once someone has done their time, they have paid their debt. With their debt paid, they should be looked at and assessed for membership in the Kindred just like anyone else, and given a fair chance.

Jotun's Bane Kindred does feel that once a man or woman has paid their debt, that they should no longer be considered an outlaw by default. Of course, the nature of their crime is a factor. Child molestation and sex offenses create a debt that cannot be paid, and I would never allow someone of this nature to be around my family or my Kindred. Violent crimes would also require a second look, in order to determine the context and circumstances surrounding the crime. After all, we are talking about making a choice to allow someone into your inner circle, into your Kindred, and into your family. Of course a man or woman's past misdeeds need to be taken fully into consideration.

STAYING EMPLOYED, OUT OF TROUBLE, AND CLEAN

Even those Kindreds who are willing to consider a convict's debt to be paid, usually take their time truly examining whether this new person has potential as a new member of their Kindred. Past illegal activity and misdeeds, can be a predictive factor in future illegal activity and misdeeds. But there are several benchmarks one can look at to determine whether the Heathen released from prison has learned their lesson, and changed.

First, do they have a job and are they staying employed? A good steady job is a great sign that a Heathen who has been in prison is determined to do better. Being steadily employed for 3 months is nice, but it is much more convincing to see someone steadily employed for a year or more. Now, it might not be at the same employer. Obviously, if the Heathen in question works hard, and actually changes jobs a few times in order to improve his position and salary, then this shows a strong work ethic and desire to legitimately succeed. If on the other hand, there are several job changes, and just as many excuses why these layoffs and firings took place, that is a very negative sign.

Obviously, not being arrested again for any reason is a great indicator that the Heathen who has been in prison has changed. Someone serious about leading a stable, law-abiding, and responsible life will keep his driver's license, license plates, and insurance up-to-date. Someone serious will pay any tickets that he or she gets, in order to avoid even the smallest warrant from being issued. Someone serious, stays out of bad situations, bar fights, and any other situation that puts them in jeopardy of going back to prison.

A big part of staying out of prison for many people, is getting clean and staying clean. So many of those that go to prison have alcohol and/or drug addictions, that actually strongly affect their personalities and decision-making to the point that going to prison was very nearly a foregone conclusion at some point. Continued alcohol and drug usage, will almost certainly lead to them going back to prison again, and again, and again until they get clean and stay clean.

Getting clean is a process, and if someone has their one month coin from AA or NA, that is a great accomplishment, but that is not yet someone with whom I would want to share a Kindred oath. Even someone with a one year coin from AA or NA, is probably not ready to make a Kindred oath. The longer an addict stays clean, the more I would be willing to put my trust in them. But, it is definitely a judgment call that you have to make on a case by case basis.

Someone who was an addict and a criminal can change. While the past can never be completely erased, a Heathen is judged by his/her deeds. So, if someone is released from prison, gets and keeps a job, rebuilds his or her family and supports them, gets completely away from substance abuse and illegal activity, and begins to lead a stable and responsible life full of honor, at some point they have transformed themselves into someone of worth. But this transformation takes time, often years, and it is only done with hard work and much difficulty. Many who try to change for the better, fail over and over again. But, there is always the brilliant exception to every rule.

RACIAL POLITICS

The prison environment is racially structured. Almost every aspect of prison life is organized around race. So, nearly every person in prison has a heightened sense of "racial awareness." The line between the races is a very stark black and white line. This can often translate to racial politics, racial hatreds, and racial beliefs that do not work very well outside of prison.

Within prison Kindreds, these racial politics can sometimes intrude into their religious beliefs. Those taught within a prison Kindred, are often surprised to find out that Heathens outside of prison do not follow these same racially-charged distortions of our Folkway. Those of us outside of prison do NOT think David Lane was a great guy and a hero. We tend to judge people by their character and deeds, rather than their skin color or ethnicity. We have neighbors, co-workers, and friends of a wide variety of ethnicities. That intense racial structuring and division that exists in prison, does not exist here in the outside world.

Kindreds outside of prison vary widely on how they approach the "Folkish" question. The Heathen who is attempting to transition from a prison Kindred to a Kindred outside of prison, will need to keep this in mind.

Within Jotun's Bane Kindred, we have often discussed that it seems like it takes at least a year for a Heathen getting out of prison to shed some of the racial baggage they bring out of prison with them. Sometimes it takes two or three years, and sometimes they never shed those polarizing racial views. While we are Folkish Kindred, that has nothing to do with the hatred of other ethnicities or races. We are not "white-separatists." We do not have 14-88 bumper stickers. We do not tolerate racial politics or hatred being mixed in with the beliefs of our Ancestors. So, until a Heathen coming out of prison has shed that racial baggage, they are not going to be seriously considered for membership in our Kindred.

SEXUAL ORIENTATION POLITICS

This one can be a bit more controversial. Most Heathens coming out of prison, have a great dislike for anyone who is homosexual, or at the very least have a great dislike for their "lifestyle" or their "choices." They will often express how "unnatural" it is, and declare that they will "never share a horn" with a gay person. I think this, much like the racial baggage is just a natural consequence of the prison environment.

While there are Heathens and Kindreds outside of prison that share this anti-homosexual sentiment, it is not nearly so common or as intensely felt as it is within prison Kindreds. So, the Heathen attempting to transition from a prison Kindred to a Kindred outside of prison, needs to keep in mind that many Kindreds outside of prison are much more interested in the character and deeds of a man or woman, than in who that man or woman is attracted to behind closed doors. As with the racial issue, the intensity of the anti-homosexual beliefs tends to fade the more time that separates that Heathen from when they were in prison. That transition period can be further shortened once the Heathen with anti-homosexual beliefs meets a homosexual Heathen with quite a bit of knowledge and worth to their Kindred.

MANY VARIABLES

I have spoken very generally in this essay, and I fully realize that my generalities do not fit every Heathen or Kindred, whether they are in prison, out of prison, or have never been in prison. I just wanted to share what I have seen and heard Heathens who have been in prison go through during their transition to a life and a Kindred outside of prison. I would much appreciate anyone who has been through this, sharing some of the issues or difficulties that came up for them during their transition.

HOW TO CARVE
A WOODEN HAMMER

I have gotten some requests to post an essay about how to carve a wooden hammer to wear as a necklace. I have learned all of this from trial and error, and so the steps listed here are just how I do it. There may be better ways to do this of course, as I am self-taught. So here we go...

CHOOSING AND ACQUIRING THE WOOD - You should probably work with a softer wood the first couple times. Both pine and basswood are fairly soft and easy to carve. You can buy small blocks of pine and basswood at most hobby stores. Hobby Lobby and Michael's for example, sell inexpensive pre-cut little blocks of pine and basswood.

Another good source of wood is Home Depot or Lowe's. Go to the section of the store where they sell nicer woods for use as trim. They will have small pieces of red oak and poplar you can buy for just a few dollars. One of those small boards could produce 6 or 7 hammers.

If you live in a medium to large sized city, you most likely have woodcarving store in-town. A quick Google search will help you locate it. Almost any woodcarving store sells small blocks of exotic woods for a fairly reasonable price. Do not carve your first hammer from ebony or lignum vitae. You will be very sorry if you use one of these enormously hard woods for your first hammer.

Once you have carved a few hammers, you will get an idea of what sort of designs to attempt to which woods. When you have a wood with beautiful colors and wood grain, a simpler design is often better. A simple design really shows off the color and wood-grain. If you are carving wood that is not particularly striking on its own, putting more detail into the shape of your design can really help make the hammer look nicer.

DRAW THE HAMMER YOU WANT TO CARVE - I try to buy wood that is the basic thickness and width of the hammer I want to carve. This cuts down on the amount of sawing you have to do. But the next step is to cut off a piece of wood that is the basic size you want to make the hammer. I use a little hand saw for this.

Once I have the block the right size, I draw the outline of the hammer I want to carve. If you can freehand this, then do it. But, if you cannot freehand and make it even, print off a hammer image from the internet, and use that for a template. Do not choose one that is enormously complex for your first hammer. Sometimes simple is better, when you are carving wood. Both in difficulty and the beauty of the finished result.

Another way to create an even/balanced template, is to fold a piece of paper in half that is the same size as your block of wood. Then draw half your hammer on one half of it. Cut that out (sort of like making a paper snowflake), and unfold the piece of paper. This will give you a hammer that is of equal proportions on both sides.

Then transfer the hammer drawing to the wood. You can cut out the hammer shape and trace around it on the wood. Or used some carbon paper to trace the shape onto the wood.

CARVE THE BASIC SHAPE OF THE HAMMER - I use a Dremel tool. You can buy one for anywhere from $60 to $100, depending on how nice the Dremel tool is. Do not buy a knock-off of a Dremel tool. In my experience, the knock-offs are under-powered and do not last as long. You can use a cutting bit on the Dremel tool, or a carbide burr shaped bit.

To save yourself time, rather than just hacking away at this big block of wood with the Dremel tool, use a hand saw to cut away the parts of the block of wood you do not need. The more wood you remove with the saw, the less carving you will have to do with the Dremel.

Once you have the block of wood trimmed down with a saw, fairly close to the hammer drawing you have made, it is time for the Dremel. Take your time. You are not in a hurry. Use the cutting or burr bit to cut away all the wood, except what is outlined by your hammer drawing.

SHAPING THE HAMMER - Once you get it cut down to the basic shape of hammer you drew, you can begin shaping the hammer. Round off the top and sides. Add details you want. Cut the hole in the top, from which the hammer will hang on a necklace. Use your imagination when shaping the hammer, but it is also important to sort of have a plan. Think about what you are doing, and do not rush it.

Keep in mind while shaping it, that you eventually have to sand the hammer. Sharp angles can be hard to sand. Lots of details are hard to sand. It is probably hard to think about this when you are carving your first hammer, but believe me when I say you will think about it when carving your second hammer! The sanding step is the most time-consuming and difficult, and how you shape the hammer during his step, will definitely have an impact on the sanding step.

Feel free to look at some of the hammers I have carved, and try to imitate one of the simpler ones. No reason to reinvent the wheel when carving your first couple hammers.

SANDING IT SMOOTH - It can take hours to properly sand and smooth the hammer. Do not get frustrated. You are making something that will last you or whomever you give it to for years and years. In that perspective, taking hours to sand it does not seem so bad.

Buy 3 or 4 levels of sandpapers. Buy and 80 or 100 coarseness with which to begin the sanding process. You will spend the most time with this sandpaper. I tear off a square about 3 x 3 inches, and fold it in half. Then I start methodically sanding the hammer. You have to take off all the irregularities, scratches, and imperfections. You need to get it as smooth as possible with this coarse coarse sandpaper, because the other sandpapers are simply meant to smooth the hammer out. It is with this very coarse sandpaper that you will bring the hammer almost to its final form. While sanding with the 80 or 100 sandpaper, this is the time when you can even things out. Often, during carving, you will have messed up. One side of the hammer is thicker, or the angle does not match the angle on the other side. With a little work, you can even these mistakes up with the coarse sandpaper.

Once the hammer is looking pretty good, move to a sandpaper that is not so course. Maybe a 220. Then go over the entire hammer, smoothing it as smooth as that sandpaper will allow. If you see scratches, you can hack away at them with the 220, or you can go back to the 80 or 100 in just that spot, until the tiny scratch or imperfection is gone. Then go back to the 220.

Finish up sanding with 400 sandpaper, and if you can find it, go ahead and hit it with 600 sandpaper as well.

The final smoothing step is steel wool. You can buy various grades of steel wool, but I was suggest the finest steel wool you can find at the store. At this point, you are basically buffing the hammer and bringing it to a shine.

LINSEED OIL - You can buy linseed oil at almost any hardware store. You might have to buy a big $20 can of it, but it is worth it. It will last forever, and it can be used on nearly any wood to make it look great. When your hammer is smooth as can be, and you have buffed it with the steel wool, put a generous coating of linseed oil all over it and let it sit for at least 10 minutes. After 10 minutes have passed, wife all the excess oil off of the wood.

Sometimes I do this step twice, just to make sure I am getting the maximum benefit from the linseed oil. You need to wipe it all off when you done, because you do not want linseed oil getting on your clothes when you are wearing the hammer.

That is the process as best I can describe it. I included some photos of recent hammers I have carved below.

SECTION SEVEN

KINDRED BYLAWS

THE PURPOSE OF KINDRED BYLAWS

Having Kindred bylaws that are well crafted, and that feature the input and understandings of every Kindred member, can help avoid a lot of confusion and conflict. Who is a member of the Kindred and who is not? How does someone become a member of the Kindred? What form of decision-making will be used within the Kindred? What positions of responsibility will be recognized, and for what are they responsible? If everyone has fully discussed these sorts of issues, and the consensus of the group is put into writing, it provides a stable and solid framework for dealing with most situations that may arise.

If your Kindred incorporates legally as a "church" in your State or your Kindred seeks 501(c)3 status from the Federal Government, then you will likely need a set of bylaws to fulfill certain legal and tax requirements. So, even if you are unsure whether you will ever pursue these two options, working on Kindred bylaws from very early on will ensure you have them when you need them.

Your Kindred's by-laws can be enormously simple or enormously detailed. The content of your Kindred bylaws will be unique to your Kindred, because each Kindred is unique.

One good thing to have included in your bylaws, is the method by which the bylaws can change. Kindreds evolve, circumstances change, and fresh challenges bring up new issues to be addressed, so having clear methods for keeping your bylaws relevant and timely is important.

Not every Kindred will choose to have Kindred bylaws, and that is certainly each Kindred's choice. But we have found that our Kindred bylaws provide us with a collective written understanding of how our Kindred should operate.

BYLAWS ARE
DIFFERENT FROM THEW

It is important to keep in mind that Kindred bylaws and Kindred Thew are two different things. Kindred bylaws are simply a written set of procedures and a statement of understanding between Kindred members as to how their Kindred will operate. Kindred bylaws are usually fairly limited as to the specific situations they address, and they are written down as rules and procedures for Kindred operations.

Kindred Thew on the other hand, is fluid and organic, and represents the collective customs, history, traditions, and expectations of the Kindred toward its members, the members toward the Kindred, and members towards each other. It is immensely varied and detailed, and is constantly developing and growing in complexity and depth. Thew is not written. Yes, a small minority of Thew may be codified in the Kindred bylaws, but the vast majority of Thew remains as unwritten understandings between Kindred members.

AN EXAMPLE OF KINDRED BYLAWS

Below, I have provided a version of Jotun's Bane Kindred's bylaws, as they exist in late 2011. Every Kindred is different, so I would expect that any Kindred using these bylaws as a beginning template, will fully customize and alter them to fit their own collective understanding of how they want their Kindred to operate.

STATEMENT OF UNDERSTANDING
for
Jotun's Bane Kindred

Article I: Identity.

Section 1. Name:
The formal name of this organization shall be Jotun's Bane Kindred (herein referred to solely as "the Kindred").

Section 2. Purpose:
The corporation is formed for the following purposes:

To be a Heathen Church organized exclusively for religious, educational, and charitable purposes as defined within the meaning of Section 501(c)(3) of the Internal Revenue Code.

Additionally, we are also organized to give reverence to the Deities of the Norse Pantheon, education regarding their nature, education regarding the Eddas and Sagas of the Teutonic peoples of antiquity as they relate to the Deities of the Norse Pantheon, education regarding the world view, spiritual thoughts, and ethical code of the Teutonic peoples of antiquity, to provide support for the investigation of these materials and their adaptation to modern life, to provide a framework for interaction with others of similar belief, to provide for the education, licensure, and ordination of spiritual leaders within this framework of belief, and to in all other ways function as a Church for the spiritual service and support of its members.

Section 3. Affiliation:
The Kindred shall begin as an, independent, and not-for-profit entity. The Kindred shall not affiliate with any political, religious, social or

246

other organization and/or entity. The Kindred may, as it deems appropriate, perform joint functions with other organizations and/or entities, but shall remain independent of them until a consensus of the current active membership agrees otherwise. This should not be taken as meaning the Kindred will never affiliate, just that the Kindred's membership must approve any proposed affiliation.

Article II: Membership.

Section 1. Eligibility:
Membership in the Kindred shall be open to any person(s) above the age of eighteen, who currently practices or wishes to practice Heathenry as a belief system or way of life.

Section 2: Acceptance for Membership:
People who are eligible for membership in the Kindred must be accepted as "applicants" to the Kindred by the unanimous consent of its current active membership. They will then undergo a defined period of acclimation and learning, after which they must be accepted as a "full member" of the Kindred by the unanimous consent of its current active membership.

Section 3: Profession of Intent:
People accepted for membership in the Kindred are required to make a profession of their intent to worship, honor and serve the deities and other spiritual entities of Heathenry in a formal ceremony before the assembled members of the Kindred. This Profession of Intent (see Appendix A) will also consist of an Oath taken to the Kindred and its members. The Northern Gods are not jealous Gods, but new members must profess their intent to be loyal to the Kindred and to their Elder Kin, their Ancestors, and the Vaettir.

Section 4: Inactive Membership Status:
If a full member of the Kindred stops attending Kindred functions over a period of three consecutive months, he/she can be determined to be an "Inactive Member" by the unanimous consent of its current active membership (excluding the vote of the member whose status is being decided). Inactive status is not a "black-mark," but simply a way of designating that a member has, for whatever reason, become "inactive" and should have some of his/her Rights and Privileges of Membership temporarily suspended. A member who has been voted into "inactive" status can ask to be reactivated, at which time the unanimous consent of the Kindred's current active membership is required to reactivate them.

If a full members knows that he/she will be inactive for an extended or unknown period of time (going to school, called up for the military, etc.), he/she can can provide the reason for his/her absence and ask to be inactivated until his/her return. Those that voluntarily inactivate their membership can become active again at any time they choose. To become active again, they must simply notify the Kindred that they have returned from their absence and will be active again.

Section 5: Types of Affiliation:
The four types of affiliation recognized by the Kindred are as follows:

A. Applicant: is a person that has been accepted as an applicant to membership in the Kindred by its voting membership, and is passing through a period of acclimation and learning.

B. Full member: is a person that as been accepted as a full member of the Kindred by its voting membership, after undergoing a period of acclimation and learning.

C. Inactive member: is a person who at one time was a full member that has for stated or unstated reasons ceased to participate in Kindred functions, but has not formally stated their intent to leave the Kindred. This inactivation can be designated by a vote of the Kindred membership or at the request of the inactivated member.

D. Friend of the Kindred: is a person who has never been a full member and does not wish to take the profession of full membership. However would like to participate in open Kindred functions.

Section 6: Rights and Privileges of Membership:
All people accepted as applicants to the Kindred will attend and participate in all activities conducted by the Kindred to which they are invited. They will not have a vote in business matters or a role in formulating any and all decisions made by the Kindred.

All people accepted as full members of the Kindred are entitled to participate in any activities conducted by the Kindred, and to participate in formulating any decisions made by the Kindred. The collected full members of the Kindred constitute what herein is referred to as the membership of the Kindred.

Inactive members will not be able to attend business meetings, hold office in the Kindred or have a vote in the Kindred. They shall be able to attend activities to which they are invited by the Kindred. See Article II, Section 4 for details of how an inactive member returns to active status.

All People who are elected by the Kindred to be Friends of the Kindred shall be able to attend activities to which they are invited by the Kindred. Friends of the Kindred will not be able to attend business meetings, hold office in the Kindred, or have a vote in the Kindred. It is up to the consensus of current active membership of the Kindred whether to include Friends of the Kindred in other events.

Section 7: Responsibilities of Membership:
In addition to making a formal profession to worship, honor and serve the deities and spiritual entities of Heathenry, all members of the Kindred shall be expected, to the best of their abilities, to participate in activities conducted by the Kindred, including any charitable and/or public and community service projects that it decides to undertake; to contribute time, money, labor and other personal resources to the Kindred as needed to the best of one's ability; to maintain Frith with and to act with good will toward all other members of the Kindred, and to never act in such manner as to bring dishonor and/or disrepute upon Heathenry, the Kindred, or any of its members.

Section 8: Revocation of Membership:
Membership in the Kindred may be revoked from any member at any time for due cause by the agreement of a consensus of its remaining members. Due cause for revocation of membership shall include, but shall not be restricted to:

- Breaking or failure to maintain one's oath to worship, honor and serve the deities and spiritual entities of Heathenry
- Failure to maintain Frith with other Kindred members
- Acting in bad faith toward other Kindred members;
- Prolonged and/or repeated failure to participate in Kindred activities without due cause
- Failure to contribute to the Kindred as needed to the best of one's ability
- Theft from the Kindred or any of its members
- Breaking of any duly agreed upon rules of conduct specified by the Kindred
- Participation in or advocacy of any beliefs and/or practices deemed by the Kindred to be antithetical to its philosophy and purpose
- Any actions and/or statements which bring dishonor and/or disrepute or other adverse consequences upon Heathenry, the Kindred or any of its members.

The membership of no member of the Kindred shall be revoked without due process, and an *opportunity* to answer the charges

249

brought against the member. The level of due process provided and the nature of the opportunity to answer the charges is to be determined solely by a consensus of the remaining Kindred Members.

Section 9: Authority of Members
The Kindred shall be an egalitarian organization, in that full members of the Kindred are of equal value and importance to the Kindred. There will be an attempt to reach a consensus of the active members of the Kindred on all important decisions. But, as in any family, there will be roles within the Kindred, and these roles will sometimes entail unique responsibilities and authority.

Article III: The Applicant Process.

Section 1: Invitation to Closed Event
Possible applicants will come to the Kindred's attention through a variety of means. Activity on our website or message board. Attendance at open Kindred Events (i.e., Open Pubmoots, Open Fainings, etc.) Referral from another Kindred or national organization. If there is a consensus of the Active Kindred Membership, a possible applicant will be invited to a closed Kindred event (i.e., Study Group, Closed Faining, Symbel, Dinner, etc.) so that the Kindred can get better acquainted with them.

Section 2: Decision to Accept them as an Applicant
See Article II, Section 2 for how this decision is made.

Section 3: Defined Period of Acclimation and Learning
The defined period of Applicant Acclimation and Learning will be at least one year in length, and will consist of the following steps.

A. Assignment of a Mentor: At the same time the Kindred is coming to a consensus about accepting a new Applicant Member, they will also come to a consensus as to which member of the Kindred will serve as a Mentor to the new Applicant. The role of Mentor is extremely important. The Mentor will:

- Serve as the direct contact between the Kindred and the Applicant.
- Communicate with the Applicant frequently, by e-mail, phone, and in person.
- Answer any and all questions the Applicant might have about the Kindred or Heathenry, or guide them to the proper source for a correct answer.
- Talk about upcoming Kindred Events with the applicant,

encouraging and welcoming them to attend.
- Monitor the Applicant's progress on completing the requirements for Full-Membership in the Kindred.

B. Regular Attendance at Kindred Events: The Applicant will be expected to regularly attend events to which the Kindred invites them. For the most part, Applicants will be invited to every Kindred Event once they are accepted as an Applicant Member. The only exceptions would be important business meetings where sensitive issues are going to be discussed, etc. A failure to regularly attend Kindred Events can and will be seen as a lack of commitment or interest in becoming a Full-Member of the Kindred on the part of the Applicant.

C. Reading the Lore: Applicants will be expected to read the Prose Edda and the Poetic Edda (both the Lays of the Gods and the Heroes), and to speak with the Kindred about what they are learning in their reading. At Kindred events and/or meeting privately with their Mentor, Applicants will be asked to describe their most recent readings, and what they thought of them and what they learned from them. The Lore is at the core of our religion and our approach to Heathenry as a Kindred. This is an extremely important requirement for Full-Membership.

D. Reading the Heathen Gods Book: Applicants will be expected to read Sections 1-4 of the Heathen Gods Book by Mark Ludwig Stinson. These Sections of the book cover Essays for New Heathens, Building a Kindred or Tribe, Maintaining a Kindred or Tribe, and Living a Heathen Life.

E. Participation on the Website: Applicants with internet-access are expected to regularly visit and read the Kindred's message board, and to contribute ideas, posts, and comments on the message board. This shows an interest in the Kindred's public presence, its efforts to educate the public about Heathenry, and its mission to be a resource for Heathens everywhere. Applicants without internet access are expected to find alternative ways to show this same interest (assist in distributing pamphlets, etc.)

Section 4: Removal of Applicant Members from the Kindred
At any time during the Applicant Process, and Applicant Member can be removed from the Kindred by a unanimous consensus of the Active Membership of the Kindred. While this can be done for one of the causes listed in Article 2, Section 8 of this Statement of Understanding, it can also be done for any reason the Kindred feels is appropriate. It is essential that the Kindred grow only through the inclusion of Trú Heathens with which the membership of the Kindred is

251

100% comfortable.

Section 5: Moving from Applicant Status to Full-Member Status.
An Applicant Member must complete all the requirements of the Applicant Process before being considered by the Kindred for Full-Membership. It is acknowledged that for some Applicants the process may take longer than one year.

See Article II, Section 2 for how the decision is made to move an Applicant Member to Full-Member status. The Applicant moving to Full-Members status will be required to make a Profession of Intent, as described in Article II, Section 3.

If a unanimous consensus of the Active Membership of the Kindred cannot be reached regarding an Applicant Member's change to Full-Member status, then the issues standing in the way of a consensus will be identified. The Kindred as a whole or the Applicant's Mentor will address these issues with the Applicant, and an attempt will be made to resolve the issues by extending the Applicant Process and attempting to come to a consensus at a later date.

Stalemated membership decisions can have a negative impact, and every effort should be made to resolve them. If a stalemate situation occurs, where the Kindred cannot attain a consensus to Remove the Applicant Member from the Kindred or to advance the Applicant Member to Full-Member status, then nine months after the Applicant Process began the Applicant is automatically removed from the Kindred. Only a unanimous consensus of the Kindred can continue the Applicant Process beyond nine months.

Section 6: The Applicant Process Reflects the Formation of the Kindred
The founding members of Jotun's Bane Kindred went through this same process prior to the formal creation of the Kindred. We gathered together often and dedicated time and interest to the Kindred, we read the Prose Edda and Poetic Edda, and we waited for a period of six months before making our Profession of Intent and our Oaths to each other. Over time, we learned that one year was a more appropriate length of time. In establishing this Applicant Process, we are asking of new members that they show the same commitment to the Kindred that was shown by those that founded the Kindred.

Article IV: Legally Ordained Clergy.

Section 1: Chieftain and Godhi:
By virtue of their positions as Chieftain and Godhi of the Kindred, and their role in its founding, Mark Stinson and Rod Landreth are automatically ordained as "clergy" for the Kindred, and shall serve as legally ordained clergy in the State of Missouri.

Section 2: Ordination Process:
All other candidates for licensing or ordination must be of necessary experience and qualifications, as set forth by the Chieftain and Godhi of the Kindred, and shall have demonstrated their ability to undertake the responsibilities of heathen clergy. No one shall be licensed or ordained until he/she shall has been engaged in the active work of our Folkway, exhibiting a strong working knowledge of our Lore and an ability to serve as heathen clergy. Credentials shall be valid only when signed by both the Chieftain and Godhi of the Kindred, and shall be renewed every three years.

Article V: Activities.

Section 1: Nature of Activities:
The Kindred shall engage only in activities of a religious, social, educational, cultural, environmental, charitable, or community and/or public service nature. The Kindred shall not engage in any form of political, military or paramilitary activity; or any activity designed to advance any racial, sexual, ethnic, social or cultural ideology and/or agenda. The individual members of the Kindred reserve the right to endorse and/or contribute financially to individual legislative initiatives which they deem to be consistent with the purposes and philosophies of the Kindred. The Kindred as an organization, however, will take no stance on political issues. However, no member of the Kindred shall ever be excluded by other members from any event or activity conducted by the Kindred.

Section 2: Rituals and Feasts:
The Kindred shall, at the appropriate times of year, conduct group rituals and feasts in observance of the Holy Days of Heathenry. Such rituals shall always be entirely of a Heathen nature, and shall not in any way involve the deities and/or spiritual entities of any religion outside of the religion of Heathenry. The Kindred may also conduct group rituals and/or feasts of a Heathen nature in observance of other Holy Days observed by any branch of the religion of Heathenry as it deems appropriate. Attendance at all such events shall be limited to members of the Kindred, their immediate families and invited guests,

contingent upon the approval of all Kindred members. Rituals and Feasts will only be made open to the general public, with the consensus of all members of the Kindred. No active member of the Kindred shall ever be excluded by other members from any event or activity conducted by the Kindred. All active members of the Kindred shall be eligible to participate in the planning, writing, organization, rehearsal and performance of any such rituals and feasts.

Section 3: Other Activities:
The Kindred may conduct other activities as it deems appropriate including, but not restricted to: moots, Symbels, Blots, Fainings, Days of Remembrance, workshops, classes, discussion groups, community and/or public service projects, or other activities consistent with its purposes and philosophies. Such events and/or activities may be open to people who are not members of the Kindred, or may be restricted to members of the Kindred only, as the Kindred deems appropriate.

Article VI: Organization.

Section 1. Decision Making Process:
The Kindred shall function by the common accord of those who are formally professed members of the Kindred. The Kindred shall always attempt to decide all issues according to consensus process, which shall be defined as an attempt to reach an agreement which is acceptable to all members, except in those instances which are otherwise specified in these bylaws. In the event that the Kindred finds that it is not possible to achieve consensus on any particular issue, the will of the majority of the members of the Kindred shall prevail. The point at which the "majority rules" shall be determined by the Chieftain, taking into consideration the importance of the question at hand, the length of the discussion thus far, and the impact the short-of-consensus decision will have upon the Kindred.

Section 2. Roles with the Kindred:
The Kindred may choose individuals from its membership to serve the following roles: Chieftain, Godhi/Gythia, Thyle, Loremaster, Secretary, Treasurer, and Large Event Planner. The Kindred shall have the authority to create additional roles, as it deems necessary. These roles are positions of responsibility and some authority, but the consensus decision-making model shall be upheld. Holding one of these roles within the Kindred does not represent a higher level of importance or privilege within the Kindred. Assigned roles within the Kindred should be spread out as much as possible, though it is possible for a Kindred member to have more than one role at a time. Depending on the current membership and the needs of the Kindred, some of these roles

may be empty at times.

Section 3. Length of Service in a Particular Role:
Persons serving in roles within the Kindred shall serve until they voluntarily relinquish such positions or until such time as a unanimous vote of the active members (excluding the vote of the member being decided upon) of the Kindred deem it necessary to replace them for failure to satisfactorily perform their designated responsibilities. No officer of the Kindred shall be removed from office without due process.

Section 4. Responsibilities of Roles within the Kindred:
The seven roles recognized within the Kindred are as follows:

A. Chieftain: The Chieftain shall maintain the Kindred's Hammer and Oath Ring, bringing both to all appropriate Kindred events. The Chieftain shall also be the Kindred Lawspeaker serving as judge whenever there is a dispute over the Bylaws of the Kindred. The Chieftain shall also serve as a spokesperson and representative to other Kindreds, organizations, and the public as the need arises. The Chieftain guides the consensus decision-making process, and can (as described in Article IV, Section 1) let the majority rule in certain circumstances.

B. Godhi/Gythia: The Godhi/Gythia shall be responsible for coordinating, scheduling and the creation of rituals and/or ceremonies to be performed by the Kindred on appropriate occasions. The Godhi/Gythia shall also be responsible for insuring that such rituals and/or ceremonies are adequately planned and insuring that all Kindred members are adequately informed of such rituals, ceremonies.

C. Thyle: The Thyle shall be the holder of the Kindred's oaths, professions, and the like. The Thyle shall record all oaths, professions, and the like that have been made by Kindred members or guests of the Kindred at Kindred functions. The Thyle shall periodically check up with those who have made oaths to see how they are progressing with said oath. At Kindred Symbels the Thyle shall insure that no false or idle oaths/boasts are made by challenging the maker to backup their oath/boasts.

D. Loremaster: The Loremaster serves as the Kindred's coordinator of education. The Loremaster shall be responsible for the coordination of lore sessions and focus activities. The Loremaster shall also be responsible for submitting educational material to be posted on the website.

E. Secretary: The Secretary shall be responsible for performing the administrative functions necessary for the routine operations of the Kindred The Secretary shall also be responsible for taking notes of all business meetings; maintaining a record of minutes of such meetings, maintaining a record of official correspondence to and from the Kindred; maintaining an official record of rituals and/or ceremonies, which shall be available on demand for inspection by all members of the Kindred.

F. Treasurer: The Treasurer shall hold and keep safe all funds held by the Kindred; shall be responsible for the distribution of monetary funds on behalf of the Kindred for approved expenditures; and for maintaining the financial records of the Kindred. The financial records of the Kindred shall be available on demand for scrutiny by the membership of the Kindred.

G. Large Event Planner: There may come a time when a large event needs to be coordinated, and the Kindred may choose to bestow the Role of Event Planner on an interested member of the Kindred. This role within the Kindred is one of coordination, and important decisions regarding the event must still be made by a consensus of the active members of the Kindred. This position can be unique to a specific event, or something that extends over numerous events, at the preference of the Kindred.

Section 5. Finances.
A. Monetary Funds: The Kindred shall maintain at least one back account, and the Treasurer shall be responsible for maintaining detailed records of all incoming and outgoing funds. These financial records shall be viewable upon request by all Full Members of the kindred. When a full member requests to view the financial records, this viewing will be facilitated by the Treasurer at the next scheduled kindred event, as long as that event is at least a week away at the time of the request.

B. Expenditure of Funds: No monetary funds possessed by the Kindred shall be expended without the prior approval of the full membership of the Kindred. Such authorization of expenditure shall always be noted in the minutes of the business meetings. The only exception to this rule is located below, in Article IV, Section 5, Part C.

C. Petty Cash Fund: The Kindred shall establish a petty cash fund that shall be used solely for the purpose of the routine operation of the Kindred. The amount in such fund shall be decided by the full membership of the Kindred and duly noted in the minutes of the meeting in which such expenditure is approved. The Kindred shall have sole access to the petty cash fund. Other members of the Kindred may request reimbursement from the petty cash fund for expenditures for the routine operation of the Kindred; however, the Treasurer shall have sole discretion as to whether such reimbursement is warranted. The Treasurer shall maintain a record of all funds placed into or expended from the petty cash fund, including receipts for all expenditures; and such record shall be available to all Kindred members for inspection. Expenditures from the petty cash fund shall not require prior approval of the full membership of the Kindred; however, the Kindred may demand reimbursement for expenditures made from the petty cash fund which it deems to be not for the routine operation of the Kindred. The full membership of the Kindred shall also have authority to overrule any decision of the Treasurer to deny reimbursement from the petty cash fund.

D. Indebtedness: No member of the Kindred, nor any other person, shall incur any debt or obligation on behalf of the Kindred, or in any way render it liable, unless authorized by the full membership of the Kindred.

Section 6: Dissolution
Upon the dissolution of the corporation, assets shall be distributed for one or more exempt purposes within the meaning of section 501(c)(3) of the Internal Revenue Code, or the corresponding section of any future tax code, or shall be distributed to the federal government, or to a state or local government, for a public purpose.

Any such assets not so disposed of shall be disposed of by the Circuit Court of the county in which the principle office of the corporation is then located, exclusively for such purposes or to such organization or organizations, as said Court shall determine, which are organized and operated exclusively for such purposes.

Section 7: Operational Limitations
No part of the net earnings of the corporation shall inure to the benefit of, or be distributable to its members, trustees, officers, or other private persons, except that the corporation shall be authorized and empowered to pay reasonable compensation for services rendered and to make payments and distributions in furtherance of the purposes set forth in Article VIII of our Articles of Incorporation and Article 1, Section 2 of these by-laws. No substantial part of the activities of the corporation shall be the carrying on of propaganda, or otherwise attempting to influence legislation, and the corporation shall not participate in, or intervene in (including publishing or distribution of statements) any political campaign on behalf of or in opposition to any candidate for public office. Notwithstanding any other provision of

257

these by-laws, the corporation shall not carry on any other activities no permitted to be carried on (a) by a corporation exempt from federal income tax under section 501(c)(3) of the Internal Revenue Code, or the corresponding section of any future federal tax code, or (b) by a corporation, contributions to which are deductible under section 170(c)(2) of the Internal Revenue Code, or the corresponding section of any future federal tax code.

Section 8: Changes to the Bylaws:
This Statement of Understanding may be amended solely by the consensus of the full membership of the Kindred.

Last Updated on 12-17-2011

APPENDIX A

Kindred Oath – Profession of Intent

People accepted for membership in the Kindred are required to make a profession of their intent to worship, honor and serve the deities and other spiritual entities of Heathenry in a formal ceremony before the assembled members of the Kindred. This Profession of Intent will also consist of an Oath taken to the Kindred and its members. The Northern Gods are not jealous Gods, but new members must profess their intent to be loyal to the Kindred and to their Elder Kin, their Ancestors, and the Vaettir. This is that Oath.

(Oath-Giver) **"{Oath-Taker's Name}, do you intend to make an oath of loyalty to the Aesir and Vanir, your Ancestors, the Vaettir, and your Kindred?"**

(Oath-Taker answers in the affirmative)

(Oath-Giver) **"Repeat after me."** *(Use this line if the Oath-Taker will be repeating his/her oath.)*

(Then the following statements are made in turn by the Oath-Giver and Oath-Taker, or an Oath-Taker can learn the oath and repeat it from memory. The Oath-Giver and the Oath-Taker should be holding the Oath Ring during the oath.)

"On this Iron Ring,

"I swear to be true to the Gods of Asgard,"

"both the Aesir and the Vanir."

"I swear to honor my Ancestors,"

"and make a life of which they are proud."

"I swear to respect and acknowledge the Vaettir,"

"of Home, Sky, Water, and Land."

"As we join together as family,

"I swear troth to Jotun's Bane Kindred,"

"and to hold aloft our Hammer against whatever may come."

"By the Gods I so swear."

"On my Luck I so swear."

"On this unbroken Oath Ring I so swear."

"Hail the Gods."

(The Kindred together) "Hail {Oath-Taker's Name}! Hail all who witness this oath!"

At this point, the Oath-Taker can make personal oaths to individual Kindred members.

Once all of the oaths have been taken, then then entire Kindred holds the ring and we proclaim:

(Kindred) "As this ring is one – we are now one. Hail Jotun's Bane Kindred!

LIGHTNING ACROSS THE PLAINS

HEATHEN GATHERING

THE LIGHTNING ACROSS THE PLAINS HEATHEN GATHERING

Heathenry is about community, gathering as a people, shaking a man or woman's hand, looking them in the eye, hearing their voice, telling stories, getting to know each other. It is letting your kids play together. Letting your spouses get to know each other. It is about laughing at dumb jokes, and telling stories from your life. It is about mingling Wyrd and taking the measure of another person, and finding them of worth.

Every September, Heathens from across the Heartland and beyond gather for 3 days and 2 nights camping at **Gaea Retreat**, a campground 40 minutes outside of Kansas City.

- ◆ Dinners Provided on Friday & Saturday
- ◆ Symbels Friday and Saturday Night
- ◆ A Blot/Faining on Saturday Evening
- ◆ Asatru & Craft Workshops all Weekend
- ◆ Viking Games Saturday Afternoon
- ◆ Children's Games and Activities
- ◆ A Heathen Auction on Sunday Morning

REGISTRATION FEES & METHODS

Registration fees include all camping fees and dinner on Friday and Saturday night. We keep these fees as reasonable as possible, and with a focus on keeping the gathering affordable for both individuals and families to attend. In 2010 **individual registration was $40, while family registration was $60.** Family registration includes a maximum of 2 adults and 3 children. You can learn more about the event and register for this year's Lightning Across the Plains at:

http://www.lightningacrosstheplains.com

ACTIVITIES AT LATP

Every Lightning Across the Plains is packed with activities in which you can participate and enjoy.

- Workshops on Heathen topics, traditional crafts, historical information about our Ancestors, modern Kindred building, tribal structure and Thew, etc.

- Religious activities, including several Fainings, two Symbels, visiting our outdoor Ve, and at every Lightning Across the Plains, a small Hof is established.

- There are children's game and activities throughout the event, with children activities scheduled at the same time as all adult workshops and many of adult activities. Hikes, sword-fighting lessons, a large foam-sword battle, storytelling, a class on the runes, Heathen craft projects, etc.

- A Heathen auction, where everyone bids on objects donated by those attending Lightning Across the Plains. There are always amazing Heathen objects

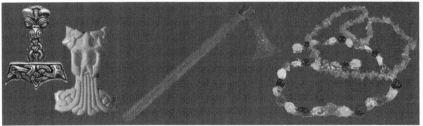

in the auction, and the money collected goes to support the LATP event and to the Heartland Hof and Hall fund.

♦ Viking games, including hammer-toss, Kindred tug-of-war, and a little game we like to call, "Steal the Wench." The hammer-toss involves throwing a large hammer made by Craig Winkler called "Skull-Splitter." The Kindred who wins the Kindred tug-of-war gets to take home the hammer-trophy for that year, and then come back the next year and defend their title.

TENTING INCLUDED, BUT CABINS AVAILABLE

The registration fees for Lightning Across the Plains cover the tent camping fees at Gaea Retreat for both nights of the gathering. Cabins are also available for a small fee, and can be reserved directly with the staff of Gaea Retreat. Details on how to do this can be found in the registration packet at the LATP website.

A REGIONAL THING IN THE HEARTLAND

We feel the growth of Heathenry is something that must happen – can only happen – at the grassroots level. Heathens find each other in their local area. Kindreds form, and grow. Regionally, Kindreds begin to gather together and face to face connections and relationships form. Over time, the trust between Tribes and tribal leaders becomes such, that the formal structure of a Regional Thing is put into place. Here in the Heartland, we have reached that point.

Strong Kindreds from across the Heartland gather at Lightning Across the Plains to hold our annual Regional Thing. Kindred Chieftains, leaders, and representatives meet together to discuss regional issues and goals. Those attending Lightning Across the Plains can bring matters before the Thing for consideration and advice. This is a process that is developing, and will continue to develop for some time.

ATTENDING LIGHTNING ACROSS THE PLAINS

If you are a long-time Heathen, a new Heathen, or someone curious about Heathenry, then you are welcome at Lightning Across the Plains. If you are part of a strong Heathen Tribe, or a small Hearth, or you are a solitary Heathen wanting more, then you are welcome at Lightning Across the Plains. If you have been to dozens of gatherings, or never been to even one, then you are welcome at Lighting Across the Plains. While this is a Heathen gathering focused on the those living here in the Heartland, all Heathens are welcome. Come and gather with your Folk. Honor our Gods, our Ancestors, and the Vaettir of the land with other Tribes and other Heathens of our region. You can learn more about the event and register for this year's Lightning Across the Plains at:

http://www.lightningacrosstheplains.com

TEMPLE OF OUR HEATHEN GODS WEBSITE

Please visit the Temple of Our Heathen Gods resource website for Heathens. It features an extensive on-line library of books related to Heathenry, an Asatru artwork archive, Heathen related articles, Mark Stinson's blog, and a message board active with interesting discussions. **Heathengods.com**

MARK LUDWIG STINSON

Mark Stinson lives with his wife and three kids in Kansas City, Missouri. Mark earned Bachelor of Arts Degrees in History, Political Science, and Philosophy from Rockhurst, a Jesuit University in Kansas City. He has worked as a police officer since 1993 and has been a Sergeant for the Kansas City Missouri Police Department since 2001.

At Thingvellir

Mark discovered Heathenry in June of 2006. A year later, in June of 2007 Mark committed himself to Heathenry and to practicing the Asatru religion. Seeking to honor the Heathen Gods in the old ways, Mark began looking for an existing Kindred in the Kansas City Area. When he discovered that there were no Kindreds in his area, he dedicated himself to finding like-minded Heathens in order to form a new Kindred.

Mark enjoys researching the history of the Asatru religion, and traditional Heathenry. Mark honors all of the Northern Gods, but has a special affinity for Asa-Thor, because Thor protects us from the monsters of this world, sets an example for how we should confront evil, and was a God for the "working class" and the thralls. But Mark has great respect for Odin's sacrifices and wisdom, as well as Tyr's courage.

Mark serves as the Chieftain of Jotun's Bane Kindred. The title of "Chieftain" denotes the leader of a Tribe. Jotun's Bane is an egalitarian organization, and important decisions are based on a consensus of its members. But the title of Chieftain reflects Mark's role as an organizer, consensus-builder, and leader, and the fact that his Luck has had a positive impact on the success of the Kindred.

Mark's middle name is Ludwig, a family name that descended to him from his Great Grandfather, a furniture-maker who immigrated to the United States from Austria. Mark's Father was Glen F. Stinson, a World War II submarine veteran. While Glen Stinson was not Heathen, he taught Mark values and a way of approaching the world that made Mark's transition to Heathenry much simpler than it could have been otherwise.

Mark is very focused on his Family, and building a solid Heathen Kindred that will stand through time and adversity.

Mark has put a lot of time and effort into encouraging the creation and growth of local Heathen communities in the Midwest, and has worked with other Heathen leaders in the Heartland to create the Regional Midwest Thing.

To contact Mark, email him at mark@Heathengods.com.

FURTHER READING

Heathenry is sometimes called "the religion with homework." There is a process of enculturation that must take place when a person returns to their Folkway. To return to the world-view and way-of-life of our Ancestors, one must read and study, and begin putting what they learning into practice. The problem of course, is making sure that you are accessing the right resources. Much of the information about Heathenry you find on the internet or in books is misleading or just wrong.

Most Heathens will recommend going to your primary sources first. These consist of the Poetic Edda, the Prose Edda, the Icelandic Sagas, Beowulf, and other contemporary source material. Then there are well-researched secondary sources that can be valuable in fleshing out your understanding. Beyond that, there are tertiary sources, such as story-books retelling the stories in the Lore, books of modern Heathen poetry, etc. Below is a list of books worth reading.

Some of the following books can be read and downloaded for free from the Temple Library at **Heathengods.com**. Many of the others can be ordered on-line or at your local bookstore. Over time, some of these books will be available from the Temple Library Collection. Some of these will be a challenge to find, but well worth it.

The Poetic Edda – This is available in various translations. Larrington's is the easiest to understand, but one of the least poetic. Hollander's is one of the most poetic, but sometime difficult to understand. Bellow's translation is a pretty fair balance of clarity and a poetic sense. Larrington and Hollander's translations come in one volume, while Bellow's translation is split into two volumes.

The Prose Edda by Snorri Sturluson – This is also available in various translations. The Byock, Faulkes, and Young translations are all fairly good.

Essential Asatru by Diana Paxon
Heathen Gods by Mark Ludwig Stinson (well, of course!)

Our Troth: History and Lore (Volume 1) by Kveldulf Gundarsson
Our Troth: Living the Troth (Volume 2) by Kveldulf Gundarsson

Elves, Wights, and Trolls by Kveldulf Gundarsson

Beowulf trans. by Seamus Heaney (I strongly suggested this trans.)
The Sagas of Icelanders (Penguin Classics Deluxe Edition)
The Saga Hoard, Volumes 1-3 (Temple Library Collection)
Egil's Saga and **Njal's Saga**
The Saga of the Volsungs translated by Jesse Byock
The Sagas of Ragnar Lodbrok translated by Ben Waggoner
The Sagas of Fridthjof the Bold translated by Ben Waggoner

The Nibelungenlied

The Agricola and Germania by Tacitus (available in various trans.)

Heimskringla by Snorri Sturluson (available in various trans.)

The History of the Danes, Books I-IX by Saxo Grammaticus

Ecclesiastical History of the English Nation by the Venerable Bede

The Culture of the Teutons (Volumes 1 and 2) by Vilhelm Grönbech
    Collected into one book from the Temple Library Collection.

Gods and Myths of the Viking Age by H.R. Ellis Davidson
The Road to Hel by H.R. Ellis Davidson
Myths and Symbols in Pagan Europe by H.R. Ellis Davidson

The Well and the Tree by Paul C. Bauschatz (hard to find)

The Mead Hall by Stephen Pollington (hard to find)

The Norse Myths: Gods of the Vikings by Kevin Crossley-Holland

The Children of Odin by by Padraic Colum

D'Aulaire's Book of Norse Myths by Ingri and Edgar D'Aulaire

True Hearth by James Allen Chisholm

Way of the Heathen by Garman Lord

AFA Book of Blotar and Ritual

The Book of Troth by Edred Thorsson

The Rune Primer by Sweyn Plowright

On Being a Pagan by Alain de Benoist

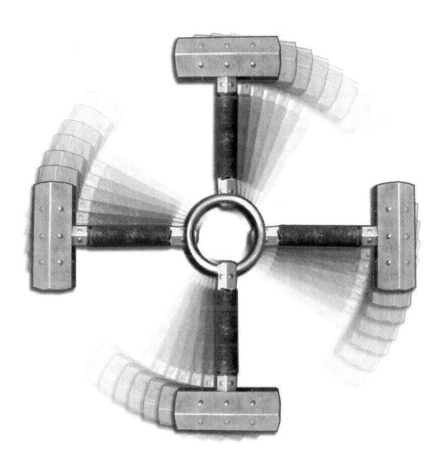